The Sport Scientists:
Research Adventures

The Sport Scientists: Research Adventures

Edited by

Gary G. Brannigan

State University of New York—Plattsburgh

An imprint of Addison Wesley Longman, Inc.

New York • Reading, Massachusetts • Menlo Park, California • Harlow, England
Don Mills, Ontario • Sydney • Mexico City • Madrid • Amsterdam

To my wife, Linda, and my sons, Marc
and Michael

Editor-in-Chief: Pricilla McGeehon
Acquisitions Editor: Rebecca Dudley
Marketing Manager: Anne Wise
Project Coordination, Electronic Page Makeup, and Text Design: WestWords, Inc.
Cover Designer/Manager: Nancy Danahy
Cover Photo: © Superstock
Full Service Production Manager: Eric Jorgensen
Print Buyer: Denise Sandler
Printer and Binder: The MapleVail Book Manufacturing Group
Cover Printer: Coral Graphic Services, Inc.

Photo credits: p. ix, Robin Brown; p. 92, University of Waterloo Central Photographic;
p. 113, Mary Levin, University Photography at the University of Washington.

Library of Congress Cataloging-in-Publication Data

The sport scientists : research adventures / edited by Gary G. Brannigan
    p.   cm.
  includes bibliographical references.
  ISBN 0-321-01345-X
  1. Sports—Psychological aspects.   2. Sports—Psychological aspects—Research.
  3. Sports sciences—Research.   I. Branigan, Gary G.
  GV706.4.S6827   1998
  796'.01--dc21
                                                          98-20915
                                                          CIP

Please visit our website at http://longman.awl.com

ISBN 0-321-01345-X

12345678910—MA—01009998

Contents

Preface

The Sport Scientists: Research Adventures provides eleven in-depth personal accounts of research on major topics in the psychology of sport. These lively stories will appeal to a wide audience because sport plays such a big part in our lives.

The book is designed to complement textbooks in undergraduate and graduate courses in Sport Psychology. For undergraduate courses, the stories can be used to illustrate principles and theories and "bring to life" the content covered in most textbooks. This approach is relatively new. Phillip DeVita has used this approach in several anthropology books, and I have produced several similar books in psychology, education, and human sexuality. Reviewers of these projects have been intrigued with this approach. The following thoughts, based on input from David Myers of Hope College, Rosemary Hornack of Meredith College, and Ann Weber from the University of North Carolina–Asheville, are representative of their feedback. Because it's easy to be intimidated by brilliant people—who seem from a distance to come up with great ideas and execute them flawlessly—you will greatly appreciate the humanness of these personal stories. As they take you backstage to view their research careers, you will read stories of uncertain initial directions, of serendipity, of false starts, of self-doubts, of job insecurity, of the importance of supportive mentors, colleagues, and students. You will also see the passion that drives these people and the ideals that guide them, values such as lifelong learning, reading published literature, working hard, making the most of all that you know from any source of experience, turning misfortune into opportunity, observing carefully, and keeping an open mind. Personal narratives also address many of the important questions that frequently go unanswered in textbooks. Who are you? Why and how did you get involved in sport research? Can I identify with you? What keeps you excited about your work? What has your experience taught you? What personal lessons can I carry away from your story? And so on. Students typically find this approach challenging and rewarding.

At more advanced levels, the stories can be used to stress the "nitty-gritty" aspects of sport research—that is, generating ideas, developing methodology, designing studies, applying results, as well as the personal and situational factors that frequently influence decision making.

Sport science is an exciting and rapidly growing area of investigation. Although it is not intended to be exhaustive, *The Sport Scientists* samples research from the major topics in sport psychology. The topics include:

- Skill Development
- Skill Performance
- Arousal
- Motivation
- Leadership/Decision Making
- Group Dynamics
- Gender Issues
- Aggression
- Drugs/Coping
- Injury
- Effective Coaching

If, as I believe, there is a lot we can learn from the experiences of others, this collection of "stories" will be informative and enriching.

Acknowledgments

This book reflects the efforts of fourteen researchers who took the time to write chapters so that others can understand and appreciate the process of sport science. I wish to express my appreciation and thanks for the quality of their work.

I owe a debt of gratitude to Becky Dudley, Executive Editor, who was instrumental in all phases of this project. Her ongoing encouragement and support are greatly appreciated. I also wish to thank Adam Rodnitzky, Editorial Assistant; Jennifer Maughan, Project Manager; and Charles Batten, Copyeditor, whose attention to the many details associated with production enhanced the success of the project.

The reviewers were invaluable to this project. They provided many helpful suggestions to improve this book. I thank:

Joe Walsh – Mankato State University
Richard O. Straub – University of Michigan – Dearborn
Richard C. Noel – California State University – Bakersfield
Susan Butt – University of British Columbia
Arnold LeUnes – Texas A&M University

Leonard Kalakian – Mankato State University
Michael C. Robinson – Texas Christian University
Raymond L. Eastman – Stephen F. Austin State University
Martha Ewing – Michigan State University
Nate Zinsser – United States Military Academy – West Point
Gregory A. Dale – Winthrop University
Ralph Vernacchia – Western Washington University
Damon Burton – University of Idaho
Michael L. Sachs – Temple University

Finally, Judy Dashnaw deserves special recognition. Her advice and counsel on editorial and word processing matters contributed greatly to the quality of this book.

Introduction

The Sport Scientists: Research Adventures grew out of my frustration with contemporary educational practices. Most textbooks are excellent repositories of information, but they tell little about the important decision-making processes that are used to collect that information. As Arthur Combs noted in *The Future Demands of Education,* this must change. "Tomorrow's citizens must be effective problem solvers, persons able to make good choices, to create solutions on the spot. That is precisely what intelligence is all about . . . Effective problem solving is learned by confronting events, defining problems, puzzling with them, experimenting, trying, searching for effective solutions."

Although *The Sport Scientists* is not intended as a replacement for first-hand experience, it provides insights into the sport research process. I asked contributors to tell how they encountered issues that were especially interesting, unique, and/or problematic, and that demanded some form of resolution. In the process, they present insiders' views of sport research by stressing the critical-thinking and problem-solving aspects of sport science.

I have chosen selectively among the varied topics sport scientists study to give you a cross section of their work. The topics range from skill learning, to group formation, to fan violence, to coping with injury.

I also have avoided chapter introductions and summaries in favor of letting the stories unfold "like good mystery novels." Enjoy the adventures!

About the Editor

Gary G. Brannigan earned his B.A. (1969) from Fairfield University and his M.A. (1972) and Ph.D. (1973) from the University of Delaware. After completing his clinical psychology internship at the Devereux Foundation, he has been serving on the faculty of the State University of New York at Plattsburgh. In addition to teaching in the Psychology Department, he served five years as Director of the Psychological Services Clinic. He also maintains a small private practice and consults with local agencies. He is a Fellow in the Society for Personality Assessment and a consulting editor on two journals. In addition to coediting *The Undaunted Psychologist: Adventures in Research, The Social Psychologists: Research Adventures, The Developmental Psychologists: Research Adventures Across the Lifespan,* and *The Sex Scientists;* and editing *The Enlightened Educator: Research Adventures in the Schools,* he has authored or coauthored numerous articles, chapters, books, and tests, including *Research and Clinical Applications for the Bender-Gestalt Test, The Modified Version of the Bender-Gestalt Test for Preschool and Primary School Children* (now in its second edition), and *Experiences in Personality: Research, Assessment, and Change.* His research is primarily on psychological and educational assessment and his applied interests have been in program development and coordination, as well as coaching, at the youth sport level—specifically baseball and basketball.

Chapter 1

Developing Sport Expertise: Transitions During Childhood And Early Adolescence

Karen E. French

Karen E. French is an associate professor in the Department of Physical Education at the University of South Carolina. She has authored or co-authored over thirty articles and book chapters related to sport expertise, motor skill acquisition, and child growth and development. Articles appear in journals such as *Research Quarterly for Exercise and Sport*, *Journal of Sport and Exercise Psychology*, *American Journal of Human Biology*, and *Journal of Teaching in Physical Education*. She is a member of the editorial board for *Journal of Teaching in Physical Education*, serves as a reviewer for *Research Quarterly for Exercise and Sport*, and is guest reviewer for *Journal of Sport and Exercise Psychology*. She is an avid basketball fan. In her spare time, she enjoys gardening, listening to music, hiking, and writing poetry.

Highly skilled athletes amaze us by making the complexity of sport performance seem so simple. Coaches and commentators often say that these athletes possess something you just can not teach. They must have some innate ability to perform the skills that most of us don't possess. Behind each of these phenomenal sport performances lie thousands of practice trials accumulated over many years. As observers, we see the outcome of the years of practice. Seldom do we catch a glimpse of performance during earlier skill development when these same athletes performed at a mere human level.

The fact that individuals reach these ultimate levels of human performance is not amazing to me. The road each athlete took to reach these levels of performance is what fascinates me. My interest in athletes' progression toward skilled performance began when my sixth grade teacher introduced me to the game of basketball. It was love at first sight. I loved everything about the game. I was fortunate to play for a high school program that was very successful. Our team won the Louisiana AAA high school state championship during my junior and senior years. Despite a knee injury, I was also fortunate to play at the college level for two years.

After college, I coached basketball for several years. Even though I had been trained in physical education, most of my early coaching decisions were based on my own experiences as a player. Some things worked very well, whereas others didn't work as well. I learned by trial and error. The entire time, I had questions. What were the best methods to facilitate long-term improvement in sport performance? Were there better ways to enhance sport performance in a shorter period of time? These were important questions to me when I entered graduate school.

When I entered Louisiana State University to pursue a doctoral degree, I was totally naive about higher education, research, or expectations for doctoral study. My first year of doctoral study was a personal struggle. I had many mixed emotions. In some ways, I was challenged intellectually and was excited that I was learning so many new ideas. I was also terrified that someone would discover how little I actually knew at the time. I also struggled because I realized I was being trained to become a scientist. I wasn't really sure I wanted to be a scientist. The doctoral program at LSU was designed to prepare students in a specialization of sport science with the research skills to become successful in faculty positions at major research institutions. I was more comfortable considering myself as a teacher and coach. My questions were related to teaching and coaching, not theoretical development.

In one of my first courses, motor learning with Richard Magill, students had to conduct two laboratory experiments and an independent research project. Each of these assignments included data collection, statistical analysis of the results, and writing the experiment in journal article format. No one in the class had ever collected data, performed statistical analyses, or written a journal article. Essentially, we learned all the steps of the research process by doing our own research.

The next semester I took courses in sport psychology with Evelyn Hall and motor development with Jerry Thomas. In each class, students had to conduct an independent research project and submit the findings as a journal article. By the end of the first year of doctoral work, I definitely knew that having a Ph.D. was not what I thought it would be. I can't tell you exactly what event prompted me to pursue a career as a researcher. I became more comfortable considering myself as a researcher gradually over a period of time.

I had begun doctoral studies with a specialization in sport psychology. After the first year, I realized I was more interested in questions related to how individuals learn and develop motor skills. I decided to concentrate my remaining studies in motor development and work closely with Jerry Thomas. Jerry was firmly committed to a mentor model of doctoral training. His philosophy was to collaborate with students in research, interact with students almost daily, and provide opportunities to socialize students into the academic field. The socialization process included providing opportunities to present papers at conferences and meet other scholars in the field. As a result of his guidance, I had the opportunity to present research papers at regional and national conferences, meet and interact with many of the leading scholars in motor learning and development, and learn many of the skills related to publishing and presenting research.

Characteristics of Sport Experts

When I attended graduate school in the early 1980s, research in sport expertise was in its infancy. We knew that expert athletes possessed superior motor skills. Studies had also shown that world class athletes in a given sport tended to have similar physiques. For example, world class divers tend to be short; centers in basketball tend to be tall. Methods for cardiovascular and strength training to enhance performance in given sports were available. Yet, few studies had been conducted to systematically identify other characteristics of elite performance.

Over the past 15 years, many studies have compared adult expert and novice performers on a variety of sport tasks. A short list of some of the characteristics exhibited by adult expert performers is given in Table 1.1. Adult experts possess the physique which allows superior performance in a sport or specific position within a given sport. Generally, elite athletes have trained over a long period of time to develop the prerequisite physiological characteristics (e.g., cardiovascular endurance and muscular strength). Athletes exhibit superior motor skill.

Experts also exhibit superior perceptual or cognitive skills that facilitate decision making during games. In sports with complex offensive and defensive tactics, players must make fast and accurate decisions regarding what skill to execute and the timing of the execution. Often response selection is as important as the ability to properly execute the motor skill. For example, successful performance in defensive play in baseball requires that you throw to the correct base (response selection) as well as execute the throw successfully (response execution). In basketball, one must choose the appropriate player to whom to pass as well as motorically execute the pass. In highly tactical sports, successful performance requires decision-making skills, such as being in the right place at the right time (positioning yourself), anticipating or predicting the actions of an opponent, planning tactics in advance, and selecting appropriate responses accurately and quickly.

Table 1.1   Characteristics of adult sport experts

Perceptual/Cognitive	Motor/Sport Skill	Physiological	Physique
Fast and accurate decisions	Consistent motor patterns	Strength	Appropriate body size and form
Superior pattern recognition	Adaptable motor patterns	Muscular endurance	
Superior visual search	Superior error detection/ correction	Cardiovascular endurance	
Superior selection of relevant cues	Superior perception of kinesthetic information		
Plans actions in advance			
Use sport specific metacognitive strategies			
Highly organized sport knowledge			

The Role of Learning in Expertise

Anders Ericcson and his colleagues present a strong argument that most of these characteristics of elite performance are not due to genetic predispositions to elite performance. Rather, these characteristics are a result of adaptations to training and focused practice over long periods of time. The one exception may be physique, especially height, which seems to have a genetic component. Thus, most of the important characteristics of elite performance result from years of focused practice and training.

In his book, *Developing Talent in Young People*, Benjamin Bloom provides a glimpse of the years of training experts in a variety of fields endure. He interviewed world-class performers in tennis, swimming, mathematics, piano, and art. All of the talented individuals spent at least 10 years training in the domain before they reached their current performance level. Three phases of learning were identified. When individuals entered the domain as children, much of the teaching and learning process was playful. The parents initially introduced the child to the talent area. The emphasis was placed on enjoying the activity and having fun. Early teachers were positive, supportive, and rewarded small improvements. At some point, near early adolescence, learning shifted into the second phase, where emphasis was placed on precision and accuracy in all aspects of the talent field. In tennis and swimming, for example, the emphasis was on mastering and refining the strokes. Frequently, a new teacher was selected. This teacher was generally a perfectionist who demanded more practice time from the student and insisted that the student reach his or her highest potential. The third phase of learning could be characterized as development of a personal style in the chosen field, and on the larger purpose and meaning of one's talent in the field. Most individuals worked with a very select master teacher to reach their highest potential during this phase.

Only a few of the one hundred twenty individuals in Bloom's study were regarded as child prodigies by teachers or adult experts. Fewer than ten percent were skilled enough at age eleven or twelve for anyone to predict they would achieve world-class status in the field during adulthood. Bloom suggests that it is so hard to predict future elite performance from early performance because one has learned at these early ages only a small portion of what must be learned. Excelling in an early phase may not have a high relation to being good at a later phase. In addition, the motivation to learn in the early phase is not the same type of motivation necessary to persist and continue learning in the more difficult later phases.

Much of my work has attempted to identify what characteristics of performance are acquired during the early phase of learning (ages 6–12) when children first enter youth sport. When children begin sport participation, their bodies are growing and developing. They are attempting to learn the motor skills, knowledge, and cognitive processes specific to a given sport. Each of these factors represents a category from the characteristics of adult expert performance (Table 1.1). Each of these factors is changing at a different rate and represents one piece of a larger puzzle. Often these factors interact across childhood to influence sport performance at a given point in time.

Cognitive Contributions to Early Skilled Performance

My interest in the development of cognitive aspects of sport performance began in graduate school. Jerry Thomas was very interested in developing a line of research to understand how knowledge stored in long-term memory may impact children's sport performance The first step in developing a line of research was to conceptualize how knowledge might affect performance. Jerry, Charlotte Humphries (another graduate student), and I met regularly over an entire summer. Our first priority was to read as many studies as possible. Most of the theories and research were from cognitive psychology and verbal learning. However, we recognized early that there were problems trying to translate verbal learning theories into models for sport performance. In most verbal learning studies, the motor output is a simple motor response (e.g., oral, written, or button push). Motor output in sport is much more difficult, complex, and variable. The models from cognitive psychology seemed to have greater power to explain *response selection processes* in highly tactical sports. Other theories of motor control and learning seemed to provide better explanations for *response execution*. Thus, we had to incorporate different theoretical frameworks in our research depending on what aspect of sport performance we were studying (response selection or response execution).

In our initial reading that summer, there were several ways to study or measure knowledge, decision making, and sport skill execution. We chose to begin our research in a field setting. We believed that the first step was to establish that response selection or decision making was an important aspect of sport performance. To do so, we had to observe response selection in "real world" sport environments. During that summer, we developed an observational instrument to measure response selection and execution of children playing in Little League baseball games. We coded the appropriateness of children's decisions (throw to appropriate base) and motor execution (success of throws, fielding, catching, etc.) during live games. By the end of that summer, we had developed a conceptual framework and a plan for a series of research studies on response selection and response execution processes in sport. The framework and initial hypotheses developed that summer were reported in one of my first published papers with Jerry. Many of those initial ideas continue to serve as a foundation for much of my research.

The first study we conducted was my dissertation. Several questions were addressed. First, we wanted to establish response selection as a component of performance in basketball. Second, we wanted to examine the relations between basketball knowledge, basketball skills, and response selection and execution components of performance. We selected high- and low-skilled basketball players at two age levels: 8- to 10-year-olds and 11- to 12-year-olds. We collected several measures on each player. We measured basketball knowledge with a paper-pencil multiple-choice test and skill performance with dribbling and shooting skill tests. We videotaped two regular-season games for each player. An observational instrument was developed to code the appropriateness of response selection and motor skill execution during game play.

The observational instrument was an event coding instrument, designed to code the actions of a player when in possession of the ball. Game actions usually take place as a series of events. A player first gains control of the ball (usually catches it), makes a decision (pass, shoot, dribble), and then executes the chosen skill. Each of these events was coded as appropriate or inappropriate. Reliability and objectivity of observation is a critical factor in using observational instruments. The researcher must develop careful descriptions of each coding category so that the researcher can code each category consistently with a second observer. Table 1.2 presents some of the definitions used for coding appropriate decisions. Definitions to determine codes for successful motor execution of dribbling, passing, and shooting were also developed. Execution for shooting was coded 1 for a successful shot and 0 for an unsuccessful shot. Passing execution was coded 1 for a successful pass to a teammate and 0 for a pass that was too high, too far behind or in front of a teammate, out-of-bounds, or at a teammate's feet. Dribbling execution was coded 1 for successfully advancing the ball and 0 for loss of control of the dribble, double dribble, or having the ball stolen. The responses

---

Table 1.2　Summary of coding definitions for decision making

Shooting

Coded as appropriate—1

　　Any shot taken within a 15-foot radius of the basket when the player was open

Coded as inappropriate—0

　　1. A shot taken outside a 15-foot radius of the basket
　　2. A shot taken off balance
　　3. Blocked shot
　　4. Charging
　　5. Not attempting a shot when open within 15 feet of the basket

Passing

Coded as appropriate—1

　　A pass to a teammate who is open

Coded as inappropriate—0

　　1. A pass made to a player who is guarded closely, defensive player positioned in the passing lane
　　2. A pass made to an area of the court where no teammate is positioned

Dribbling

Coded as appropriate—1

　　1. Appropriate penetration
　　2. Advancing the ball upcourt
　　3. An appropriate change of direction away from a defender or to open court

Coded as inappropriate—0

　　1. Charging
　　2. Dribbling into double team
　　3. Dribbling out-of-bounds
　　4. Dribbling away from the goal, dribbling without advancing the ball or attacking

---

of each player during videotaped game play were coded. From these codes, percentages of appropriate game decisions and successful skill executions were determined.

　　During game performance, the high-skilled players had higher percentages of appropriate decisions and successful skill executions than low-skilled players. Skill levels influenced decision making more than they influenced skill of execution. Thus, we established that decision making was an important component of game performance, even at young ages. Furthermore, the basketball knowledge test was significantly correlated with decision making, whereas the dribbling and shooting skill tests were correlated with skill execution during game play.

In the second experiment, we were interested in the improvement of decision making and skill execution across the season. Jerry had observed his own children in youth sport. Based on his observations, he thought that young children improved their decision making over the course of a season but did not make much improvement in their motor skills. To test these predictions in basketball, we performed our testing (observation of game play, skill tests, and knowledge tests) at the beginning of the season and at the end of the season for 8- to 10-year-old players. High- and low-skilled players did improve decision making from the beginning to the end of the season. They did not improve skill execution during games or performance on both basketball skill tests. Both groups of players improved scores on the knowledge test, and the post-season knowledge test scores were significantly related to decision making during games at the end of the season. These results suggested that as basketball knowledge improved, decision making in games also improved. Our observations of team practices also suggested that coaches had organized practices to primarily teach tactics. Coaches were trying to organize the offense and defense of their team for competition. As a result, less time was devoted to practicing individual sport skills.

These two studies were very important at the time because they established that cognition was a very important component of successful performance in real world sport environments. Furthermore, overall performance in games could be enhanced by improving decision making or the underlying knowledge related to decision making.

After I finished graduate school, I began my career at the University of South Carolina. I have continued to pursue questions related to sport expertise. Colleagues (John Spurgeon, Michael Nevett) and I have been studying the development of cognitive processes related to decision making in youth baseball for the past several years. I want to share three studies, each of which contributes a separate piece of the puzzle concerning how children learn baseball tactics. The first study we conducted attempted to determine the contribution of cognitive (decision making) and sport skill components of performance to skillful baseball performance at ages 7 to 10. We videotaped five games for every team and developed an observational instrument to code appropriate response selection (percentage of appropriate decisions) and baseball skill execution (percentages of successful fielding, catching, throwing, and batting) during games. We compared the measures of game performance for high-, average-, and low-skilled players. The highly skilled players exhibited better performance on all the baseball skills during game play. There were no differences in decision making.

Several factors may explain why the level of expertise did not influence the accuracy of decisions during games. Many of the game situations in baseball involved simple decisions. There were no runners on base in approximately 30% of all game situations. All children made better decisions when there were no runners on base (one choice, throw to first). The percentage of correct decisions was much lower (around 60 to 70%) in more complex situations with runners on base (more potential choices). Differences between high- and low-skilled children may only become apparent in more complex game situations. In addition, coaches and spectators often prompted correct decisions before and sometimes during a play. Coaches and spectators would often yell to players where to throw for infield and outfield plays. Therefore, some of the correct decisions were a result of prompting or telling the child a response rather than the child selecting a response on his or her own. We suspect that prompting may be beneficial to immediate game performance, but it may actually be detrimental to long-term learning of decision making, because the player may become dependent on the coach for correct decision making.

In the next study, we interviewed children to determine if they could identify what game actions were appropriate for five different game situations. All interviews were audiotaped, transcribed, and analyzed systematically. We used interviews for two reasons. First, young children may have difficulty answering a paper-pencil test. Second, thinking out loud while solving the baseball game problems provided more valuable information on the processes players used to generate an answer. We chose game situations which varied in complexity, importance to the outcome of the game, and the frequency with which they may occur during normal games. The five situations were:

1. a double play, a runner at first base and the ball hit to the second baseman;
2. an outfield play, ball hit to centerfield with a runner at first base;
3. a nonforce situation, runner on second base, ball hit to third;
4. a potential run, the ball hit to left field with a runner on second; and
5. a critical run situation, score tied, bottom of last inning, runners at first and third, no outs, and the ball hit to first base.

Highly skilled players answered the more complex situations correctly (3, nonforce, and 5, critical run) more often than low-skilled players. Therefore, high-skilled players do possess more knowledge of correct baseball defensive decisions, even though there were no differences apparent during game performance in the previous study. Overall, all players' responses were low for the complex situations (3, 4, 5). Only about 50 percent of the high-skilled players were correct in the nonforce and critical run situations.

The most important findings from this study, however, were the mistakes and patterns exhibited by children as they solved these defensive game situations. Children often had difficulty predicting potential defensive actions that were possible within normal time frames of the game. For example, some children said the cutoff player should throw to first base to get the batter out when the ball had been hit to the outfield (situations 2 and 4). The batter would already be safely at first. Children also had trouble predicting the actions of base runners. Coaches seldom practiced game situations with runners on base. These mistakes in players' solutions may have been due to seldom practicing running bases or seldom practicing defense with runners on base.

Players also sometimes reversed their answers. They began their response with one answer, recognized they were wrong, and changed to the correct answer. This mistake indicated that players had the correct answer in memory but had trouble retrieving the correct answer quickly. If they had to retrieve the answer in a game, they would not have had time to correct or reverse their solution and still make the correct play.

The other interesting pattern in the responses was the role that the skill of teammates played in their defensive solutions. In several situations, players stated that a teammate would move to a different cutoff position depending on the teammate's ability to throw or a different player would make the throw because he or she could throw farther. Thus, players were adapting their solutions depending on their own motor skill ability or the skill of a teammate.

Overall, this study showed that young players often do not know what the best defensive solutions are to complex game situations. They are likely to make errors in retrieving solutions, predicting baserunners, and game actions within the time frame of the game. In addition, the ability to execute some motor skills may limit some potential game actions at these ages.

Even if players do know what actions are appropriate in baseball, there is no guarantee that players will use their cognitive resources effectively to mediate decision making in games. Some useful cognitive processes in baseball would involve directing attention to relevant game information, using relevant information to predict potential player actions or game events, and planning defensive actions before the ball is put in play. Previous research with adult experts and novices had shown that experts were more likely than novices to process relevant game information, attach probability levels to potential game events, use the probabilities to predict game actions, plan responses in advance, and modify and update their plans based on new information.

The third study was Michael Nevett's dissertation. One of the ways to examine cognitive processes is to record and analyze an individual's verbalized thoughts during performance. Michael asked the players to wear a microcassette recorder during live baseball games and say out loud what they were thinking between pitches. The recorder was worn in a small pack on the player's back at waist level. A pin microphone was connected to the player's collar. This arrangement did not interfere with the player's movements at all. During game play, players were given two prompts before the pitch to a batter. They were, "What are you thinking? and "Keep talking." Michael used these prompts because previous research suggested that they were more likely to elicit the natural thought processes of the individual. One experimenter stood behind the shortstop and stated the prompts before each pitch. When the ball was put in play, the experimenter moved out of the way so he would not interfere with play.

Michael also videotaped each game so that he could identify all the critical information for each game situation (i.e., outs, score, runners on base, other game context). He selected some of the same game situations as used in the interviews for analysis. Selection of situations was important to standardize players' responses in similar game situations as well as compare responses to interviews in the previous study. The subjects were highly skilled shortstops at ages 8, 10, 12, and high school age. I will just briefly summarize some of the results.

Often the younger players (8 and 10) did not generate a plan before the first pitch to the batter or on any subsequent pitch to the batter. The twelve-year-olds were beginning to generate a number of plans for special plays, such as bunts or steals, but often they did not plan what to do if the ball was hit to them. Even if the younger players did generate a plan, generally it was a lower quality plan. For example, throw to first to get an out versus throw to second to start a double play in a double play situation. Only the high school players consistently planned what to do in advance and generated higher quality plans.

Over the course at bat (several pitches to the same batter), high school shortstops were modifying their plans based on new information (i.e., batter fouled ball down the left field line). Younger players tended to focus on the plan they generated for the first pitch and never changed or modified the plan even though some new information would have been valuable.

In addition, younger players (8–12) tended to verbalize chatter, such as hey, batter, batter. None of the high school shortstops verbalized chatter. The high school player's verbalized comments were almost entirely plans for the upcoming play, positive motivational statements directed toward teammates, or instructional types of comments to teammates to aid in concentration or tactics for the game situation. Basically, the chatter statements used by the younger shortstops are a waste of cognitive resources. Chatter does little to distract the batter. Most coaches teach children to make chatter statements as a form of an attentional strategy. Coaches will say something like, "let me hear you out there" to try to get players focused on the next play. Children need to be paying attention to game information, planning for potential actions if the ball comes to them or special plays like bunts or steals. Obviously, the older players had learned to focus their attention and direct their cognitive resources to areas that improved their performance or that of their teammates.

The high school shortstops had played an average of 10 years, twelve-year-olds 7 years, 10-year-olds 5 years. The cognitive processes to effectively attend to critical game information, plan potential actions in advance, and modify the plans based on new information develop very slowly. I suspect that most coaches do a very poor job of teaching players how to plan for upcoming plays between pitches. Repeatedly practicing game situations with runners on base so that players have to choose which decisions are appropriate is one way to facilitate knowledge of tactics and cognitive processes associated with planning. Teaching players a more appropriate attentional strategy than chatter would also help. For example, first, pay attention to all the important game information (runners, outs, score, etc.); second, plan what to do if the ball is hit in your direction or special plays (bunts, steals); third, communicate with teammates to be sure everyone knows what to do; fourth, after the pitch relax for a moment (if you do not have to cover in a steal); fifth, repeat the process by attending to any new information. A coach could teach this planning process to players by having players verbalize their plans to teammates during practice and games. The coach could also gain insight into which tactics and planning processes need more practice. Coaches need to be patient and be willing to repeat the same play over and over again because younger children do not remember as well as adults. Often the decision mistakes that children make in games are caused by never practicing in ways that would facilitate learning appropriate tactics.

Body Size, Practice Time, and Skill Development

Three of our studies (by John Spurgeon, Michael Nevett, and myself) attempted to piece together potential relations between body size, accumulated practice, and baseball skill development. In the first study, we measured body size and form of youth baseball players ages 7 to 12 cross-sectionally and longitudinally over a three year period. Two earlier studies from the 1950s suggested that the most highly skilled players in Little League World Series (ages 12–13) tended to play first base, shortstop, and pitcher. These players were all early maturers who exhibited postpubescent characteristics. Postpubescent children would have entered the growth spurt and probably had larger body sizes than pubescent or prepubescent children. Because body size is moderately related to motor skills involving force production, such as throwing, larger body size would be an advantage in these types of sport skills. We wanted to know if highly skilled players at younger ages also were early maturers or had larger body size.

The more highly skilled players in our study also tended to play first base, pitcher, and shortstop. Players who played these positions at each age had larger overall body size than other same-age players. For example, these players were taller, heavier, had wider shoulders, wider hips, longer arms, and longer legs than other similar age players. The differences in body size were apparent as young as eight and increased slightly at each successive age. From this data, one cannot determine if the differences are due to genetic predispositions to larger body size or if the differences reflect faster maturational rates. We did establish, however, that the more highly skilled children, as young as eight, had larger overall body size.

We were also interested in the contribution of practice and maturational factors to early skill development. To examine these factors, we asked parents of 7- to 10-year-old baseball players to estimate the number of hours their children practiced per week outside of official team practices (current practice time) and record the years of experience their children had in organized baseball (accumulated years of practice). We also measured throwing distance, throwing accuracy, fielding a ground ball, and obtained batting averages for every child. We conducted separate correlational analyses with the scores of the 7- and 8-year-old players and with the 9- and 10-year-old players to determine relationships among age, current hours practiced, years experience, and baseball skills.

Age and hours practiced significantly predicted throwing accuracy, throwing distance, and fielding for 7- and 8-year-olds. No variable predicted batting. Thus, for young beginning players, practice time was a significant predictor for skill development in throwing and fielding. Chronological age could be considered an indication of maturity. Age was probably significant because it is also highly correlated with body size.

The findings were very different for 9- and 10-year-olds. Age and years experience playing baseball were significant predictors of throwing distance, throwing accuracy, and fielding. Age (body size, maturity) contributed much less to the prediction of these skills at ages 9 and 10 than it did in the younger age groups. Years of experience (accumulated practice) was the best predictor of these skills. Practice time was the only significant predictor of batting.

When children first enter organized sport, the amount of focused practice outside of normal practice settings seems to be very important for skill development. Children who enter sport at later ages (9 or 10) are not generally as skilled as same-age peers who began practice of the skills at a younger age and have accumulated more practice. Body size seems to be a more important contributor to performance of throwing and fielding skills early in skill development than it does after children have accumulated more practice of the skills.

The findings with batting were also interesting. Younger children played coaches-pitch baseball. Age, practice, and years experience did not predict batting in coaches-pitch baseball (ages 7 and 8). Additional years of experience batting in coaches-pitch did not significantly help older players make the transition to player-pitch batting. For batting a player-pitched ball, practice time was the only significant predictor. This illustrates that not all types of previous practice positively transfer to better performance on a more complex task. Sufficient practice time at the next level of task complexity may be necessary to progress further toward skillful performance.

In the previous study, parents estimated practice time of all baseball skills. No attempt was made to identify how much practice time was devoted to a specific skill. We also wanted to determine which skills were practiced most often. In our next study, we interviewed high- and low-skilled 7- to 10-year-old players to determine which of four baseball skills (throwing, catching, fielding, batting) they practiced most and least often and the reason for their choices.

High-skilled players in this study tended to play in the infield whereas low-skilled players tended to play in the outfield. The practice choices for specific skills were influenced by player positions. Low-skilled outfielders, ages 7 and 8, chose to practice catching and batting most often.

High-skilled players (infielders) practiced batting most often. At ages 9 and 10, low-skilled outfielders practiced catching most often whereas high-skilled infielders practiced fielding most often. These findings are not surprising but are further evidence that being assigned to a specific player position affects the skills that children practice during organized practices and outside of organized practices as well.

The reasons players chose to practice a skill more often were interesting. Most players chose to practice a skill more often because they were not good at the skill or they wanted to improve in the skill. The reason most players cited for practicing a skill less often was because they thought they were already good at the skill. Very few of the players avoided practice of a skill at which they were not good or did not like. The other interesting pattern was the number of responses that indicated that some of their practice choices were limited due to equipment or space limitations. Some players did not practice batting because they didn't have a bat, they might break a window, or the space or equipment was not available for them to practice the skill more often. One of our favorite responses was, "My mom doesn't pitch too good so I don't practice batting very much." Some players indicated that they practiced a skill (usually throwing or catching) more often because they could practice by themselves. Thus, many of these players may have practiced some skills more often if the resources were available (equipment or space).

Taken together, these three studies suggest that coaches may be identifying players as young as 8 who are more skilled because they are larger or more mature. The selection of players for infield positions, especially firstbase, shortstop, pitcher, based on physical stature and early performance may lead to more opportunities to practice important skill tasks. For example, players who play these positions often receive more opportunities to field, catch, and throw in organized practices and games. The additional practice may further improve their skills. These players may also receive more encouragement, feedback, and support because of early success. This in turn may motivate them to accumulate even greater amounts of focused practice outside of regular team practice sessions.

This type of early selection and practice specificity for a given player position probably works very well in terms of a team's *won-loss record*. The problem is that every individual matures at a different rate. The 8-year-old outfielder may be the best shortstop at 16 if given the encouragement, opportunity, and motivation to practice the important skills over a long period of time. Coaches and parents need to be very careful to make sure that every player, regardless of physical maturity, has sufficient opportunities to practice all baseball skills. The contribution of body size to throwing and fielding skills decreased as players accumulated more practice. By 9 and 10, accumulated years of practice contributed much more to performance than physical maturity. Most of the players practiced because they wanted to improve their skill level. Many would have practiced some skills more often if they had the resources to do so. We need to find ways to encourage children to practice the skills outside of organized practices, provide the equipment and space for practice, and increase the number of practice trials for each of these skills during organized practices.

Thoughts for Parents

Many of you will become parents and may one day be asked to coach your child's team. Most mistakes by youth-sport coaches are caused by using coaching methods developed for use with adult players (often from their own playing days) that may not be appropriate for younger players. We need to think about long-term motivation and skill development. Every study has clearly shown that the number one reason to participate is to have *fun*, followed closely by improving one's skills. For every individual who developed into an expert, the early phase of learning was fun. Although each child enters sport with different skills, knowledge of the game, and maturational status, they all desire to learn and improve. As our studies have shown, all the children practiced to improve and would have practiced even more if they had the equipment and space. The biggest problems related to long-term skill development are expecting skilled performance too quickly, emphasizing winning to the detriment of long-term motivation and learning, and criticizing errors when often the mistake is not the child's fault (i.e., never practicing decision making).

For those who aspire to raise the next expert in a given area, I suggest you read Bloom's book on developing talent. You may rethink your aspirations when you understand the sacrifices each of the families made to develop the talent of one child. There were sacrifices related to finances, time, energy, family activities, and often the attention and resources devoted to other children within the family.

Concluding Thoughts

I have been very fortunate over the years to have worked with many talented colleagues. Colleagues, from graduate school at

Louisiana State University (Jerry Thomas, Richard Magill, Sue McPherson), have been instrumental in developing many of my ideas over the years. One person cannot carry out this type of field research without assistance. I have been blessed by the support and assistance of graduate students and fellow faculty members at the University of South Carolina. John Spurgeon (University of South Carolina) and Michael Nevett (University of Alabama) played major roles in the studies reported in this chapter. In addition, none of this work would have been possible without the cooperation of hundreds of parents and players who gave freely of their time. Sometimes research can be scary for coaches because the results have evaluative implications. Gaining cooperation from league officials, parents, coaches, and children can be a challenge sometimes. Much of the knowledge gained from any study must be credited to the participants of the research.

I promised myself a long time ago that I would always *choose* a career that I enjoyed. When it was no longer fun, I would find something else to do. I hope you will make the same choice. Research is fun and a challenge. The rewards are not immediate. The research process is very slow. The big picture emerges slowly from the findings over a series of studies. Considerable progress toward understanding transitions from novice to elite performance has been made during the past ten years. Hopefully, future research will provide more of the pieces and insight into the kinds of instruction that facilitate every child's sport performance.

Suggested Readings

Bloom, B.S. (Ed.). (1985). *Developing talent in young people.* New York: Ballentine Books.

Ericcson, K.A., Krampe, R.T., & Tesch-Romer, C. (1993). The role of deliberate practice in the acquisition of expert performance. *Psychological Review, 100,* 363–406.

French, K.E., Nevett, M.E., Spurgeon, J.H., Graham, K.G., Rink, J.E., & McPherson, S.L. (1996). Knowledge representation and problem solution in expert and novice youth baseball players. *Research Quarterly for Exercise and Sport, 67,* 386–395.

French, K.E., Spurgeon, J.H., & Nevett, M.E. (1995). Expert-novice differences in cognitive and skill execution components of youth baseball performance. *Research Quarterly for Exercise and Sport, 66,* 194–201.

Helsen, W. & Pauwels, J.M. (1993). The relationship between expertise and visual information processing in sport. In J.L. Starkes & F. Allard (Eds.), *Cognitive issues in motor expertise.* (pp. 109–134). Amsterdam: Elsevier.

McPherson, S.L. (1994). The development of sport expertise: Mapping the tactical domain. *Quest, 46,* 223–240.

Starkes, J.L., & Allard, F. (Eds.). (1993). *Cognitive issues in motor expertise.* Amsterdam: Elsevier.

Thomas, J.R., French, K.E., & Humphries, C.A. (1986). Knowledge development and sport skill performance: Directions for motor behavior research. *Journal of Sport Psychology, 8,* 259–272.

Chapter **2**

Movement Preparation: The Role of Attention and Cognitive Strategies

Craig A. Wrisberg

          Craig A. Wrisberg is a Professor of Sport Psychology in the Cultural Studies Unit in the College of Education at the University of Tennessee, Knoxville. Dr. Wrisberg is past president of the North American Society for the Psychology of Sport and Physical Activity and a fellow of the American Academy of Kinesiology and Physical Education. Since 1985, he has also supervised the provision of mental training services for athletes in the Departments of Men's and Women's Athletics at the University of Tennessee. Dr. Wrisberg has served on the editorial board of the *Research Quarterly for Exercise and Sport* and is a regular invited reviewer for the *Sport Psychologist,* the *Journal of Sport and Exercise Psychology,* and the *Journal of Motor Behavior.* He has written over sixty publications in the areas of anticipation and timing performance, knowledge of results and motor learning, warm-up decrement in sport performance, and the quality of life of male and female athletes. Living less than 50 miles from the Great Smoky Mountains, he enjoys canoeing, hiking, jogging, and tennis.

I was introduced to sports and games at an early age. Growing up in St. Louis, my childhood dream was one day to play professional baseball for the Cardinals. My father (who actually rooted more for the old St. Louis Browns than he did for the Cardinals) taught my younger brothers and me how to throw, catch, and hit a baseball at about the same time that we were learning how to walk. As an athlete, my father possessed modest physical skills but was fiercely competitive and had a keen sense of the mental nuances of sport. Consequently, he schooled his sons on the importance of the "mental edge" in competition almost as much as he helped us develop our physical skills. One of the first "mental tips" I remember my father giving me is probably the one I have used the most during my own competitive sport experiences. "Regardless of who your opponents may be," my father would say, "watch carefully for the things they seem to do the best and then try to make them do something else." As I look back on it now, I realize that my father's mental approach to sport competition emphasized the two aspects of movement preparation that I have spent much of my career as a sport scientist investigating—attentional focus and cognitive strategies.

After graduating from high school I entered Greenville College, a private liberal arts institution in southern Illinois, where I proceeded to explore several academic majors before finally settling on physical education. My baseball coach, Robert Smith, who was also a faculty member in the physical education department and a person I greatly admired, convinced me that my professional future was too important to settle for something that wasn't going to be fun. Since the prospect of playing baseball for the Cardinals was by this time remote, I decided that teaching high school physical education and coaching baseball might be an enjoyable alternative. However, that plan evaporated during the last semester of my senior year when I did my student teaching internship at a nearby high school. Suffice it to say, the experience convinced me that trying to teach high school students was something I might not survive, much less enjoy, for any length of time.

Thus, I embarked on a course of action that has always been popular with college graduates who are not yet prepared for life in the real world—I entered graduate school. Interestingly, my decision was made with no more than a few weeks left in my senior year of college. I was sitting in the office of the athletic director when a friend of his came in. The friend was an associate dean at Indiana State University who was prepared to offer a graduate teaching assistantship in physical education to a qualified student. At that point, the athletic director turned to me and said "What are *you* doing next year, Craig?" When I replied, "I'm not really sure," he said "Would you like to go to graduate school?" Without giving it much thought, I responded, "I guess so." Within minutes I had accepted the assistantship and started thinking about the move to Terre Haute.

While I had been exposed to a rigorous curriculum during my undergraduate degree program, taking classes had, for me, been an exercise in information absorption rather than critical inquiry. However, in graduate school I came face to face with the rigors of the scientific method and learned how it could be used to study the effects of exercise on the body. I was particularly intrigued by the subject matter in exercise physiology. My coursework was stimulating and, outside of the classroom, I began to read some of the published research exploring the mechanisms of physical activity. It became clear to me that graduate school was not about the absorption and regurgitation of textbook information but about the critical analysis of experimental literature. If I wanted to say something in class I was expected to provide supporting rationale and documentation for my arguments. For the first time in my life, I genuinely enjoyed being a student and was convinced that I had found my niche.

With the encouragement of my major professor, Robert McDavid, I completed a master's thesis exploring the energy costs of various physical education activities. I then applied for admission to the doctoral program in exercise physiology at the University of Michigan, which also happened to be McDavid's alma mater. I was admitted, but soon after was drafted and spent the next two years in the U.S. Army. Upon completing my term of military service, I arrived in Ann Arbor in December, 1970, where, once again, I experienced a chain of events that radically altered the course of my career preparation.

During my master's degree program, I had focused on the experimental literature dealing with the physiological effects of movement activity on humans. At Michigan, a more basic scientific model was in place and much of the research going on there was being conducted with animals. For a variety of reasons, this orientation was less appealing to me and, after several unsatisfying experiences, I decided to explore alternative subject matter. Among the classes in which I enrolled was one taught by Richard Schmidt on the topic of motor learning. Although I didn't realize it at the time, Schmidt had already made his mark on the field of motor behavior and was, over the next two decades, to become one of the pivotal figures in the evolving field of motor learning and control. I was immediately captured by Schmidt's teaching style and by the subject matter in motor behavior. At that time, the field of experimental psychology was dominated by information processing approaches to the study of human behavior. In the subdiscipline of motor behavior, it was assumed that much of human movement was accompanied by purposive attentional and cognitive activity that included a search of the environment for relevant information and the determination of appropriate plans of action. In an interesting way, this reminded me of some of the points my father had emphasized during our conversations about sport competition. *Pay attention to what's going on around you and then think about the things you need to do to achieve success.*

I began to realize that, while my brief experience in the domain of exercise physiology had served to open my eyes to the power of the scientific process, it had not satisfied my desire to understand the psychological mechanisms underlying human motor behavior. Near the end of my first year at Michigan, I informed Dick Schmidt (he preferred for his students to call him by his first name) that I was thinking about switching my program of study to motor behavior and asked him if he would consider becoming my major professor. He said he thought I should give the matter further consideration in order to be sure that I felt the same way after a week or so. In short, I did, and when I shared this with Schmidt, he agreed to add me to the ranks of his graduate students. In retrospect, I believe this was the most significant decision I made during my educational preparation.

Dick Schmidt was a model mentor for graduate students. He exposed us to the most recent thinking in our field, challenged us to build a strong case for our arguments, and actively involved us in all phases of the research process. My initial collaboration with him was in a laboratory experiment designed to test the activity-set hypothesis for warm-up decrement that he and one of his former students, Jacques Nacson, had proposed. A common occurrence in many motor-skill situations is the appearance of a temporary lull in performance (referred to as warm-up decrement) following a brief rest period. A sport example might be a double fault by a tennis player during the first service point following a change of sides. Nacson and Schmidt reasoned that warm-up decrement was due to maladaptive adjustments in underlying support systems (e.g., arousal level, attentional focus, expectancies for certain events) that occurred during a rest period. They hypothesized that warm-up decrement should be reduced or eliminated if participants engaged in activities, interpolated at the end of a rest interval, that served to readjust support systems to levels that were appropriate for resumed task performance. In our experiment, Schmidt and I found that participants who only rested during a brief break in the performance of a rapid, preferred-hand arm movement displayed a typical pattern of postrest warm-up decrement while those who rested and then briefly engaged in an activity that had requirements similar to those of the criterion task (e.g., rapid movement with the nonpreferred hand), demonstrated no postrest decrement.

This research whetted my appetite for further investigation of the role of preparatory activity on subsequent motor performance. For my doctoral dissertation, I performed another test of the activity-set hypothesis in order to determine whether appropriate rest interval activities could reduce or eliminate warm-up decrement in tasks that were not highly practiced (i.e., those in which only a small number of practice trials were given). The experimental task I chose to use was the linear positioning apparatus which was popular with investigators that conducted motor short-term memory experiments during the 1970s. A small carriage comprised of a magnesium plate and ball-bearing bushings was mounted on parallel metal rods that were attached by supports to a wooden base (see Figure 2.1). By gripping a plastic handle attached to the carriage, blindfolded participants were able to make a slow, smooth movement to a target position that was defined by a stop peg which was inserted in the path of the carriage by the experimenter. Following a rest interval, the stop peg was removed and the participant was asked to return the carriage to the previously-defined position. The results of my

Figure 2.1 Front View of a participant operating the linear positioning apparatus with the right and left hands.

dissertation revealed that warm-up decrement in the recall of a right-hand limb position was the same for a group of participants that performed an appropriate warm-up activity (i.e., left-hand positioning movements) as it was for a control group that performed no warm-up activity. Thus, it appeared that for movements which are not highly practiced, warm-up decrement is not reduced or eliminated by performing relevant warming-up activities.

While this finding provided additional clarification of the warm-up decrement phenomenon, it was not the most important outcome of my dissertation. In the two experiments that comprised the dissertation, blindfolded participants were given 12 and 10 trials, respectively, in which the same right-hand limb position was presented. In the first experiment, participants were not made aware that the location of the position would be the same on all trials, while in the second experiment they were told that the location "may or may not be the same" from trial to trial. In neither experiment was information regarding participants' accuracy of limb positioning given by the experimenter. In spite of these rather impoverished feedback conditions, all groups improved both the accuracy and consistency of their positioning movements over trials. These results were consistent with the then popular notion that humans were active information processors who attempted to devise mental strategies for accomplishing tasks even when very little sensory information was available.

Following the completion of my doctoral degree, I accepted a faculty position at Virginia Tech where I was asked to design and teach courses in motor behavior and develop a laboratory for the investigation of factors influencing the learning and control of motor skills. During the 1970s, motor behavior was a booming area and many universities with programs in physical education were adding faculty and coursework in motor learning and sport psychology. The first experiment I conducted in the new lab at Virginia Tech was a collaborative effort with one of my colleagues, Martin Pushkin, who also happened to be the track and field coach. In this experiment, we utilized a reaction-time paradigm which allowed us to examine the effects of mental preparation strategies on the production of rapid movements.

We attempted to determine whether reaction time for a simple (linear) movement and a complex (multidirectional) movement was influenced by different mental preparation activities. For both types of movements, participants were instructed to focus mentally either on the upcoming stimulus (an auditory tone) or on the to-be-executed movement (simple or complex). The results revealed that, for the simple movement, reaction time was significantly shorter when participants focused on the upcoming movement than when they focused on the upcoming stimulus. However, for the complex movement, no difference in reaction time was found as a function of preparatory focus. Thus, we concluded that performers who prepare for a movement by mentally focusing on its mechanics react more slowly as the movement becomes increasingly more complex. Our results also seemed to be consistent with the popular notion in sport psychology that for the execution of more complicated motor skills, participants should adopt a "let it happen" focus rather than one that entails an analysis of the mechanical properties of the movement.

Among my early faculty experiences was the initial opportunity to mentor a doctoral student. Charles Shea was an eager scholar who was extremely interested in learning as much as he could about the field of motor behavior and the process of scholarly inquiry. During the three years that I was on the faculty at Virginia Tech, Charlie and I collaborated on several studies exploring shifts in attention demands and motor program utilization which occur during the course of motor-skill learning. In what I believe was our most significant experiment, participants were given extensive practice on a primary task that involved a ballistic movement of the right hand a distance of 86 cm from a start position to a hinged target. On each trial, participants attempted to strike the target at the exact moment that a sweep hand on a 1-second timer completed a single revolution and returned to the 12 o'clock position. Striking the target caused the sweep hand to stop, thus providing visual feedback regarding the amount and direction of timing error.

A secondary task required the left-hand depression of a reaction key in response to an auditory stimulus (termed a probe stimulus) that was presented at various points before, during, and after the primary task movement. Control groups performed either the primary or secondary task in isolation while a dual-task group performed both tasks on each trial. The results revealed that the attention demands of the primary task (assessed by comparing secondary task reaction times for the experimental group to those of controls) decreased significantly over the four days of practice. However, during all trials, attention demands were found to be significantly higher when the probe stimulus was presented immediately prior to movement initiation than when it occurred at other points in the movement. Thus, while it was clear that the control of a discrete, ballistic, timing movement required less attention over extended practice, it was also obvious that more attention was devoted to the movement preparation phase than to other parts of the movement. Our results indicated that participants were involved in some form of cognitive activity during the moments prior to execution. The question was "what?"

In 1977, I was invited to apply for a faculty position at the University of Tennessee. After an enjoyable interview, I was offered the position and decided to accept it. Upon arriving in Knoxville, my research focus shifted to the examination of practice structure effects on the acquisition, retention, and transfer of motor skills. A paradigm shift had occurred in the field of motor behavior and most of the researchers in the prominent motor behavior laboratories at that time were investigating the role of practice structure in motor learning. However, it also seemed to me that if the movement preparation period represented an important interval for mental operations, as most of the research I had conducted up to that point seemed to suggest, then it might be assumed that practice conditions which influenced those operations would also have an effect on the performance and learning of a motor task.

Stimulated again by the theorizing of my former major professor, Dick Schmidt, I conducted several studies that tested the variability of practice hypothesis, which was a key feature of Schmidt's schema theory of discrete motor skill learning. According to this hypothesis, learners who practice a variety of movements during skill acquisition should demonstrate superior learning compared to that of persons who repeatedly practice a single movement. The theoretical rationale for Schmidt's prediction was that varied practice presumably enhanced the development of a generalized motor program that the learner could then flexibly apply to future situations requiring similar types of movements.

In a series of studies with several colleagues and graduate students at Tennessee, I tested Schmidt's hypothesis by using a laboratory task in which participants viewed a light pattern that was produced by the sequential illumination of a linear series of runway lamps. During training trials, participants practiced under conditions of either low or high stimulus variability (i.e., a single stimulus velocity was presented across trials or an equal number of trials were given with each of four different velocities) and either low or high response requirements (i.e., participants merely viewed the light pattern or they attempted to depress a response key with the nonpreferred hand at the same moment that the last lamp on the runway illuminated).

Following training, all participants were given transfer trials in which they viewed a stimulus velocity that had not been previously presented and then attempted to "time" its arrival by depressing the response key with their preferred hand at the precise moment the target lamp was illuminating. The results indicated that the transfer performance of persons who had experienced higher levels of *both* stimulus variability *and* response requirements during training was significantly more accurate than that of participants in the other combinations of training conditions. Thus, partial support was produced for Schmidt's variability of practice hypothesis. However, since superior transfer only occurred when high-stimulus variability during training was accompanied by the requirement to produce a response, we concluded that the mental operations associated with the *act of movement preparation* were an important component of motor skill practice. Once again, it appeared that the movement preparation period was a crucial aspect of motor performance and learning. The challenge now seemed to be one of determining the types of mental preparation activities that were most appropriate for the performance of various types of motor tasks.

About that time, another serendipitous event shifted the emphasis of my teaching and research in a more applied direction. The head women's volleyball coach at Tennessee asked for my permission to sit in on my graduate course in sport psychology. Since I thought it would be good for my students to hear a practitioner's perspective on the concepts we were talking about, I approved his request and welcomed him to the group. From the initial class period that semester, it was clear to me that this coach was very interested in the practical application of many of the theories we were discussing. He regularly reminded the class that, at the collegiate level, the primary determinant of the outcome of sports competition was the mental preparation of athletes. Most athletes, he would say, have refined their physical skills to a high level and, therefore, what separates the best from the good is what he called "the mental edge."

Throughout that semester, this coach engaged me in a number of out-of-class conversations and "grilled" me as to what I thought were the best methods for mentally preparing athletes for competitive situations. At the conclusion of the semester, he asked me if I would be willing to meet with his team to discuss mental preparation techniques and strategies. I told him that I had had no prior sport psychology consultation experience and that I couldn't promise anything but that I would do the best I could. What ensued was a working arrangement that I found to be both enlightening and challenging. During periodic team sessions, the players would share with me the thoughts and emotions they experienced during their competitive experiences, both good and bad. Before too long, it was clear to me that, among other things, the thoughts that occupied athletes' minds prior to important moments in competition had a significant influence on their subsequent performance.

About that time I became aware that the experimental paradigms I had been using to examine questions dealing with the performance and learning of movements under highly-controlled laboratory conditions might also be appropriate for the examination of factors that influence the performance of sport tasks in ecologically-valid environments. For several years I had regularly attended motor behavior conferences that included the presentation of papers in both the areas of motor learning/control and sport psychology. However, there seemed to be an implicit assumption at those meetings that scholars in motor learning/control had nothing of interest to say to scholars in sport psychology and vice versa. Now, for the first time in my professional life, I began seriously to question that assumption.

Soon after this, I received a letter from Mark Anshel who was a colleague in motor behavior from New Mexico State University. In his correspondence, Mark informed me that he had just accepted a position at the University of Wollongong and would shortly be moving to New South Wales, Australia. For some time, Mark and I had shared an interest in the movement preparation issue and now he asked me if I would be receptive to doing some collaborative research with him in order to explore the efficacy of various types of warm-up activities on the sport performance of athletes.

The timing of Mark's letter could not have been better. Not only had my recent experiences with the women's volleyball team at Tennessee whetted my appetite for applied research, but financial support for many research programs at the University of Tennessee was beginning to wane, making it increasingly obvious that the Motor Behavior Laboratory would not be acquiring the kind of state-of-the-art technology that was becoming increasingly important for the types of basic experiments in motor control and learning that I had previously been doing. Needless to say, I eagerly accepted Mark's offer and embarked on what has since become a most satisfying program of collaborative scholarship.

In all of our research, Mark and I have employed the warm-up decrement paradigm to which I was initially introduced by Dick Schmidt during my doctoral program at Michigan. Interestingly, if we had looked to the field of sport psychology for a paradigm to do our research, we might still be looking. Fortunately, the one we "borrowed" from motor control/learning was ideally suited for the study of an issue of vital importance to all high-performance athletes—adequate movement preparation. In each of our experiments, Mark and I have sought to determine the impact of a variety of warm-up activities in reducing postrest warm-up decrement. Participants are given a number of trials of a well-learned, sport task in order to determine their baseline levels of performance. Once this is done they are given a brief rest period of 5 to 7 minutes.

Near the end of the rest period, participants either continue resting or they briefly engage in a designated warm-up activity that is either relevant or irrelevant to the sport task. Immediately after this, all participants perform additional trials of the sport task. In all of our experiments, the classical warm-up decrement phenomenon (i.e., diminished postrest performance compared to baseline levels that usually lasts for 3 or 4 trials) has been observed for control and irrelevant warm-up activity participants. On the other hand, participants performing relevant warm-up activities have demonstrated differing levels of diminished warm-up decrement, with the performance of some showing no decrement at all.

Over the past 8 years, we have found that warm-up activities which serve to increase the arousal level of performers (e.g., running in place or riding a stationary bicycle), simulate the motor plan and proprioceptive feel of the sport task (e.g., practice swings or eye-hand coordination activities), or provide mental images of relevant task characteristics (e.g., a baseball batter's image of the ball in the pitcher's hand or the moment of bat-ball contact) are the most effective in reducing postrest warm-up decrement. Consistent with contemporary thought in sport psychology, our results have consistently suggested support for the notion that successful performance preparation is most often characterized by increased emotional intensity and a task focus that is *process-oriented*. That is, the participant's attention and cognitive strategies are directed to an energizing of the body for activity and to cues and behaviors that contribute to effective movement production, regardless of the environmental circumstances under which the movement is performed.

In our most recent study, we tested the hypothesis that warm-up activity must not only be relevant to primary task performance but must also create a positive focus that reminds participants of behaviors they should attempt to *do* upon performance resumption rather than behaviors they should attempt to *avoid doing*. It is common for sport psychology practitioners to encourage athletes to prepare mentally for task performance by focusing on positive, performance-relevant things they intend to do. In our study we compared the postrest warm-up decrement of advanced field hockey participants who reviewed a list of relevant *positively-worded* performance reminders (e.g., "keep my head down and watch the ball") at the end of a rest period with that of participants who reviewed a list of relevant but *negatively-phrased* reminders (e.g., "avoid using awkward foot, body, and grip positions"), as well as that of participants who engaged in nonrelevant warm-up activity (e.g., reading from a field hockey manual). Our results revealed an absence of warm-up decrement for the relevant positive-reminders group in both the accuracy of the field hockey penalty shot and the mechanics of the shot (as assessed by expert judges' ratings). However, classical patterns of warm-up decrement were found for the other two groups on both measures. While further study is warranted to determine the extent to which these results are generalizable to other sport activities, our findings provide the first empirical substantiation of the notion that mental preparation activities which encourage a focus that is *both* positive and performance-relevant facilitate subsequent movement execution.

When athletes are asked about the thoughts and feelings that accompany their best performances, they usually report things like a narrow focus of attention, a feeling of being in complete control, a focus on the present, a positive attitude, an expectation of success, a sense of inner calm, and a feeling of total immersion in the activity. An important assumption underlying the concept of mental training for sport performance is that the systematic practice of appropriate mental preparation activities should allow participants to experience peak performance on a more consistent basis. The results of my research over the past 23 years clearly indicate that the nature and substance of movement preparation activities has an impact on subsequent motor performance. Future longitudinal research in applied settings should begin to reveal the extent to which the development and implementation of appropriate mental plans contributes to consistently successful athletic performance in a variety of sport settings.

What is particularly exciting for me today is the fact that the research I am doing represents more than an interesting intellectual exercise. Rather, it stems from questions that arise during the course of my consultations with athletes and coaches. For, as it turned out, my experience with the women's volleyball team eventually led to an opportunity to consult with the men's basketball team. Then, in 1992, I was asked by the Men's Athletic Director to submit a proposed plan for the systematic provision of mental training services for all intercollegiate sport teams at the University of Tennessee. The proposal was subsequently completed and approved and, since that time, my duties have been expanded to include the provision of mental training services for all athletes and coaches in the Departments of Men's and Women's Athletics as well as the supervision of graduate students in sport psychology who are seeking practicum opportunities with high-performance athletes.

Not only are these students gaining valuable consultation experiences during their program of studies, but they are realizing first-hand the vital connection between research and practice. Problems they confront during their consultation experiences are explored in group discussion and some become research questions that are examined in subsequent projects. Most importantly, students at Tennessee are challenged to identify the *connections* between bodies of knowledge and the potential usefulness of experimental paradigms in the various disciplines that comprise departments of exercise and movement science, particularly the areas of motor learning/control and sport psychology.

When I was in graduate school, I was often told that, for people to make a name for themselves in the research literature, they must identify a particular topic and then conduct a long line of experiments that converge on answers to the important questions in that area. As I reflect on my 23 years of research, I don't believe that this is the approach I have taken. There were times when I chose to conduct an experiment chiefly because it was in line with what other prominent investigators in the field were doing at the moment: thinking that such experiments had a better chance of being published. Obviously, some of these choices were driven more by the need to achieve tenure and promotion or to obtain merit pay increases than by an intrinsic interest in the research question. In spite of this, what I have come to realize during the writing of this chapter is that the majority of studies I have conducted and published throughout my career have focused in some fashion on the common theme of movement preparation. The findings of those studies have led me to the conclusion that the *act of preparing for movement* is a significant activity at all stages of motor skill practice and that this activity is most beneficial when it serves to activate the emotions of participants and direct their attention to positive, performance-relevant cues. Upon final reflection, I find it interesting and in some ways fitting that my scholarly activity has essentially represented a systematic examination of several themes associated with mental preparation for sport performance that were conveyed to me long ago by my dad: Carefully assess the situation and then devise a plan for success.

Suggested Readings

Anshel, M.H., & Wrisberg, C.A. (1988). The effect of arousal and focused attention on warm-up decrement. *Journal of Sport Behavior, 11,* 18–31.

Anshel, M.H., & Wrisberg, C.A. (1993). Reducing warm-up decrement in the performance of the tennis serve. *Journal of Sport and Exercise Psychology, 15,* 290–303.

Keele, S.W. (1973). *Attention and human performance.* Pacific Palisades, CA: Goodyear.

Orlick, T. (1990). *In pursuit of excellence*. Champaign, IL: Human Kinetics.

Orlick, T., & Partington, J. (1988). Mental links to excellence. *The Sport Psychologist, 2*, 105–130.

Schmidt, R.A., & Wrisberg, C.A. (1971). The activity-set hypothesis for warm-up decrement in a movement-speed task. *Journal of Motor Behavior, 3*, 318–325.

Wrisberg, C.A. (1974). *Interference and warm-up factors in motor short-term memory*. Unpublished doctoral dissertation, University of Michigan, Ann Arbor.

Wrisberg, C.A., & Anshel, M.H. (1989). The effect of cognitive strategies on the free throw shooting performance of young athletes. *The Sport Psychologist, 3*, 95–104.

Wrisberg, C.A., & Anshel, M.H. (1993). A field test of the activity-set hypothesis for warm-up decrement in an open skill. *Research Quarterly for Exercise and Sport, 64*, 39–45.

Wrisberg, C.A., & Anshel, M.H. (1997). The use of positively-worded performance reminders to reduce warm-up decrement in the field hockey penalty shot. *Journal of Applied Sport Psychology, 9*, 229–240.

Wrisberg, C.A., & Pushkin, M.H. (1976). Preparatory set, response complexity, and reaction latency. *Journal of Motor Behavior, 8*, 203–207.

Wrisberg, C.A., & Ragsdale, M.R. (1979). Further tests of Schmidt's schema theory: Development of a schema rule for a coincident timing task. *Journal of Motor Behavior, 11*, 159–166.

Wrisberg, C.A., & Shea, C.H. (1978). Shifts in attention demands and motor program utilization during motor learning. *Journal of Motor Behavior, 10*, 149–158.

Chapter 3

The Achieving Personality: From Anxiety to Confidence in Sport

Robin S. Vealey

Robin S. Vealey is a professor in the Department of Physical Education, Health, and Sport Studies at Miami University in Ohio. Dr. Vealey has published two books and over 30 articles and book chapters, and has presented over 90 professional lectures nationally as well as internationally in the areas of self-confidence, competitive anxiety, coaching effectiveness, and mental training in sport. She has worked as a consultant for the U.S. Nordic Ski Team, U.S. Field Hockey, various elite-level golfers, and athletes and teams at Miami University and in the Cincinnati area. Dr. Vealey has served as Editor of *The Sport Psychologist*, is a National Instructor for the American Sport Education Program, and received the 1995 Australian Sport Psychology Award. She has been recognized as a certified consultant and fellow of the Association for the Advancement of Applied Sport Psychology. A former intercollegiate basketball player and coach, Dr. Vealey now enjoys golf, reading, fitness activities, travel, and her work.

January, 1976, Bowling Green, Ohio

I stood at the free-throw line all alone waiting for the referee to hand me the ball—I had been here before. In spending many hours working on my shooting in our driveway as I grew up, I had often envisioned myself in just this situation. I was a senior playing for a Division I college basketball team. I was also the captain, leading scorer and rebounder, and the best free-throw shooter on the team. My team was down one point to the opponent. There was no time left on the clock. I had been fouled while driving to the basket and now stood at the free-throw line with a one plus one opportunity. If I made the first shot, I would tie the score and we would at least go into overtime. Also, if I made the first shot, I would get a second shot, and if I made *that* one, I would win the game for my team. Perfect. . . the stars had aligned to provide this golden opportunity for me—the opportunity I had wished for since I was a small child dreaming big dreams in my driveway. But quite unexpectedly, my mind began to race with worrisome thoughts about failing, looking bad, and letting down my teammates. I told myself not to act nervous, but I was keenly aware that I was more nervous than I had ever been and that my right arm felt frozen and stiff. The referee handed me the ball. . . I shot quickly—too quickly—in my attempt to act as if this was a routine experience for me. I missed the shot badly—the ball clanged off the front right side of the rim. The opposing team exploded into joyous shouts of victory, and I walked off the floor to the locker-room with my teammates patting me and telling me that it was okay.

November, 1979, Nampa, Idaho

I stood on the sideline and said a small prayer ("Please, God, don't let us be embarrassed") as I watched the team I coached take the floor for the Northwest Region Small College Volleyball Championship match. The winner of the match would automatically qualify for the National Tournament in Los Angeles—a glamorous prize and seemingly unattainable objective for our team. We were huge underdogs. We had beaten our arch-rival in the semi-final match and my players had celebrated deliriously, as this rival team had beaten us twice during the regular season. The semi-final victory had *made* the tournament for us. The team we knew we would face in the final was so much better than all the other teams in the tournament that it was a fait accompli that they would be crowned champions. However, we had scouted the team extensively and put together a solid game plan. My players were loose and relaxed, even though I had to start a freshman in place of my best front line player who was injured in the semi-final match. Then, a funny thing happened—we won the match. Everyone was stunned—the crowd, the opposing players, my players, and, most of all, me. It was one of those extremely rare occasions when an entire team plays almost perfectly. Each player performed flawlessly and most performed beyond what I had assessed as their ultimate potential. It was the greatest example of peak performance that I had ever witnessed—and as the coach of the team I had absolutely no idea how or why it had happened nor how I might attempt to make it happen again.

I have a passion for sport psychology. As far back as I can remember, I've loved sport and the thrill of competition. I love the excitement and nervous anticipation prior to competing, and I firmly believe that the feelings I've experienced from competition (e.g., winning important championships, making the big shot to win the game, sliding into home under the catcher's tag to score the winning run) are more intoxicating than any drug I could ever take. Throughout my development as a player and then as a coach, I became entranced with the mental side of sport. Even as a child, I always picked out the most intense, mentally-tough players as my favorites and I remember wondering why other players lacked intensity and confidence and mental toughness.

The two scenarios described previously contributed heavily toward my decision to begin graduate work in sport psychology. As a player, I never thought I would choke in a pressure situation. It was a rude awakening for me, and I began to realize for the first time that sometimes my passion and intensity weren't enough. In fact, I realized that sometimes my passion and intensity worked against me! In retrospect, just a little bit of specific sport psychology knowledge would have helped me—take your time and follow your routine, a slow deep cleansing breath to relax physically, repetition of a key trigger thought ("soft over the rim"), and a nice visual and kinesthetic image of the perfect shot. Bingo—intoxication! Unfortunately, it was instead embarrassment and depression. If a genie ever gives me a chance to do one thing over, I would definitely shoot that free throw again.

The scenario I described as a coach is the reason I left coaching. Riding home on the bus from that championship victory, I pondered the incredible power that I had witnessed within my team. It was a total team flow experience as described by Mihalyi Csikszentmihalyi—I never had any other team come close to achieving so near its maximum potential.

The players could describe how they felt, but were unsure why it had happened and did not feel that they could conjure up that level of performance and focus again at will. It made me think. . . perhaps we're being too haphazard about this. Maybe we can "push the envelope" actually to control or at least pursue the achievement of one's potential. I knew I had to study it. I entered the University of Illinois the following August to begin doctoral work toward a Ph.D. in sport psychology. I was in search of the achieving personality.

In Search of the Achieving Personality

The purpose of this chapter is to describe my personal journey as researcher, teacher, and consultant in the field of sport psychology. I chose the title "Achieving Personality" because it best describes my interests and the driving motivation behind the different types of research and writing in which I engage as a sport psychology professional. I am interested in the personal characteristics of individuals that enable them to pursue and achieve excellence in a manner that sets them apart from other people. Why do some people persist and continue to work harder in the face of numerous obstacles? Why do some people have the self-discipline to forego short-term gratification and seek out significant and meaningful long-term rewards? What is it about certain athletes that allows them to shine at just the right moment while other athletes wilt under the pressure of expectations? What are the necessary ingredients to develop and maintain an achieving personality? Are those ingredients the same for everyone and, if so, can they be taught and learned? Or is the achieving personality hard-wired in through genetic programming and early socialization experiences? These questions were all in my mind as I began my graduate career in the field of sport psychology.

I describe my journey based on what I view as the five developmental stages through which people go in their pursuit of knowledge through research. The first stage is *Naive Engagement,* which is where I was upon entering graduate school in the fall of 1980. It's an exciting stage because you are filled with wonder and curiosity about your chosen area of study. The second stage I call *Research Reality,* which involves the slow realization that realistically it is very hard to answer those exciting questions generated in the Naive Engagement stage, due to the extreme difficulty in measuring psychological phenomena. As I will discuss, this stage is crucial as many people become cynical about the nature of research at this point and decide to do something else. However, those individuals who view this as a personal challenge move on to the next stage. (Isn't it interesting that the achieving personality becomes a factor here as it weeds out those who wish to study it? We are what we study, don't you think?)

I like to call the third stage *Surfing the Mainstream*. Typically, young researchers lack the conceptual and empirical abilities to do anything except become immersed in the mainstream culture of research and catch the latest wave in the form of the current hot topic or zeitgeist in the field. I do not view this as a bad thing; rather, it is a rite of passage and perhaps even a necessary step to experience the mainstream before you can ever envision leaving it. The idea of leaving it occurs with stage four, which is *Personal and Professional Dissonance*. It is my opinion that those who truly want to know in the scientific sense must reach and traverse this stage. The dissonance refers to a growing realization that the Naive Engagement stage perhaps wasn't so naive and maybe you've been too preoccupied catching mainstream waves to remember why you wanted to study sport psychology in the first place. This leads to the final stage, *Meaningful Engagement*, which is the peak of professional life and personal fulfillment. Am I there? I'm not sure, but at least I know that I'm working to get there.

September, 1980, Champaign, Illinois

As she handed me her completed questionnaire, the volleyball player smiled at me and said, "Boy, those are some interesting questions. I really had to think about it." She had just participated in a research study I was conducting as part of the requirements for my first graduate course in sport psychology. When the professor, Dr. Glyn Roberts, explained the assignment, I panicked a bit as I had no clue how to conduct a research project. So I sat at home and started writing down questions that I thought were interesting. Glyn had emphasized the need to choose a simple question to pursue in this, our first research experience.

As a team-sport athlete, it always irritated me when coaches said "there is no I in team." As an athlete, I knew quite well that there was. Thus, my research question focused on the amount of satisfaction, pride, and perceived competence that athletes feel as a result of their team outcome *and* their individual performance. That is, who feels most satisfied, proud, and competent—athletes on winning teams who individually performed below average or athletes on losing teams who individually performed better than average? I smiled back at the volleyball player and beamed inside as her comment confirmed to me that I had asked an important question. In that moment, I knew I was heading for the first Nobel Prize awarded to a sport psychologist. I got a B– on the paper (close to a failing grade for a graduate student) and Glyn told me that I needed a better conceptual rationale and a crash course in statistics since I had totally blown the data analysis.

Naive Engagement

What I really like about my first research experience was that it was pure inquiry driven only by my interest in answering a question that I thought was very important. To this day, I believe that the results of that study (had I not "blown" the statistical analysis) were significant if only to explain to coaches that there *is* an I in team. Despite the statistical limitations of the paper, the results clearly indicated that athletes' overall degree of satisfaction was related to team outcome, but their pride and perceived competence was indelibly linked to their individual performances. In retrospect, I can see clear conceptual links with attribution theory, competence motivation theory, and achievement goal theory. It makes total sense that athletes develop and enhance their perceptions of competence and pride from their individual performance, which is much more personally controllable than team outcomes. However, it also makes sense that overall satisfaction is tempered by whether one's team wins or loses. Thus, it is entirely possible (and even warranted) to experience these seemingly contradictory responses which really are not contradictory at all. I believe coaches should acknowledge that athletes can still feel pride and confidence in their performance even if the team loses. But, as a responsible and committed team member, the team outcome of losing, of course, elicits dissatisfaction with the experience, and it is socially appropriate and desirable to demonstrate your solidarity with the team by expressing negative emotion.

I was excited about my results and I remember thinking that I was really going to like this research stuff. Although my grade on the paper somewhat tempered my enthusiasm, to Glyn's credit he met with me and lauded my research idea and my skill in developing a questionnaire to operationalize appropriately the constructs that I wanted to study. He explained that my conceptual and statistical prowess would develop as I matured as a scholar. I believed him, and his support and pep talk enhanced my motivation even more to study the achieving personality.

I remember fondly my time in the Naive Engagement stage. Also during my first semester of graduate school, part of my assistantship assignment was to work on the production of a youth sport coaches' newsletter called *Sportsline*. Although I spent many hours attaching mailing labels to hundreds and hundreds of newsletters, I also got to write a short article on developing confidence in children. I believed in the newsletter as a vehicle to disseminate practical knowledge to coaches throughout the state, and it sparked my interest in coaching education, in which I am still involved today.

November, 1980, Champaign, Illinois

It was well past midnight as I sat at my kitchen table with a stunned look on my face. Scattered across the table in front of me were stacks of various personality inventories measuring what I believed to be important dimensions of the achieving personality, such as self-confidence, intrinsic motivation, anxiety tendencies, self-esteem, self-concept, attributional style, attentional and interpersonal style, and competitiveness. These inventories had been completed by the members of the U.S. National Ice Hockey Team and my job was to take the information and compile a personality profile of each athlete. Our office had been commissioned to conduct this project so as to provide a baseline understanding of each athlete's personality characteristics in relation to competition so that intervention programs could be specifically tailored for them. Although held in strict confidentiality, the names of the athletes were written on the inventories so we could match them together to create the profiles. It was a name that had precipitated the stunned look on my face.

Nine months earlier, I sat in front of my television and watched this athlete with great admiration as he performed skillfully and courageously for the United States in the 1980 Winter Olympic Games. His outstanding performance and clutch play in no small part contributed to the "miracle on ice" as the underdog U.S. team beat the powerful Russians on their way to the gold medal in ice hockey. As I watched him play in the Olympics, I knew that he indeed possessed the achieving personality about which I was interested in knowing more. Nine months later, I sat in my kitchen and stared unbelievingly at the results in front of me. His profile was a disaster—on paper he possessed very few of the characteristics that I associated with the achieving personality. In fact, if you didn't know who this athlete was, you might take one look at his profile and decide that he was quite ill-suited for the competitive demands of elite sport.

Research Reality: Cynicism or Personal Challenge?

As a college professor and advisor of graduate students, I constantly observe students hitting the Research Reality stage. As defined previously, this stage is a bit of "paradise lost" because the wonderment of asking tantalizing questions generated in the Naive Engagement stage becomes tempered by the frustration of attempting to measure validly and reliably the constructs of interest. Many students become discouraged and/or cynical and leave the research field at this point. Although my first research experience described previously gave me a sense that things were going to be harder than I had anticipated, my experience in developing personality profiles for the U.S. Ice Hockey Team was the real milestone that jolted me into the Research Reality stage. I was dumbfounded with the realization that the best battery of sport psychological inventories that we could compile had a miserable predictive validity with regard to sport performance.

The next day, I reported my findings to my advisor, Dr. Rainer Martens. He listened calmly as I expressed my bewilderment and disillusionment with the profiling process. He then told me that he was not surprised with the results. He explained that when the National Team contacted him and asked him to oversee the profiling, he suggested to them that they may want to consider some other alternatives because, typically, profiling did not provide a great deal of useful information. The National Team officials insisted on the profiling, probably because the National Hockey League uses personality tests and believes that they provide useful information. Rainer explained to me that the problem was that most inventories developed in sport psychology were research tools developed to test and advance theory. They often provided little practical knowledge about individual athletes. He assured me that I would understand all of this much more next semester when I took his advanced graduate class in sport psychology.

Rainer was right. Upon reviewing the personality research published in the sport psychology literature, I reached several conclusions that influenced my future choices of research areas. No distinguishable "athletic personality" has been shown to exist, and I realized it was pretty certain that one would not appear in the future. There were no consistent research findings showing that athletes possess a general personality type distinct from the personality of nonathletes. Also, no consistent dispositional personality differences between athletic subgroups (e.g., team vs. individual sport athletes) have been shown to exist. Although some differences have been reported in the literature, the findings are inconsistent overall.

Was my idea of identifying and understanding the achieving personality a pipe dream? Maybe. But the literature provided some other interesting information. Success in sport seems to be facilitated by positive self-perceptions and productive cognitive strategies. The research indicated that successful athletes had greater self-confidence and ability to persist after setbacks than less successful athletes, and, while no differences were found between groups in trait anxiety, the successful athletes were much more skilled in coping and adapting to precompetitive anxiety. Also, we know a great deal about specific personality characteristics studied in research areas that have developed sound theoretical frameworks and valid measurement instrumentation (e.g., competitive anxiety). That is, researchers who have isolated and studied specific personality characteristics, such as competitive anxiety or self-esteem, have progressively developed a knowledge base in those areas.

Armed with this knowledge, I came out of the Research Reality stage with four professional objectives. First, I realized that I could not study the achieving personality in a totally integrated sense because no one set of characteristics had been supported as an achieving personality in sport. Thus, I began to move into the Surfing the Mainstream stage by hitching my wagon to the star of Rainer Martens and his work in the area of competitive anxiety. This seemed perfect for me to study as I had experienced anxiety as a player (remember?), and my casual observations over the years had convinced me that one of the most important attributes of the achieving personality was an athlete's ability to control and manage anxiety and pressure to stay focused on the task at hand. Second, I chose the area of self-confidence for my dissertation topic for the same reason—I knew it was one of the most important characteristics of the elusive achieving personality. I had begun to understand the wide scope of human thought, feeling, and behavior as well as the necessity of choosing small parts of the achieving personality to study. I believed that anxiety and confidence were two of the most integral parts to understanding achievement thoughts and feelings related to sport competition.

Third, I became extremely interested in psychometric research largely based on my previous frustration with available psychological inventories that assessed critical sport-specific personality or cognitive constructs. I also was totally intrigued by the challenge of psychometric research which is to develop a way to measure how humans think. Physical scientists attempt to interpret an object (e.g., liters of oxygen, roentgens of gamma rays), while social scientists interpret a subject or an interpretation (e.g., amount of self-esteem, level of self-confidence). To me, the ultimate intellectual challenge is to conceptualize theoretical models of human cognition, emotion, and behavior as well as to struggle with ways to operationalize human constructs from the models. It's not as intoxicating as those sport highs that I experienced, but it is very rewarding. As I will discuss in the next section, I became very involved with psychometric projects in both competitive anxiety and sport-specific self-confidence.

The fourth professional objective to which I committed in coming through the Research Reality stage was a focus on applied intervention work with coaches and athletes. Ironically, the Research Reality stage taught me that research was often divorced from practical application in sport psychology. The irony is that I thus bought into the research-practice gap that everyone spends so much time talking about bridging. Graduate school demonstrated to me that research and practice in sport psychology were quite disparate and at that time, in the early 1980s, applied work was not at all popular and even ridiculed. This was mainly due to the inferiority complex that the young field of sport psychology had at that time, and the field's need to follow the experimental psychology empirical paradigm to gain scientific respectability and prestige. Most sport psychologists had no interest in applied work as it threatened their standing as serious researchers. However, I had come to the field of sport psychology from an athlete-coach background, and I was clear about my objective of wanting to become involved in psychological skills training. Also, Rainer, as my advisor, was one of the pioneers in terms of offering intervention programs for athletes, and he was highly esteemed in the field based on his research accomplishments. I'm sure I would not have so vigorously pursued this objective without his sponsorship and support.

February, 1983, Urbana, Illinois

Drops of sweat splashed all over the paper as the nervous wrestler attempted to read and complete the questionnaire with the pencil bobbing in his shaking hand. As part of a research team developing an inventory to measure competitive-state anxiety (the Competitive State Anxiety Inventory-2 or CSAI-2), my colleagues and I were at a high school wrestling meet collecting field data. The CSAI-2 assesses how physically and cognitively anxious athletes are about the upcoming competition. It is a self-report measure, which means that athletes need to engage in honest self-assessment and then report this accurately and honestly on the form. This wrestler was in the holding area waiting for the current match on the center mat to conclude—his match was to fol-low immediately. Suddenly a sharp slap could be heard and the wrestler who was working on our questionnaire jumped a foot in the air and threw the half-completed paper form and pencil at me. The sound was the official slamming his hand on the mat to indicate that the match was over (one wrestler had been pinned by another, which ends the match immediately). I picked the sweat-soaked paper off the floor and to my dismay noted that this wrestler, who was a nervous wreck and who had jumped out of his skin at the sound of the match ending, had responded to every item on the CSAI-2 in a totally socially desirable manner (i.e., not at all nervous, totally confident, not concerned about my perfor-mance, etc.). In other words, he lied.

Surfing the Mainstream: Zeitgeists and Epistemopathology

After dealing with Research Reality, I now immersed my-self in Surfing the Mainstream. This is very typical of graduate students because we become engaged within the ongoing research program of our respective mentors. I was very fortunate to work for Rainer who was a highly esteemed researcher in the area of competitive anxiety. This re-search area was "hot" in the 1970s and 80s, thus my access to participa-tion in this zeitgeist or powerful research trend was helpful to my career. Much of my graduate school research experience was spent with Rainer and his other students developing a conceptual rationale and method-ological operationalization of competitive-state anxiety.

We developed the CSAI-2 based on emerging theory from general psychology that indicated that anxiety is multidimensional in nature. Multidimensional anxiety theory posits that anxiety is manifested in a cognitive component, including worry and self-rumination, as well as a somatic component comprised of bodily characteristics of nervousness, such as increased heart rate, profuse sweating, or muscle tension. Thus, cognitive and somatic anxiety reflect two independent systems of re-sponse to stressors. Prior to multidimensional anxiety theory, anxiety was measured in sport psychology research using unidimensional scales—the idea was that people score high or low on anxiety as a single construct. Multidimensional anxiety theory was intuitively appealing to me as I know I had experienced both cognitive and somatic anxiety and I be-lieved that they were separate and elicited by different precursors, as the theory suggested.

Our research program in this area involved 15 studies by the time we completed the project. I gained a deep appreciation for the multiphase approach to research, and gained valuable experience and knowledge as to the rigor involved in psychometric work. The CSAI-2 was originally constructed to include subscales to measure, not only cognitive and somatic state anxiety, but also fear of physical harm and generalized anxiety. The objective of the initial studies was to support the reliability and validity of the inventory, and several samples of athletes (e.g., college football players, college swimmers, college track and field athletes, high school wrestlers, road racers, and junior golfers) participated in our research. Various statistical procedures provided evidence for three constructs or CSAI-2 subscales: cognitive anxiety, somatic anxiety, and state self-confidence. The self-confidence subscale emerged as a serendipitous finding, meaning that we didn't expect it to appear.

After the initial set of studies to develop the items and subscales of the CSAI-2, we began theory testing, which involved using the CSAI-2 to test various conceptual predictions emanating from multidimensional anxiety theory. Our research demonstrated that individual sport athletes, female athletes, and athletes in subjectively-scored sports (e.g., gymnastics) experienced higher precompetitive cognitive and somatic anxiety than team sport athletes, male athletes, and athletes in objectively-scored sports (e.g., basketball), respectively. We also found that cognitive and somatic anxiety differentially changed in athletes as time to compete neared. Cognitive anxiety was elevated a few days prior to competition, while somatic anxiety became elevated once athletes arrived at the competition site. This was an important finding as it supported multidimensional theory that says that cognitive anxiety is related to expectancies about outcomes or performance, while somatic anxiety is often a conditioned anxiety response to precompetitive stimuli, such as warm-ups, getting dressed for competition, or arriving at the competitive site.

The most critical conceptual predictions to examine involved the relationship between cognitive anxiety, somatic anxiety, and performance. Our results supported multidimensional theory in that cognitive anxiety was inversely related to performance, meaning that the lower the level of cognitive anxiety, the better athletes performed. Self-confidence was the opposite—the higher the level of self-confidence, the better athletes performed. As hypothesized, somatic anxiety was related to performance in an inverted-U manner, meaning that performance increased as somatic anxiety increased up to an optimal point, after which further increases in somatic anxiety hurt performance. Overall, then, our systematic progression of research studies provided evidence to support the reliability and validity of the CSAI-2 as a measure of sport-specific cognitive state anxiety, somatic state anxiety, and state self-confidence.

We presented our completed research program at a national conference in 1983—it was my first major conference presentation. Because multidimensional anxiety theory was new and a current "zeitgeist" in the field, our symposium was received most favorably by the audience, and I will always remember the pride and satisfaction that I felt in achieving this prestige as a researcher. I realized that I was very motivated to obtain that prestige, so of course I targeted my career in a way that I believed would allow me to do that. Our entire compilation of research in competitive anxiety was published as a book titled *Competitive Anxiety in Sport* in 1990. The book incorporated Rainer's earlier work in competitive *trait* anxiety as well as our latest research on competitive *state* anxiety, and was a useful integration of the conceptual and psychometric rationale for the study of anxiety in sport. We also included a review of all published research in the area, computed norms for the inventories from this research, and ended the book with an emerging conceptualization of sources of stress in sport. Although the book was not my answer to explaining the achieving personality which I had set out to do, in some small way it did satisfy my need to study the personality-sport connection in a systematic manner. I believed that our extended program of systematic research at least provided important information about how anxiety is manifested in athletes, how this anxiety influences their behavior and performance, and even provided preliminary information as to how various interventions may enable athletes to manage or decrease their anxiety.

Along with my work in competitive anxiety, I began my conceptual and psychometric journey to study self-confidence in sport. It seems interesting to me that, although I found that I could not study the achieving personality in its totality, I chose to study what many people describe as the opposite ends of achieving personality continuum—self-confidence and anxiety! Perhaps I thought that by studying the opposite ends of the personality continuum, I could better understand the remaining parts of the achieving personality in between. At that time in the early 1980s, self-confidence in sport had largely been studied in relation to Bandura's self-efficacy theory. However, I believed that sport-specific self-confidence was unique, based on the competitive, socially evaluative nature of the sport subculture. Rainer had written a very provocative article in 1979 titled "About Smocks and Jocks" in which he argued that sport psychology needed to adopt research paradigms that more appropriately studied the phenomenon of sport as opposed to isolating human behavior in experimental laboratory-oriented research. The central thesis of the article was that Rainer was shedding his laboratory "smock" for a more field-based research "jock" in his attempts to understand human behavior in sport. I agreed with his arguments (although the "jock" analogy didn't thrill me), and even though self-efficacy theory was an elegant and intuitive model within which to study confidence, I wanted to conceptualize confidence a bit differently based on the unique nature of sport.

To this day, many individuals ask me to compare my self-confidence work with Bandura's self-efficacy work and at times people juxtapose my approach with Bandura's to argue which is right or better. To do this is really missing the point. All conceptual ideas are merely extensions. Even if they are radically different from previous work, they must take into account how previous work has been conducted even to state that theirs is a radical departure from current research! Clearly, I incorporated ideas gleaned from reading self-efficacy theory (as well as other theories, such as competence motivation and expectancy theory) in my conceptual model of sport-confidence. Thus, my work is not a radical departure from nor a competing perspective with self-efficacy theory—rather, it is an extension from which I attempt to study sport-specific confidence, which I named sport-confidence.

My dissertation and the line of research emanating from the dissertation involved not only the conceptualization of sport-confidence, but also the development and validation of three measurement instruments to assess the constructs set forth in my conceptual model. It was a huge undertaking, but it paid off in that I established a conceptual model for others to ask questions regarding confidence in sport, and I developed the instrumentation with which researchers could pursue their questions. I and others have conducted several studies using this conceptual framework and instrumentation. We found significant relationships between confidence and other psychological constructs (e.g., achievement goals, anxiety, satisfaction, and perceived success in sport), as well as various differences (e.g., age, gender) between groups in confidence, but I began to question the relevancy of this research. Sure, I could demonstrate statistically significant relationships within the conceptual model, but I started to think "So what?" This was the first time I had questioned whether Surfing the Mainstream was logical or significant in terms of the goals that I had established for myself and for the reasons I became interested in sport psychology in the first place.

The scenario of the wrestler who was a participant in our competitive anxiety research described at the beginning of this section demonstrates a common criticism of the type of research conducted when one is Surfing the Mainstream in sport psychology. It is based on a positivistic epistemology (way of knowing), where inquiry is restricted to observable units of behavior collected "objectively" and "impersonally." It typically uses nomothetic (group-oriented) measurement targeted to measure general responses assumed to be relevant for all individuals. Often, the measures used have been derived from theory from general psychology (e.g., multidimensional anxiety theory, self-efficacy theory). The high school wrestler described in the scenario *clearly* was extremely anxious, but our measure failed to capture that. I had a similar experience when assessing precompetitive sport-confidence at the U.S. Olympic Trials for gymnastics. Virtually no variability in confidence scores appeared across the sample of elite gymnasts, and it was obvious to me why this occurred after talking to one of the gymnasts about the study. He said, "It's not that we're lying to you that we're confident. It's just, at this stage of competition, any elite gymnast trying to make the Olympic team is not going to consciously process that they are not optimally confident."

Thus, this was not a social desirability problem in the traditional sense of subjects lying to create favorable impressions. Rather, it was a timing and measurement issue related to the positivistic (and naive) notion that I could get these physically and mentally elite athletes to be hypercritical about their cognitions and feelings about success just prior to the biggest performance of their lives! Of course they reported they were confident— if they hadn't, they would not be in that situation. In retrospect, I believe I had fallen prey to what Koch calls "epistemopathology" which describes the ways in which scientific paradigms and methods become entrenched to the point of actually limiting our vision and development of knowledge.

Therefore, I began to have doubts about the social relevance of Surfing the Mainstream. My doubts were preliminary and fleeting as it was hard to denigrate or even challenge the basic assumptions that I had just studied and embraced for my four years of doctoral work. At this point in my career I was job-hunting for a position as a university professor, so I stayed in the Mainstream because I believed that it would further my career to do so. In August, 1984, I accepted an assistant professor position at Miami University to continue my study of the achieving personality.

September, 1985, Oxford, Ohio

Dave, a graduate student of mine, leaned across my desk and in a soft voice not much louder than a whisper asked me, "What are we trying to discover?" He was deadly serious, and his eyes were wide with anticipation as he stared intently at me waiting for my enlightening response. He posed his question just after I had briefed him on his responsibilities for an upcoming research study we were conducting. The study focused on how achievement goals of adolescent athletes might be related to their self-confidence. I was amused by the melodrama of his question, and although touched by his sincerity, I thought that he was quite naive about the research process.

Personal and Professional Dissonance

I didn't realize it at the time, but *I* was the one being naive, not Dave. I had been Surfing the Mainstream so long, riding the zeitgeist waves firmly entrenched in my epistemopathology, that I had lost sight of the bigger question. Why do I do research? Dave was at the Naive Engagement stage to be sure, but he did ask the most significant question possible, "What *are* we trying to discover?" Our planned research study attempted to make a conceptual link between sport-confidence and motivational goals. Perhaps the research focus had some merit with regard to understanding how underlying achievement orientations or goals influence sport-confidence, but it was also another example of research that I had begun to call the "psychology of the obvious." My Dissonance began to grow stronger.

I'm not sure that I would have reached this stage of Personal and Professional Dissonance if I had not taken my first academic position at Miami University. Dr. Hal Lawson, the chair of the department, was an important mentor to me in gently nudging me toward a broader and more critical approach to research and scholarship. The curriculum at Miami was designed around a cross-disciplined approach to studying sport phenomena, and I was part of a Sport Studies faculty that included several colleagues with expertise in the sociocultural study of leisure and sport.

My professional discourse with colleagues at Miami was very stimulating as they often challenged what they saw as questionable assumptions upon which traditional sport psychology research was based. The main assumption questioned was the naive belief by sport psychologists that we could study human cognition, affect, and behavior without accounting for the social context within which humans exist. I remember being defensive about these questions early in my career, and my patterned response was "I'm not concerned with history and culture. That's what *you* study—I study psychology, which focuses on individual behavior." Yet at some level, I knew they had a point. Now I can see that the cross-disciplined approach to inquiry in a refreshing sort of way takes us back to the Naive Engagement stage where the focus is on the relevance and social impact of the question being asked, without becoming tangled up in Research Realities and Mainstream zeitgeists that dictate and gatekeep *who* can study *what* phenomena in *which* settings using *what* methods.

Thus, it was in my early years at Miami that my Dissonance began to crystalize because I was now in an environment where attempts to Surf the Mainstream were challenged, as opposed to my doctoral studies where Surfing was expected and rewarded. Although these challenges to my work were sometimes painful, I firmly believe that all scholars should be challenged to defend their work if for no other reason than to develop the introspection necessary to understand clearly the epistemological assumptions and limitations of their work. I believe that the Dissonance stage involves an important integration of personal and professional goals, where scholars pause in their rat-race pursuit of academic prestige through books and journal articles to assess critically and honestly how relevant and useful their accomplishments are to society. Clearly, what drives the Mainstream zeitgeists is the knowledge that careers are made via approval of members of our disciplinary community, not that of the target population affected by their work. You learn this quickly in graduate school, and it becomes more reinforced in seeking tenure and promotion at most universities.

Another milestone in my Personal and Professional Dissonance stage involved the evolution of my applied sport psychology consulting philosophy. Applied intervention programs targeted to athletes, often called psychological skills training (PST), became popular in the 1980s. Obviously, I was interested in PST because my interest in sport psychology had emanated from my experiences as an athlete and coach. I was fortunate to be at the University of Illinois working with Rainer in the 1980s when he and colleague Damon Burton were developing their first PST program. I received numerous consulting opportunities from Rainer and became involved with the U.S. Nordic Ski Team, U.S. Field Hockey, and several teams and athletes at Illinois. The main objective of PST at that time was to enhance performance. Sport psychologists became part of an army of sport scientists who left no stones unturned in their attempts to enable athletes to perform optimally.

Upon my arrival at Miami in 1984, I met and began extended dialogue with Dr. Jim Slager, who was a counseling psychologist for the Student Services division at Miami. Jim argued extensively with me about the narrow focus of sport psychology on performance enhancement and the fact that this objective was typically pursued only with elite athletes who represent an infinitesimal portion of the human population. He helped me gain a broader, counselor-oriented perspective to my PST work by arguing that intervention requires taking into account *all* aspects of that individual instead of naively trying to focus only on performance parameters. Jim was "right on," and I began to notice that his arguments were validated by the amount of time I spent in consultation with athletes about personal development issues as opposed to performance issues.

This evolution of my consulting philosophy crystallized in an article I published in 1988 titled "Future Directions in Psychological Skills Training." In the article, I present a holistic PST model based on the objective of personal development of athletes. Performance skills are one part of the model, but they are not the only focus of intervention, as I included the need to develop foundation skills, such as self-esteem and self-awareness, as well as personal facilitation skills, such as lifestyle management and interpersonal communication skills. In the article, I also argued that sport psychology should broaden its focus toward a holistic life skills approach that is relevant for the entire population as opposed to elite sport.

Overall, my experiences in the Personal and Professional Dissonance stage stimulated tremendous personal development and professional maturity. In fact, I believe that, to some degree, I am still in this stage. But the difference is that now I am comfortable with being there—in fact, I even expect to be there. Experiencing Dissonance on occasion is necessary to prompt the introspection that focuses you toward Meaningful Engagement.

June, 1994, Clearwater Beach, Florida

Tara gave me a big hug, then looked at me intently and said, "That was a peak performance. You're in a new place now, aren't you?" I smiled and nodded. It meant the world to me that she "got it." Dr. Tara Scanlan was a leading scholar in the field of sport psychology and had served as a valuable mentor for me since graduate school. I had just finished my invited presentation titled "Tired of Gulfs, Gaps, and Schisms?: Beyond Epistemological Dualism in Sport Psychology Research" at the annual North American Society for the Psychology of Sport and Physical Activity (NASPSPA) conference and it *was* a peak performance—at least for me. In the talk, I publicly voiced my dissatisfaction with Surfing the Mainstream and I passionately described my growing Dissonance over what I felt was our inability and even unwillingness to examine the social relevance and societal impact of our work in sport psychology. I had worked obsessively on the paper, and my reading in philosophy of science and epistemology had created a feverish intensity that culminated in a passionate presentation. Never before had I presented a paper that I believed in so much. It was a significant personal and professional milestone for me, and the overwhelming and laudatory support I received after the talk from various colleagues indicated to me that others too were experiencing a similar Dissonance. I became more motivated than ever to sharpen my professional focus with an eye toward Meaningful Engagement.

Meaningful Engagement: The Peak of Professional Life

The thesis of my NASPSPA talk was that our field has ignored the underlying epistemological issues that create and perpetuate the research-practice dichotomy about which we spend so much time talking at the more superficial method and design levels. Most of our dualistic debates and calls for integration focus on questions, such as: What do we do (basic vs. applied research)? Where do we do it (lab vs. field)? How do we do it (deduction vs. induction)? I argued that addressing the dualism in our field required asking questions at the epistemological level, such as: Why do we do it (prestige vs. relevance)? Who benefits from it (maintaining current social order vs. pursuing social equality)? What *is* IT (facts vs. values)? I then attempted to outline ways that I thought our field could begin to address these questions within various research areas. I advocated that we should continuously engage in discourse on the sociology of psychological knowledge in sport and that we should put greater emphasis on creative discovery as opposed to the certification of the "known unknown" or psychology of the obvious.

How did my arrival at the Meaningful Engagement stage influence my personal pursuit of understanding of the achieving personality? At this point, I think my experiences have honed the question that I am interested in to this: How can I help athletes realize the potential of their individual achieving personalities that is optimal for them based on their unique physical, psychological, and sociocultural make-up and experience? The question sounds broad, and it is, but when I narrow in to study specific offshoots of the question, at least I attempt to keep in mind that my narrower inquiry is really part of this broader question. That helps me stay focused on what for me feels like Meaningful Engagement.

Currently, I am involved in two lines of research inquiry emanating from my interest in anxiety and self-confidence that represent important anchors of the achieving personality. First, I have extended my previous work in competitive anxiety to conceptualize competition activation as an athlete's psychobiological state of specific cognitions, affective feelings, and somatic reactions activated in response to the perceived incentives, threats, and demands of sport competition. Our current work involves the development of an idiographic (individualized study of a specific person) assessment system to identify individual athletes' unique and personalized responses to competition, termed the Competition Activation Profile or CAP. A social constructivist perspective is taken by developing a CAP for each athlete which focuses on personalized or individualistic competition activation. Social constructivism in this sense means that each athlete constructs his or her own way of responding to competitive stressors based on his or her unique socialization experiences, cultural influences, and personality characteristics. Assessment using the CAP involves a longitudinal process within which the athlete, through repeated interview discussions with the researcher, actually develops and continually revises his or her unique profile.

This is in direct contrast to previous nomothetic (group-oriented) inquiry where researchers design measurement instruments from theory that represents a collectively applicable "template" that is assumed to be relevant for all athletes. From an epistemological standpoint, the purpose of the project is *not* to develop knowledge that may apply to groups of individuals (e.g., whether high or low levels of competition activation enhance performance, what types of cognitions or emotions help and/or hurt performance). Rather, the purpose is to construct an individually and socially relevant profile to better understand the intra-individual nature of individuals within the competitive environment. CAP profiles may be used to increase athletes' awareness of their responses to competition, monitor change across time in profiles (e.g., in response to intervention programs), provide an assessment tool for case study research, and motivate athletes to take more ownership of their mental training and personal development.

For example, I am currently working with a college volleyball player whom I will call Janet. Janet and I have worked together to create a CAP for her based on her unique thoughts and feelings prior to and during competition. Based on emerging theory in anxiety and emotion, researchers now realize that anxiety and unpleasant emotions/feelings can help some athletes to perform better. This is evident from Janet's CAP profile as she likes to put pressure on herself not to let her teammates down. This pressure prompts her to energize effectively and focus her attention on her specific game responsibilities. We also identify key situational occurrences that help and hurt Janet's activation level. For example, Janet finds it very helpful to receive brief, technical advice from the coaches during time-outs. These brief tips make Janet feel she is on top of her game and focused on what is relevant for her during competition. Janet also identifies negative situational occurrences that cause her to lose her focus or confidence, such as teammates telling her to "relax" or Janet herself thinking that her team is stuck in a weak rotation (fixed player positions on the floor as determined by the rules of the game).

All of the specifics of Janet's profile are compiled on a scoresheet and she assesses her competition activation levels after each match based on her own unique profile. From her CAP profile, we then design specific mental training goals for Janet and even talk to the coaches about ways they can facilitate Janet's mental approach to competition. We use such techniques as imagery and self-talk so Janet can visualize and feel herself getting into her optimal competition activation state just prior to competition. For example, in Janet's position of middle blocker, it is very important to have good footwork in moving quickly around the net to block opponents' attacks. A big part of Janet's CAP is feeling "quick" and "light" on her feet, explosive in the legs, and strong in her block at the net. She energizes herself using these cues and likes to visualize the sound (ba-BOOM) of the block as it hits off her arms back into the opponent's court. Thus, Janet's mental game plan emanates from her unique CAP, which is an ongoing self-awareness/self-reflection exercise for her to consider how she may best achieve optimal activation prior to and during competition. I like to think of the goal of the CAP work as helping individuals achieve a *momentary* achieving personality based on the situational demands of their sports and their own individual uniqueness as athletes at that point in their development.

Our CAP project attempts to avoid two limitations that have been traditionally inherent in research on psychobiological states. First, previous research in the dominant anxiety paradigm has not been able to demonstrate consistently how and why anxiety influences performance. Second, traditional research has exacerbated the research-practice dichotomy in that most measures and approaches to studying psychobiological states are not useful in applied settings for athletes and coaches. I believe that my dissatisfaction and even chagrin with positivistic approaches that surfaced during my attempts to profile the U.S. Ice Hockey Team and collect CSAI-2 field data with wrestlers ultimately led me to pursue this CAP research. Thus far, the research has been extremely rewarding as the participant athletes demonstrate sincere motivation to develop and refine their CAPs to understand more fully their own achieving personalities. This is a welcome change from the day that high school wrestler threw his half-completed, totally falsified CSAI-2 at me to make the point that it clearly had no relevance or meaning for him.

My work in the self-confidence area has evolved into inquiry into the sources of sport-confidence and an expanded conceptual model of sport-confidence that includes the influence of sociocultural influences and the organizational culture of sport. We are currently conducting questionnaire and interview research to examine the social, developmental, and cultural influences on how females develop confidence in sport. This has particular relevance for me and other educators, as a major threat to girls' and women's achievement is the sudden drop in self-confidence and self-esteem that occurs at adolescence. Thus, this research studies how an important aspect of the achieving personality (confidence) is developed and/or debilitated at various developmental stages in girls and women in sport. Our follow-up study to this will be an intervention study to test the effects on girls and women of a confidence-enhancing program that is developed from the knowledge we gain in the current study.

A Final Word

Along with the valuable mentoring I've received from thoughtful colleagues and my own personal attempts to work through the five developmental stages of scholarly inquiry, my favorite comic strip, The Far Side, has on occasion provided humorous material to inspire my introspection and professional development. The best Far Side I've seen is a picture of a flock of sheep standing around contentedly grazing and minding their own business. One sheep suddenly stands up and says, "Wait! Wait! Listen to me! We don't HAVE to be just sheep!"

That is the most important lesson that I've learned from my research, teaching, and consulting experiences in sport psychology. We *don't* have to be just sheep. We don't have to remain fixated in Surfing the Mainstream. I am certainly not arrogant enough to claim that I am totally immersed in Meaningful Engagement and have successfully traversed the other stages. I believe that my movement through the stages is constant and cyclical depending on the type of work I am doing and my level of thinking about particular phenomena at that moment in time. I am sure that my studies of the achieving personality will continue to take me back and forth from Naive to Meaningful Engagement and that I will constantly face the challenges of Research Reality and Personal and Professional Dissonance.

But my experience has allowed me to understand *how* to move toward Meaningful Engagement, and the goals that I have as a researcher are now related to pursuing inquiry in this fifth stage. I won't win the Nobel Prize nor will I definitively operationalize the exact essence of the achieving personality in sport. But I will contribute positively to society by developing useful knowledge related to individuals developing and maximizing their unique achieving personalities within sport and physical activity contexts.

And. . . I know why I choked at the free throw line back in 1976. It's because I didn't understand *my own* achieving personality. I tried to respond and act like other people whom I believed had the most effective achieving personalities instead of understanding myself well enough to successfully adapt my personality to the situation. I know that I will achieve personal and professional fulfillment by helping athletes understand their own achieving personalities, and forget the genie (!)—I can exorcise my memory of choking on my own, by applying knowledge gained from that object lesson to contribute something of worth to society.

But. . . I still can't explain why my volleyball team achieved a total and magical peak performance at just the right moment in time. That's the other reason I will continue to experience personal and professional fulfillment in studying the fascinating world of sport—there will always be elusive questions and perplexing phenomena to chase. I can't imagine being in a career without such constant stimulation and challenge.

Suggested Readings

Martens, R., Vealey, R.S., & Burton, D. (1990). *Competitive anxiety in sport.* Champaign, IL: Human Kinetics.

Vealey, R.S. (1988). Future directions in psychological skills training. *The Sport Psychologist, 2,* 318–336.

Vealey, R.S. (1992). Personality and sport: A comprehensive view. In T.S. Horn (Ed.), *Advances in sport psychology* (pp. 25–59). Champaign, IL: Human Kinetics.

Vealey, R.S., Walter, S.M., Garner-Holman, M., & Giacobbi, P. (in press). Sources of sport-confidence: Conceptualization and instrument development. *Journal of Sport and Exercise Psychology.*

Chapter **4**

The Motivation to Study Motivation: Goal Perspectives and Their Influence

Joan L. Duda

Joan L. Duda is a Professor of Sport and Exercise Psychology in the Department of Health, Kinesiology and Leisure Studies and the Department of Psychological Sciences at Purdue University, West Lafayette, Indiana. Dr. Duda has been a member of the executive boards of the North American Society for the Psychology of Sport and Physical Activity, the Sport Psychology Academy, the International Society for Sport Psychology, and a Fellow of the American Academy of Kinesiology and Physical Education. She was editor of the *Journal of Applied Sport Psychology* and is on the Editorial Board of the *Journal of Sport and Exercise Psychology*. Dr. Duda has over 90 publications focused on the topic of sport motivation and the psychological dimensions of sport and exercise behavior. She has been an invited speaker in 15 countries around the world. For over 10 years, Dr. Duda has been involved in applied work with athletes and coaches in a variety of sports at all competitive levels. She is certified by the Association for the Advancement of Applied Sport Psychology and is listed on the U.S. Olympic Registry. Since 1992, she has been the sport psychology consultant for the USA Gymnastics Women's Artistic Program and National Team. Dr. Duda's hobbies include music, traveling, watching all sports and playing tennis.

In this chapter, I will present some of the major predictions and findings stemming from a contemporary approach to the study of sport motivation, namely goal perspective theory. Through this discourse, however, I have two other points that I hope to make. First, I want to demonstrate (with a personal example) that the topics that individuals decide to investigate, especially those aspects of the topics which they find most compelling, are not random occurrences. Rather, the focus of a major line of research usually links to the researcher's values, interests, and life experiences. Second, this is also true of the primary theoretical framework that is chosen to guide an individual's work. This theory reflects a personal theory of the topic—maybe even a personal theory of life. That is, individuals select certain conceptual models because they capture what they perceive is important about the area of study *and* represent (to some degree) their comprehension of how the process of interest operates. In other words, they become captivated by certain theories because they attempt to predict what they believe is worth predicting and explain things in a manner consistent with their perceptions of how this world functions.

The Motivation to Study Motivation

I have been interested in the topic of motivation for a long time. Even as a student, I was interested in why some of my peers hated school while others enjoyed being in the classroom. There was also considerable variability in the willingness to study and openness about how hard one worked. For example, I was struck by how some students would engage in academic activities (e.g., reading, writing poetry or prose) over and above requirements imposed by their teachers. Other students did nothing unless made to, and, sometimes, avoided the task in question even when instructed to do so. The teacher's role in such motivational differences was thought provoking, too.

When I became involved in organized sport (at the age of 11), my intrigue with the variability in motivation among athletes and the impact of others on participants' motivational levels became more pronounced. Somehow, whether individuals were motivated or not, or the way outside forces had an impact on their motivation, seemed more apparent in the athletic setting. In contrast to the educational context, sport involvement was generally a voluntary enterprise—thus, one could readily witness the act of "dropping out." Further, when compared to academic pursuits, athletic activities provided more information about people's motivational states and degree of accomplishment and prowess. In sport, not only can we observe the outcome (and read the statistics associated with this outcome), but we can also more easily witness the process. In other words, we can see the results of one's performance as well as how one performed when engaged in a physical task.

I started taking classes in psychology during my first year at Rutgers University and these courses enhanced my awareness of the nuances and potential antecedents of human behavior. I was hooked, and soon became a psychology major.

Although I enjoyed most of my course work, little information (in my opinion) was revealed about the nature and dynamics of motivation. In particular, the classes I took, which were heavily behaviorally oriented, did not offer the type of explanation I seemed to be looking for. My heavens, I couldn't even get a rat motivated enough to run a maze for an assignment in my experimental psychology course! The only class that allowed a glimmer of hope for some insight into motivation was entitled the "Psychobiology of sex differences." Motivational differences between males and females (in intensity as well as direction) were something I had noticed—particularly in the physical domain. Class lectures and readings that pointed to social situational factors and psychological attributes as major contributors to gender-related differences in motivated behavior were most critical to my thinking. This was an approach I was to adopt in my later research activities.

One evening in the Rutgers' library, a fortunate fluke helped me realize that there was a field out there that combined two of my loves: sport and psychology. I was searching for some books to help with a term paper for a sociology class when my eyes fell on a text called *Involvement in sport: Somatopsychic rationale for physical activity* (written by Dorothy Harris). Although not an exciting title, the words "psychic" and "physical activity" caught my attention. Could it be a content, . . . a body of knowledge, . . . a scientific discipline oriented toward the psychological aspects of sport-related behavior? After reading the book from cover to cover that evening, I knew where my academic road was leading me—graduate work in the field called "sport psychology."

Although I was motivated, I discovered in the weeks to come that information on graduate programs in sport psychology was hard to come by. My search, which was far from organized and systematic, finally pointed me to Purdue University and I enrolled in its master's degree program.

When I arrived at Purdue, I quickly discovered that the Department of Physical Education, Health and Recreation Studies did not actually have a faculty in sport psychology. However, this turned out OK. I was able to take many interesting courses in the sport sciences (talk about relevant information if you are an athlete and had experience as a coach), such as exercise physiology and motor learning. I also was able to take classes in social psychology, in which we covered theories of motivation (especially achievement motivation) and, thus, my long-standing captivation with this topic was rekindled.

After reading the (very long!) works of McClelland, Atkinson and some of their scholarly compatriots, I came across a concept that appeared to have some potential in explaining gender differences in motivation—particularly as displayed in achievement activities which were not deemed "gender typical." The concept was "fear of success" (coined by Matina Horner) and my master's thesis topic was born. The basic premise is that some people exhibit motivational deficits, not because they possess a weak motive to approach success or have a pronounced motive to avoid failure, but because the thought of achievement causes them great anxiety.

My research question was: Would there be differences in "fear of success" imagery when female non-athletes, female athletes who were involved in "gender-inappropriate" sports, and female athletes who participated in "gender-appropriate" sports were asked to write about female athletes who succeeded in stereotypically classified "masculine" and "feminine" athletic activities? In an attempt to answer this question, the subjects were presented with hypothetical situations, such as "Jane scored the most points for her women's basketball team" and/or "Anne has been selected for the Women's All-Regional Tennis Team." They were then asked to write a story which: (1) described the person in the hypothetical scenario, (2) indicated what had led up to the present situation, (3) speculated on what the target person was thinking and wanted, and (4) indicated what the probable consequences would be.

Well, as I discovered as soon as I could figure out how to analyze the complex statistical research design I used (which I did the night before my thesis defense!), there were no significant differences between the three subject groups or as a function of whether the achievement described took place in a "masculine" or "feminine" sport. However, my subsequent critical look at the stories these women wrote, and the criteria by which I scored them, suggested that there was something rather biased in what was considered success and what was classified as reflecting a "fear" about achievement. For example, if story themes suggested a group-oriented or cooperative (in contrast to individualistic) slant on accomplishment, such a referral increased one's overall fear of success score. Perhaps women didn't necessarily feel anxiety about success? Perhaps women tended to define success in a different way than men (and the prevailing theories of achievement motivation at that time)?

My master's degree studies proved to be an effective stepping stone to a doctoral program which did focus on sport psychology. I started my pursuit of the Ph.D. at the University of Illinois and will never forget my first two years of course work there. Not only was I taking courses which dealt specifically with sport psychology content (from two esteemed sport psychology professors named Glyn Roberts and Rainer Martens), but these courses had a strong social cognitive bent which felt right to me. Without knowing it, this was the perspective I had always employed to try to understand my world of human action and interaction. Most incredibly, though, I was fortunate to be at the U of I at a time that gave me the opportunity to take courses from some of the leading thinkers in (what else?) my favorite topic—motivation. In terms of my own scholarly interests, classes with John Nicholls, Carol Dweck and Marty Maehr changed me forever.

Through such fortuitous and influential encounters, I developed my predominant area of research—the study of motivation in sport and physical activity from a social cognitive perspective. Specifically at that time, I was enamored with attribution theory (which was also the favorite topic of my advisor, Glyn Roberts). I believed that if I knew whether athletes attributed their wins and losses to ability, effort, luck or task difficulty, I would have tremendous insight into their motivational patterns. But two circumstances occurred that made me question this assumption and move toward another model of motivation. First, I heard a presentation from Maria Allison, a sport sociologist, who became a good colleague and friend. From an ethnographic perspective, she discussed her work on Navajo basketball. In so doing, she described interesting differences between this ethnic group and the Anglo mainstream in how they approach and process competition. What she conveyed was fascinating to me and I couldn't help but think that the Navajo value system and way of thinking about the world seemed contrary to what was assumed in the attributional framework. For example, in contrast to the

Anglo culture, Navajos tend to be more group-oriented and cooperative than individualistic and competitive. The Navajo culture also is
marked by less concern with controlling the world which surrounds us;
rather, the focus is on being in communion with nature. Based on such
differences, it didn't seem likely that Navajo athletes would employ
the same causal explanations for their performance outcomes or clas-
sify those attributions (in terms of their locus of causality, stability, or
controllability) in a manner similar to Anglo athletes. Most importantly, it appeared very unlikely that participants in Navajo sports
would equate success and failure to the competitive outcomes of winning and losing (which was the state-of-affairs in most sport attribution studies at the time). Thus, I wondered whether attribution theory
might be culturally limited.

Maria Allison's presentation (and related writings) was the impetus
to my dissertation, namely a cross-cultural comparison of achievement
motivation in sport and the classroom among Navajo and Anglo inter-
scholastic athletes. The dissertation research fostered a long-term commitment to appreciating and investigating cultural variation, as well as
gender-related differences, in the sport experience.

A paradigm shift in the conceptualization of motivation was also
taking place at the U of I right before my eyes. In a collaborative chapter published in 1980, Maehr and Nicholls pointed out that *subjective*
success and failure may not be equivalent to indices of *objective* success
and failure (like wins/losses). They spoke of different achievement orientations or approaches to defining accomplishment and suggested that
people feel successful (or unsuccessful) if they perceive that they demonstrated (or did not demonstrate) a desirable attribute. It was John
Nicholls, in particular, who extended this line of thinking into a theory
of achievement motivation that has had the most influence on my work.
His goal perspective framework was crystallizing during my years at Illinois and he published his first major papers describing this approach to
understanding motivational processes in 1984.

After completing my Ph.D., I accepted a 3-year visiting assistant
professorship at UCLA. There were some good folks there in both psychology and education who were interested in motivation (including the
"major player" in terms of the application of attribution theory to the
study of achievement motivation, Bernie Weiner). I was able to exchange
ideas with colleagues on the latest developments in theoretical approaches to motivated behavior. Moreover, given the wonderful diversity
that marks the population of Los Angeles, the possibility of conducting
cross-cultural research was readily available.

Beaches and nice weather soon get tiring (only kidding!). In 1985 I found myself looking at an attractive job offer from Purdue University. Somehow, this position was like coming home. Ironically, I was asked to develop the sport psychology specialization which did not exist when I passed through this academic community a number of years before. Further, my path once again crossed with John Nicholls, who was a member of the Purdue faculty in education at that time. This presented some possibilities for collaborative work and many wonderful exchanges of ideas. In my opinion, one of John Nicholls' many strengths was that he viewed the athletic setting as a fascinating milieu for the study of motivational processes; sport was not a "second class citizen" to the academic setting.

Fortunately, my regular exchanges with John continued through the years as he moved up the road to the University of Illinois at Chicago Circle. We were still discussing motivation, and debating the similarities and differences between sport and the classroom, up to his untimely death in 1994.

Selecting a Theory: A Personal Choice

John Nicholls once stated that "differences among scientific theories involve differences in the purposes of those who construct the theories. People with different priorities ask different questions and tell different stories about the world. Scientific theory is, in this view, very much a personal, social, human affair" (1992, p. 268). Thus, science is a product of our needs and values, and theoretical frameworks are (as William James would say) a "conceptual shorthand" for representing and reflecting our conceptions of real life. This argument implies that there is a subjective side to even the most objective science. I don't think this subjectivity takes away from the integrity or significance of scientific inquiry; rather, this realization brings an energy and sensitivity to scientific endeavors and certainly helps maintain the motivation of the researcher! How sad it would be to study something which is not meaningful to you.

My research on motivation over the past 15 years has been grounded in goal perspective theory. Now, I would like to highlight what it is about this conceptual framework that I find appealing. This discussion will reveal some specifics about this theory's tenets and summarize some pertinent findings in the athletic domain. Given the points just expressed, the discussion will probably reveal something about me as well.

Goal Perspective Theory: Its Attractive Features

The Significance of Cognitive Interpretation

Although I don't discount the influence of biological factors, I guess I have always been a social cognitive theorist at heart. Goal perspective theory places central importance on people's cognitions within particular social situations. The key assumption is that individuals' goal perspectives, or the ways in which they define success and failure and judge their level of competence, influence how they think, feel and behave in achievement settings such as sport. That is, people's actions, reactions and interpretations make sense only when considered in terms of their goals. The theory holds that there are two major goal perspectives, termed task and ego involvement. In terms of the former, subjective success and perception of competence result when one believes that he or she has personally improved, mastered the task at hand and/or exerted effort. If ego involvement prevails, a person feels successful and competent when superior ability has been demonstrated. Beating others is the goal in this case.

According to Nicholls, one's goal perspective is a critical component of his or her own personal theory of achievement activities. The other major facet of such theories is our beliefs about the determinants of success or ideas about "what does it take to get ahead?" Therefore, theories—whether scientific theories of human behavior or personal theories of particular realms of endeavor—inform us about what is conceived to be most relevant and what is perceived to be the requisite mode of operation.

Over the years, my collaborators and I have investigated this link between goals and beliefs in sport settings. Individual differences in the former are measured by the Task and Ego Orientation in Sport Questionnaire which was developed by John Nicholls and me in 1985. People who tend to manifest a task perspective are more likely to think that hard work (e.g., training, studying) results in achievement. Individuals who score high in ego orientation are more likely to feel that the possession of superior ability, external factors and/or deceptive tactics lead to success. We have found such personal theories to generalize across the classroom and sport. As implied above, I often wonder whether such theories allow any intuition into what people study in sport motivation research and how they approach the investigative and interpretive dimensions of the research process.

Don't Forget the Joy

Besides representing a social cognitive approach to the study of motivation, the goal perspective framework does not ignore the motivational significance of affect. My point here is very much consonant with Susan Harter's (another social cognitive motivation theorist) position. At the meetings of the North American Society for the Psychology of Sport and Physical Activity several years ago, she gave a keynote address entitled "Understanding motivation in children's sport: Where is the joy?" Her central thesis was that we will not fully comprehend motivated behavior unless we consider the impact of affective responses on people's current and subsequent actions as well as the factors influencing whether or not individuals intrinsically enjoy what they are doing.

A perusal of the sport psychology literature will quickly show that fun is not a trivial concept. It is a salient motive for participation and a predictor of persistence at all competitive levels. Moreover, sport psychology research has shown us that enjoyment and anxiety are like "oil and water"—they do not mix very well and seem to be incompatible affective states. My collaborators and I (and others, too) have conducted a number of studies examining the associations between goal perspectives and individuals' emotional reactions. These investigations have involved athletes, ranging from youth sport or recreational participants to elite competitors, from the U.S. and abroad. Typically, the athletes sampled are requested to fill out the Task and Ego Orientation in Sport Questionnaire and then a measure of intrinsic motivation (such as the Intrinsic Motivation Inventory) specific to the athletic activity in question. The findings have been very consistent, i.e., this work indicates that a focus on task-involved goals corresponds to greater enjoyment of sport. There are at least three explanations for this result. It has been suggested that task involvement implies that people experience activities as an end in themselves rather than as a means to an end. This should make these activities more intrinsically enjoyable. The theory also holds that people are less likely to feel incompetent when task-involved. This is because their perceptions of ability are self-referenced rather than dependent on others' performances. When individuals feel competent, they tend to enjoy what they are doing. Finally, task-involved goals are more within the personal control of the person than ego-involved goals. Research emanating from the intrinsic motivation literature tells us that enjoyment is enhanced when we have a sense of self-determination.

Beyond Performance

Another attractive feature of goal perspective theory is that the framework aims to predict behavioral patterns (e.g., effort exerted, task choice, persistence) that are short-term as well as long-term. Given that the primary dependent variable in many motivational frameworks is current performance (whether operationalized as scores on an achievement test, class grades, win/loss, or number of free throws made), one has to wonder what this says about our society at large or, more specifically, the academic community. Performance is very ability-dependent and knowing something about who performs well tells us little about how he or she achieved that performance. Moreover, a person's outstanding short-term performance reveals almost nothing about whether he or she will achieve overall excellence and lifetime accomplishment.

Goal perspective theory holds that the consideration of a person's goals and level of perceived competence provide insight into behavioral variability. It is assumed that the adoption of a task-involved perspective, whether the person thinks he or she is good or not, will lead to adaptive behaviors. That is, this individual will consistently try hard, prefer tasks which are optimally challenging and "hang in there when the going gets rough." Oh yes—this person will also be more likely to perform up to his or her capability—which is all we can ask, isn't it? In contrast, when people are ego-involved, maladaptive behaviors are more likely to emerge. A negative achievement pattern is often revealed, especially when the individual has some doubts about the adequacy of his or her competence. In such a scenario, it makes sense (in terms of a rational/intentional approach to human behavior) not to "give it your best shot," but to give up when you face obstacles, and select activities which are not most conducive to improving (such as tasks which are too easy for you, or activities which are far beyond your abilities). Such a constellation of actions might compromise immediate performance, and if the long-term implications of such behaviors are taken into account (and we remember that it is difficult to maintain high perceptions of ability when ego-involved), there is no question that this goal perspective should prove costly.

To date, sport research has produced results consonant with these predictions. For example, my previous Ph.D. student, Likang Chi, and I conducted a laboratory experiment involving male undergraduates who were either high task- low ego-oriented or low task- high ego-oriented. Two at a time, these students came into the lab where they were asked individually to complete an exercise ergometer fitness test. They were given bogus feedback, i.e., the students were told either that their capacity at this task was high or that their fitness capabilities were very low. The students were then brought together in the same testing room and requested to race against each other for 6 minutes. The measure of performance was the distance covered during the race. Two back-to-back races were conducted and the subjects were once again given bogus information, i.e., they were told that they won both races or lost both races (NOTE: a divider was placed between them so they couldn't see how well their opponents performed). Questionnaires were completed before and after the two races. The worst performance, lowest degree of confidence in one's abilities, and desire to race against an easier opponent were observed among the high ego students who had low (manipulated) perceived competence and found themselves in the loss-loss condition.

As epitomized in the Chi and Duda study, the findings in general indicate that, whether tested in laboratories or in correlational field studies, task involvement seems conducive to optimal motivation. However, it should be noted that the majority of investigations to date have assessed self-reported rather than actual or objective behaviors. Further, which seems to be the case for so many areas of research, the literature so far has little to say about the behavioral implications of goal perspectives when examined over time. In essence, there are far too few longitudinal investigations.

Motivation and Morality

In my opinion, the research on achievement motivation is limited because it primarily deals with possible antecedents of achievement. Our achievement activities are not isolated entities, however. What we do in these contexts and how we process such activities have repercussions for other facets of our lives. As a result, I look for a model of motivation that gives attention to the prediction of differences in people's values, moral reasoning and ethical and health-related behaviors in sport, and not merely their achievement-related strivings. As proffered by Nicholls and extended by others, goal perspective theory provides a foundation for addressing such significant issues. For example, research has revealed a conceptually consistent interdependence between individuals' goal perspectives and their views about what is considered acceptable to do in order to be successful. Sport studies have indicated that task and ego goal perspectives differentially relate to athletes' sportspersonship attitudes and judgments about the legitimacy of aggressive acts. Specifically, athletes who place greater emphasis on ego-involved goals are more likely to agree with doing whatever it takes to win, including breaking or stretching the rules and purposely injuring an opponent.

We have also conducted research indicating that whether athletes tend to be task- or ego-involved relates to their views about the overall purposes of sport participation. In regard to this work, it is interesting to note that only a task perspective is associated with the view that an important purpose of sport is to build character. On the other hand, an emphasis on ego-involved goals is coupled with more extrinsic values (e.g., to increase social status, provide recognition, and make money).

Recently I have been interested in the implications of goal perspectives for understanding health-related outcomes in the athletic domain. I pose the question, how moral is sport if people risk serious health consequences for the chance to achieve athletic greatness? For example, with my colleague Dan Benardot in sport nutrition, I have been examining whether the goal perspectives emphasized by coaches and parents predict established psychological (e.g., self esteem, body image, perfectionism) and energy balance (e.g., ratio between energy requirements and energy intake) correlates of eating disorders. We know that eating disorders can kill and, at best, remain long-term battles for individuals. In short, our research suggests that strongly ego-involved athletes are at risk for much more than achievement-related problems, while task-involvement is associated with a healthier athletic attitude.

Individual Differences and Situational Factors

Another strength of the goal perspective framework is that it incorporates the potential impact of individual differences and variations in the current and long-term social environment in regard to motivational patterns. People vary in their tendency to be in a state of task or ego involvement within the sport setting. We refer to these differences as their degree of task and ego orientation and individuals can be high on both, high on one and low on the other, or low on both orientations. To further the investigation of the motivational significance of task and ego goals in the athletic domain, I noticed quite early that a measure of dispositional goal orientations was needed. In 1985, working with John Nicholls, I developed the Task and Ego Orientation in Sport Questionnaire (TEOSQ) to assess this individual difference variable. A typical item on the task orientation subscale would be "I feel successful when I work really hard." In contrast, items like "I feel successful when others can't do as well as me" are contained on the ego orientation subscale.

Social situations, which are created by significant others, such as the coach, parents, peers, etc., also can be distinguished in the degree to which they emphasize a task or ego goal perspective. Collaborating with a number of my graduate students (Jeff Seifriz, Mary Walling, Maria Newton and Likang Chi) over the years, I have formulated the Perceived Motivational Climate in Sport Questionnaire (PMCSQ) to assess the goal perspective deemed to be prevailing on an athlete's team. In the development of the PMCSQ, we have learned a lot about the characteristics of sport environments which are more or less task- and/or ego-involving. For example, it seems that when coaches constantly punish athletes for mistakes, recognize only the more talented athletes and foster a sense of rivalry among teammates, an ego-involving atmosphere is manifested. When coaches reinforce effort and collaboration among teammates and when athletes feel that everyone on their team makes a contribution and errors are part of learning, then the environment fosters task involvement.

Our research group at Purdue has examined the potential interplay between dispositional and situationally emphasized goals in two ways. First, we have looked at what happens when athletes who are predominantly task- or ego-oriented find themselves in a climate which is primarily task- or ego-involving. Although still in its infancy, this work suggests that motivationally all is OK as long as athletes are strongly task-oriented and/or these individuals participate in an environment which is strongly task-involving. Second, we examined the socialization of individual differences in goal perspectives. It is assumed that one's goal orientation is a result of his or her experiences over time in motivational climates. Thus, in a number of studies, we have determined the associations between individuals' degrees of task and ego orientation and their perceptions of the degree to which their significant others (such as their coaches, parents, physical education teachers) define success in a task- versus ego-involving manner.

What about Cognitive Maturity?

Please don't interpret this as reflecting a Freudian perspective, but it has been my personal observation (and I believe the empirical research will back me up) that the motivational problems of adults emanate from motivational difficulties encountered when they were considerably younger. As a consequence, I would argue that any theory of achievement motivation that is worthwhile acknowledges differences in how children (at different age levels) interpret achievement activities when compared to adults. Besides, it is important to be sensitive to where children are coming from for their own sake. It is wrong to think, for example, that young athletes are miniature adults in smaller uniforms!

I subscribe to Nicholls' goal perspective theory because there is an incorporation of the impact of developmental change in cognitive capacity and experiences in the theory's central concepts and tenets. For example, Nicholls and his colleagues have shown in a series of studies the more sophisticated (although more motivationally maladaptive) type of thinking that is required for one to be in a state of ego involvement. To be ego-involved, you must be able to differentiate ability and effort as causes of performance outcomes (e.g., realize that effort will only get you so far if you don't have the ability, and recognize that if someone can perform well with little effort, he/she must be very talented). You also must comprehend that a difficult task is one that few people can successfully complete. In terms of such differences, children go through a series of stages in their understanding. They begin at a stage in which ability is not differentiated from effort, i.e., young children think that if you try, you must possess ability and vice versa. When they are a little older (around 7 to 9 years of age), children believe that effort is the major determinant of outcomes. Finally, as they move closer to 12 years of age, children comprehend that ability is a capacity and success without effort reflects very high competence. When these developmental transitions are examined in the physical domain, the results parallel what Nicholls and his collaborators have observed in the cognitive domain.

Making Sense of What We Already Know

There is a lot of "good stuff" out there in the sport psychology literature. An impressive amount of this knowledge base falls into the "consistent finding" category. The problem (from both a theory building and practical standpoint), however, is that much of our work is isolated. Goal perspective theory allows for the assimilation and explanation of existing empirical findings in the sport psychology literature which seem pertinent to motivation but have typically been addressed tangentially to this topic (e.g., research on stress and burnout, sportspersonship and aggressive tendencies, health behaviors in sport).

I am suggesting other applications for a useful model of motivation. A favorite theory should not mean that we put on blinders, adopt a confirmation bias, and/or stop observing life as it is. Rather, conceptual frameworks should help us "put on our glasses"—making it easier to pull together what we know from other lines of work, and/or see facets of human experience that we did not see before. In my view, an alluring theoretical framework not only holds up in terms of its empirically-substantiated validity but it also serves a most valuable integrative purpose while enhancing our observational skills.

Conceptual Convergence

I like "bigger pictures" and, even though I am grounded in the goal perspective approach, I'm cognizant enough of the complexity of human action to know that one framework cannot do it on its own. In our study of sport motivation, "let's get together." Goal perspective theory is amenable to conceptual convergence across other models of motivation (e.g., Bandura's social cognitive theory, Deci and Ryan's cognitive evaluation theory). In this way, we are more likely to account for a higher percentage of variance in indices of motivation, which should prove important from both a theoretical and practical standpoint.

From Theory to Practice

As has been repeatedly stated in the sport psychology literature, any theoretical framework holding promise for the field must address the real issues facing practitioners/participants in the athletic context. In evaluating the value of a conceptual model, we should ask whether the theory in question provides solutions to (or at least insight into) important problems. However, I would take this point one step further by stating that, through applied work, we also garner information concerning the validity of our conceptual frameworks. Confirmation and corroboration comes in many ways.

In short, I concur with my good friend and colleague Bert Carron, who has reinforced the interdependencies between knowledge and theory building, utilization of this knowledge through intervention, and improvement in the quality of life. Kurt Lewin once said that "there is nothing as practical as a good theory" and it also has been proposed that there is nothing as theoretical as good practice. A model of motivation needs to provide the bases for and direction to interventions with athletes and the significant others who have an impact on the sport competitor. This type of effort then gives feedback about the veracity of the theory and provides direction to theoretical refinement and extension.

The goal perspective literature has provided a compelling rationale for how success should be defined if we wish to maximize motivation in the physical domain. Drawing from the classroom-based work of Carole Ames, some initial studies have emerged which are directed at changing the goal perspective characterizing sport environments. When conducting such manipulations, researchers need to realize that the motivational climate is both multidimensional and dynamic—we cannot change just one thing at one time if we hope to modify people's goals.

In my activities as a sport psychology consultant, I have drawn heavily from goal perspective theory (as well as other knowledge bases in sport psychology). For example, as the sport psychology consultant to the USA Gymnastics Women's Artistic Program and National Team, this line of inquiry has provided the foundation for many of the educational materials created, workshops conducted (with coaches, parents, and judges) and one-on-one work with athletes.

In sum, here are the goals when we attempt to apply goal perspective theory to the sport world. We want to enhance the quality of the athletic experience for all participants and maximize their motivated behaviors. This means assisting the talented so they maintain motivation and move toward excellence. We also need to help the more typical individual so that he or she enjoys sport and adopts a physically active lifestyle. To accomplish such aims, we need to get the message out to coaches, parents, sport organizations, and the athletes themselves.

Concluding Thoughts

According to Paul Meehl, "theories rise and decline, come and go, more as a function of baffled boredom than anything else." I disagree. Working over time in accordance with a theoretical framework should entail a mutual growth process. There are ebbs; there are flows; there are a number of curves in the road. If theories are selected and developed as a function of our own values and motivational perspectives, our models should not become boring unless we ourselves are boring and we look at the richness of human behavior as a boring activity. Like the topic itself, motivational research should be energetic and evolving.

Will the goal perspective framework guide my work forever? Probably not. As we test, contrast, integrate, and apply this theoretical framework, it might just evolve into another theoretical paradigm. Such work may lead to the posing of totally different research questions about the nature, scope, and implications of motivation. I think that the future study of motivation will be an exciting and hopefully fruitful adventure. I am very motivated to continue.

Suggested Readings

Ames, C. (1992). Achievement goals, motivational climate and motivational processes. In G. Roberts (Ed.), *Motivation in sport and exercise* (pp. 161–176). Champaign, IL: Human Kinetics.

Duda, J.L. (1992). Sport and exercise motivation: A goal perspective analysis. In G. Roberts (Ed.), *Motivation in sport and exercise* (pp. 57–91). Champaign, IL: Human Kinetics.

Duda, J.L. (1993). Goals: A social cognitive approach to the study of motivation in sport. In R.N. Singer, M. Murphey, & L.K. Tennant (Eds.), *Handbook on research in sport psychology* (pp. 421–436). New York: Macmillan.

Duda, J.L. (1994). A goal perspective theory of meaning and motivation in sport. In S. Serpa (Ed.), *International perspectives on sport and exercise psychology* (pp. 127–148). Indianapolis, IN: Benchmark Press.

Duda, J.L. (1995). *Mental readiness and the motivational climate* [Video]. Indianapolis, IN: USA Gymnastics.

Duda, J.L., & Allison, M. (1990). Cross-cultural analysis in exercise and sport psychology: A void in the field. *Journal of Sport and Exercise Psychology, 12,* 114–131.

Dweck, C.S. (1986). Motivational processes affecting learning. *American Psychologist, 41,* 1040–1048.

Harris, D.V. (1973). *Involvement in sport: A somatopsychic rationale for physical activity.* Philadelphia. Lea & Febiger.

Maehr, M.L., & Nicholls, J.G. (1980). Culture and achievement motivation: A second look. In N. Warren (Ed.), *Studies in cross-cultural psychology* (pp. 221–267). New York: Academic Press.

Nicholls, J.G. (1989). *The competitive ethos and democratic education.* Cambridge, MA: Harvard University Press.

Nicholls, J.G. (1992). The general and the specific in the development and expression of achievement motivation. In G. Roberts (Ed.), *Motivation in sport and exercise* (pp. 31–56). Champaign, IL: Human Kinetics.

Chapter 5

Leadership and Decision Making in Sports

Packianathan Chelladurai

Packianathan Chelladurai is currently Professor of Sport Management at Ohio State University. Former Editor of the *Journal of Sport Management*, he is currently on its editorial board and that of the *European Journal of Sport Management*. He is a frequent reviewer for the *Journal of Sport and Exercise Psychology* and the *Journal of Applied Sport Psychology*. He was honored by the North American Society for Sport Management as the first recipient of its prestigious Earle F. Zeigler award. He has over 75 publications in the areas of physical education, sport psychology, and sport management including the books *Sport management: Macro perspectives* and *Sport management: Micro perspectives* (in press), and the monographs "Leadership" (Co-authored with A.V. Carron) and "Group cohesion and sport" (Co-authored with P. Donnelly and A.V. Carron). He and his wife, Ponnu, enjoy playing with their five grandchildren through two sons.

As I was writing this chapter I was reminded of two statements attributed to different scientists—Albert Einstein's statement that "The whole of science is nothing more than a refinement of everyday thinking," and Kurt Lewin's view that "There is nothing so practical as a good theory." My narration of the chapter highlights how my work on leadership was guided to some extent by my own experiences and thinking. But I do not have any illusions that the models and research results I have outlined in the chapter constitute "a good theory" as Kurt Lewin had suggested. There is much more work to be done before such a claim can be made.

My interest in leadership and decision making in sports coaching stems from my experience as a player, referee, and coach in basketball, and from my professional career as a physical educator in the fifties in India. At that time, professional training in physical education centered largely around "bouncing the ball and blowing the whistle." That is, we were taught how to teach the skills of various sports and how to officiate in those sports. We had to read a set of "how to" books and follow a uniform pattern of lesson plans. The characteristics that distinguished a good physical educator from a bad one were his or her physical prowess and a commanding presence. I was considered good because I could execute the skills of the sport as the textbooks prescribed.

In addition, my membership on the national basketball team contributed much to my status as a physical educator, which, in turn, engendered in me a sense of competence and confidence. I had been a quite successful coach at the university level, and I suspect that my coaching record may compare favorably with the records of many coaches in America. Yet despite that record I had very little knowledge about the physiological and psychological aspects of athletics. That awareness came to me much later in my life when I migrated to Canada at the age of forty one. My decision to migrate to Canada was prompted by my sense of stagnation in life (call it mid-life crisis!). I wanted to do something more than coaching but there were not many opportunities for a physical educator in India. Luckily for me, my friend and teammate in volleyball, Peter Sivanandi, who had already found a teaching job in Canada, urged me to join him. My move to Canada was quite smooth, thanks to his help and friendship.

My first job in Canada was as a physical education teacher and coach at St. Mary's High School in Prince Albert, Saskatchewan, a small city in the far north. For a man who had not seen snow, it was quite an experience to live in a such a cold place. I continued to be successful as a coach and referee of both basketball and volleyball. I was also asked to teach accounting and bookkeeping for the senior grades. I made good use of what I learned in my college degree in commerce and accounting in that aspect of my job. Thus, apart from the change in locale, my first job in Canada was quite similar to the one I left in India.

The real turn in my career took place when I began taking courses toward a master's degree in physical education (it was necessary to get a Canadian degree to make any progress in my career) at The University of Western Ontario. That was a period of great revelation, frustration, and enormous excitement. I found out that, at the age of 42 years, I was almost totally ignorant of sport science. My classmates, the young turks in their twenties who had four years of intense training in sport and exercise sciences behind them, knew much more than I did. That was the frustration. The excitement was that I liked the subject matter so much and I decided to play catch-up. I recall all the days and nights I spent at the university libraries and classrooms. I slept so many nights at the university itself that I cultivated great friendships with the night-time caretakers. In short, the bug of scholarship got into me and I enjoyed it. I did well in all my courses and compared favorably with the brightest of the younger students.

Earle F. Zeigler and Garth Paton, the Dean and Assistant Dean, respectively, of the Faculty of Physical Education at The University of Western Ontario, were impressed enough with my work that they offered me a lecturer's job at the university. I am forever indebted to them for their confidence in me, and I hope that I have not failed them. I am also grateful to my friend and classmate, Terry Haggerty, who taught me the craft of being a good student, and stood by me in my efforts at scholarship.

Even as the threat of "publish or perish" was hanging over my head, I was quite excited about the enterprise of research. As eager as I was about it, I was also doubtful and fearful of entering a new field of endeavor. But something kept me going. (There was always the option of going back to India should I fail in these efforts!) My research has always followed my teaching responsibilities. For example, my experience as a volleyball teacher led me to write an article titled "Spike the second hit." A novel proposition in 1972, it suggested increasing the variability of attack in terms of both time (i.e., whether the second or third hit will be the spike) and space (i.e., the location from which the ball will be spiked). I must also note that the present practice of spiking the second hit had nothing to do with my article because it was published in an obscure and narrowly circulated volleyball publication. I am still proud of the publication because of the realization that my thinking was not far off the mark. This confirmation, that one's thinking is sound, is critical for everyone.

One of my first assignments was to teach fitness and fitness measurement. In that experience, I noticed that the definition and measurement of agility did not capture the essential dimensionality of the concept. So, I wrote a paper on the spatial and temporal dimensions of agility and it was published in a widely circulated journal in Canada. While having published in the journal gave me encouragement, I was most thrilled when Albert Carron, a colleague and an internationally renowned sport psychologist, stopped me in the corridor to tell me that he enjoyed the article, and that he appreciated how I conceptualized the problem and articulated the solution. That was the shot in the arm I needed to realize that I could do scholarly work. It was also the beginning of a long and friendly relationship. It is one of the few occasions when a much younger person mentors an older person, and it illustrates that it is not age or experience but the insights, intelligence, and devotion to the field that are critical to the scholarly domain. At any rate, I am forever grateful to Bert.

Leadership

My thrust toward the study of leadership in sport began during my doctoral studies, thanks to my advisor, Shoukry Saleh, who guided me most admirably during that stage of my life. While there was considerable interest and effort in the study of leadership in industrial and business contexts, I was amazed at the dearth of studies of leadership in sport, especially since almost everyone in America and around the world is aware of the exploits of famous and even not-so-famous coaches who mold disparate and self-centered individuals into collaborative and high-performing units. Obviously, I was quite intrigued by my own success as a coach—that is, intrigued by the fact that I was not aware of the mechanisms through which my actions and behaviors influenced team performance. Thus, my interest in the study of leadership in sports began.

One of the notable theories on leadership at that time was Fred Fiedler's contingency model of leadership, which focused on (a) the *leader's personality* (defined in terms of task orientation versus interpersonal orientation), and (b) *situational favorableness* (defined in terms of leader-member relations, structure of the task, and power residing in the leader's position). In contrast, Robert House's path-goal theory of leadership suggested that it is the characteristics of the members (e.g., personality, abilities, and preferences) that are critical to leadership. In House's view, the leader's role is to (a) clarify for the members how their personal goals can be attained if they follow certain paths (i.e., organizationally relevant paths), (b) help the members traverse those paths, and (c) remove the road blocks that members may encounter. A third theory that impressed me was that of Richard Osborn and James Hunt, who argued that a leader was expected to abide by the requirements of the situation (e.g., the goals of the organization) and at the same time be attuned to the needs and preferences of the members. In their view, a leader's style is composed of a set of *adaptive behaviors* (i.e., adaptations to the situational demands) and a set of *reactive behaviors* (i.e., reactions to members' needs and preferences). It appeared to me that these three apparently different approaches to leadership could be synthesized into a more comprehensive model. Accordingly, my doctoral research was focused on developing that model and testing the propositions arising out of the model. The model has been revised subsequently and the latest version is shown in Figure 5.1.

The Multidimensional Model of Leadership

Briefly, the Multidimensional Model of Leadership focuses on three states of leader behavior—*required* (i.e., the prescriptions and proscriptions defined by the organization and the situation), *preferred* (i.e., member preferences) and *actual*. The antecedent variables that determine these leader behaviors are classified into *situational characteristics* (e.g., goals and norms of the group, its size, its tasks), *member characteristics* (e.g., personality, ability), and *leader characteristics* (e.g., experience, needs, personality). The consequences (outcome variables) in the model are group *performance* and *satisfaction*.

In the multidimensional model, the coach is assumed to be flexible and capable of altering his or her behavior according to changing conditions. If a coach finds that his or her behavior has not resulted in increased performance of the group, the coach is likely to alter the actual behavior with a view to enhance performance (e.g., the coach may spend more time and effort in training and instructing the players). By the same token, if the coach finds that his or her group is not cohesive and integrated, the coach could begin emphasizing those aspects of his or her behavior that would foster warm interpersonal relations within the team.

The multidimensional model takes into account the characteristics of the situation, the leader, and the members, and conceptualizes three states of leader behavior—required, preferred, and actual leader behaviors.

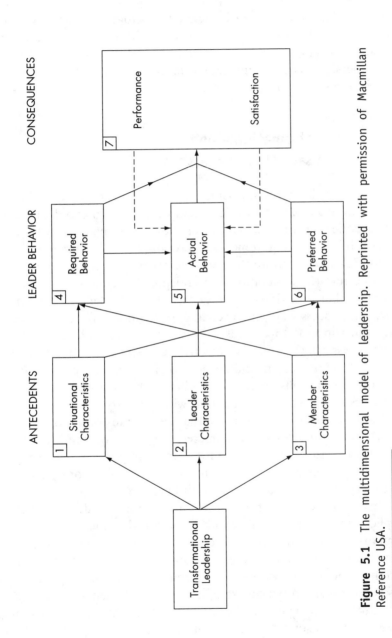

Figure 5.1 The multidimensional model of leadership. Reprinted with permission of Macmillan Reference USA.

The degree of *congruence* among these three states of leader behavior is assumed to affect group performance and member satisfaction. While a portion of the leader's behavior is dictated by situational characteristics, that portion of behavior at the discretion of the leader is expected to have greater impact on member performance and satisfaction. Thus, the coach's leadership plays a significant role in effective utilization of the human resources at his or her disposal.

Transformational and Transactional Leadership

The latest revision of the multidimensional model adds the perspective of *transformational* leadership that has emerged in recent years. The earlier versions conceived of the coach as operating within the confines of situational requirements, exercising his or her limited discretionary influence to motivate the team members. The coach is perceived to exchange rewards for compliance and punishments for noncompliance to his or her directions and requests. Thus, leadership is strictly a *transactional* process—i.e., the exchange of member efforts for coach's approval and support. In contrast, transformational leadership aims to (a) change drastically the team's objectives and strategies, (b) gain commitment to those revised and enhanced objectives, and (c) change the attitudes and assumptions of team members. The basis for transformational leadership is a general discontent with the status quo. In terms of the multidimensional model outlined above, a transformational leader attempts to alter the situational characteristics (i.e., goals and strategies) and the characteristics of team members, including lower level leaders/ managers (i.e., their beliefs and attitudes). These effects of transformational leadership are shown on the left in Figure 5.1.

In many of the descriptions of transformational leadership, there is the implication that such leadership begins with the chief executive officer of an organization and that it filters down to lower levels through the empowerment of successive levels of subordinates. The notion of transformational leadership can also be operative in smaller organizations such as a sports team. A typical example is that of a coach who transforms his or her team from a perennial doormat, as they call it, into a winning team. Such a coach sows discontent with the current image of the team, articulates a vision wherein the team is performing in a winning fashion, and convinces the members that the vision is attainable and that they have the abilities to be a winning team.

Leader Behaviors in Coaching

The descriptions of both transactional and transformational leadership emphasize leader behavior and its effects. The focus is more on what the leader *does* than on what the leader *is*. In fact, the multidimensional model describes leadership in terms of three sets of leader behaviors and the congruence among them. Therefore, any research designed to understand leadership dynamics has to delineate the various forms of a leader's behavior, and develop adequate methods of measuring such behaviors. It is also important that such efforts focus on those categories of leader behavior relevant to a particular context (in this case, sports).

The *Leadership Scale for Sports* (LSS) consists of five factors (described in Table 5.1). It parallels some of the existing scales, and is consistent with the process of individual motivation shown in Figure 5.2. To be more specific, an individual is motivated toward the rewards offered by the team and puts forth certain effort. As this effort can be translated into performance only if the athlete has the ability and perceives his or her task role on the team correctly, the coach's training and instruction behavior would facilitate the athlete's performance. Once the expected performance is achieved, the rewards that should accrue may not all be forthcoming because of the unique nature of athletics. First, athletic competitions are zero-sum games meaning that for every winner there

Table 5.1   Dimensions of Leader Behavior in Sports

Dimension	Description
Training and Instruction	Coaching behavior aimed at improving the athletes' performance by emphasizing and facilitating hard and strenuous training; instructing them in the skills, techniques and tactics of the sport; clarifying the relationship among the members; and by structuring and coordinating the members' activities.
Democratic Behavior	Coaching behavior which allows greater participation by the athletes in decisions pertaining to group goals, practice methods, and game tactics and strategies.
Autocratic Behavior	Coaching behavior which involves independent decision making and stresses personal authority.
Social Support	Coaching behavior characterized by a concern for the welfare of individual athletes, positive group atmosphere, and warm interpersonal relations with members.
Positive Feedback	Coaching behavior which reinforces an athlete by recognizing and rewarding good performance.

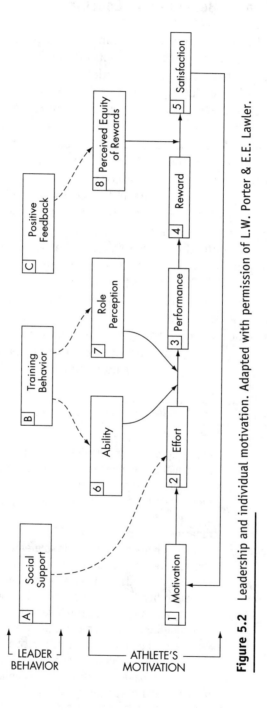

Figure 5.2 Leadership and individual motivation. Adapted with permission of L.W. Porter & E.E. Lawler.

must be a loser. Thus, the effort and performance by the team may not yield the reward of victory in a contest. Further, the contributions of every individual in team sport may not be evident or acknowledged. For instance, the quarterback and the running back may get all the accolades when the efforts of the linemen were equally important.

Under these circumstances, the coach must offer his or her own personal rewards (e.g., praise, encouragement) equitably based on the relative performance of the members. Social support behavior is critical in the context of athletics because athletics is characterized by disproportionately long periods of preparation while the performance periods are considerably shorter. Even in high school athletics, a basketball team may practice for two hours a day for five days for a game that lasts for 40 minutes. (In contrast, I spent about four years to get my Ph.D. and I have been riding on that training for nearly 30 years!) Further, the effort during those training periods is quite agonistic and painful and therefore the coach's social support behavior is critical to maintaining motivation. Incidentally, I am proud to say that the LSS has been translated into 12 languages.

Research related to the multidimensional model, using the LSS as the measure of leadership, has largely employed a simple methodology which requires that one or more of the versions of the LSS be administered to the selected sample of subjects. The three versions of the LSS are (a) athletes' preferences for leader behavior, (b) their perceptions of that behavior in the coach, and (c) the coach's perceptions of his or her own behavior.

One set of studies investigated the effects of individual difference factors on preferred leadership. In the first study of 160 physical education students, Shoukry Saleh and I found that males relative to females preferred their coaches to be more autocratic, yet more supportive. This finding was subsequently replicated by Frank Erle, my student, in his study of intercollegiate and intramural hockey players. For my doctoral dissertation, 216 athletes from Canadian university teams (basketball, wrestling, and track and field) responded to the preferred and perceived versions of the LSS and four single-item measures of satisfaction with individual performance, team performance, leadership, and overall involvement. As hypothesized, those high on cognitive structure (i.e., the need for more information and structure) preferred significantly more training and instruction than those low on that personality variable. Frank Erle showed that those high on *task motivation* preferred more training and instruction while those high on *affiliation motivation* and *extrinsic motivation* preferred more social support.

Following Paul Hersey and Kenneth Blanchard's suggestion that leadership should vary as a function of members' maturity level, Bert Carron and I administered the preference version of the LSS to athletes at four levels of maturity represented by high school midget, high school junior, high school senior, and university-level basketball players. We found that preference for training and instruction progressively decreased from high school midget to high school senior levels but increased at the university level. The preference for social support progressively increased from the midget level to the university level. The explanation for these findings is that as athletes seek independence in their adolescent years they prefer less training from the coaches, but later in the university years they recognize the importance of training, and ask for more of it. As more and more time is taken up by athletics as individuals develop from midget-level to university-level players, their sources of social support narrow down to the athletic team, including the coach, and thus the progressively increasing preferences for social support.

My research also showed that preferences for various forms of leader behaviors varied with the task characteristics of the sport—basketball, wrestling, and track and field. These three sports differ in terms of variability (basketball and wrestling being more variable than track & field) and dependence (basketball is composed of interdependent tasks, whereas wrestling and track & field are independent tasks). As expected, athletes in interdependent tasks (i.e., basketball) and in variable tasks (i.e., basketball and wrestling) preferred more training and instruction than their counterparts in the study. Further, preference for democratic leadership behavior was higher among those athletes in independent tasks (wrestling and track & field) and nonvariable tasks (track & field).

One of the situational characteristics that influences the dynamics of leadership is said to be national culture. In order to verify this proposition, my Japanese colleagues Hiroaki Imamura, Yasuo Yamaguchi, Yoshihiro Oinuma, Takatomo Miyauchi, and I collected data from 115 Japanese and 100 Canadian university-level athletes who responded to the preferred and perceived versions of the LSS, and a set of items eliciting their satisfaction with leadership and personal outcome. We found that the Japanese athletes preferred more autocratic behavior and social support, whereas the Canadian athletes preferred more training and instruction. In addition, the Japanese perceived higher levels of autocratic behavior in their coaches, whereas the Canadians perceived higher levels of training and instruction, democratic behavior, and positive feedback. Finally, the Canadians were more satisfied with leadership as well as their personal outcomes. We concluded that cultural influence was more dominant in leadership dynamics than the contingencies of athletics.

The essence of the multidimensional model is the notion of congruence among the three states of leader behavior leading to the outcome variables. The research investigating this proposition has been largely restricted to assessing the congruence of preferred and perceived leadership, with athlete satisfaction being the outcome of interest. A curvilinear model is proposed in the multidimensional model; that is, if perceived leader behavior differs from preferred leader behavior in either direction, satisfaction should be lowered. My research involved the assessment of the effects of this discrepancy on satisfaction with *leadership, individual performance, team performance,* and *overall involvement.* A significant result of my research was that perceptions that *exceeded* preferences in training and instruction were associated with greater satisfaction with leadership. While this result negates the notion of congruence, it also supports the view that athletics is a task-oriented enterprise and, therefore, the behavior of the leader that emphasizes task accomplishment will meet with approval and satisfaction.

Another significant finding was that discrepancy in any of the dimensions of leader behavior was unrelated to satisfaction with individual performance, while it was related to satisfaction with team performance. The explanation for this finding is that team performance is often judged by external standards (e.g., winning percentage) which tend to be rather objective and stable for some time. On the other hand, an individual's perception of personal performance is judged by the internal performance standards set by the athlete himself or herself, and that such internal standards keep escalating as performance improves. Thus, satisfaction with individual performance is unrelated to what a coach does or how well the team performs.

Decision Making in Coaching

Decision making is perhaps the most important part of coaching. In this regard, the coach has to be concerned with both the rationality of the decisions and the extent to which members participate in making the decisions. The coach can arrive at rational decisions only after defining problems clearly, identifying relevant constraints, generating possible and plausible alternatives, evaluating and ranking the alternatives according to some selected criteria, and then selecting the best alternative in terms of those criteria. In this view, generating alternatives and evaluating them become crucial to rational decision making.

In the other perspective, the coach may allow the team members to participate in decision making. Such participation may vary from consultation with one or a few members, consultation with all members, and group decision making, to delegation of responsibility to one or more team members. We call these variations the *decision styles* of the coach. Participative decisions may enhance the rationality of a decision because the group generally has more information and insight than the individual. Equally, if not more, important is that members will (a) understand the decisions better, (b) feel a sense of ownership of the decisions and, therefore, (c) execute the decisions better. For all these reasons a leader is expected to engage the members in decision making.

Despite the advantages of participative decisions, coaches are said to be very autocratic, and they are criticized for that approach. Some scholars equate a coach's autocratic style with inhuman treatment of the athletes. Further, coaches tend to be defensive about this style. One coach, when questioned about his autocratic style, is purported to have said "Hey, I was asked to run a football program, not a democracy." The implication here is that, somehow, running a football program is not consistent with democratic practices. As I alluded earlier, there is a tendency even among athletes to prefer their coaches to be "benevolent autocrats."

When I examined my own experience, I realized that I had been autocratic in my decisions as a coach. As I read the literature on this issue, vacillating between the two positions (the arguments for participative and autocratic decisions in coaching), I came across Victor Vroom and Philip Yetton's work on member participation in decision making. Their fundamental argument was that instead of dubbing a leader as autocratic or democratic, we must look at the problem situation and its attributes, and decide on the appropriateness of the type and extent of member participation in decision making. That approach suggested to me that perhaps coaching is characterized by situations that warrant more autocratic style than participative style, and that is why coaches tend to be more autocratic in making decisions. This view contradicted the notion that coaches' autocratic style was a function of their personality.

After lengthy discussions with Terry Haggerty, we proposed the *Normative Model of Decision Styles in Coaching* shown in Figure 5.3. The attributes of a problem situation are listed as questions at the top of the diagram. The decision maker answers each of the questions sequentially and follows the path as indicated by his or her yes or no responses to find the feasible style(s) of decision making to a given configuration of problem attributes. Our scheme included (a) autocratic style (where the coach makes the decision by himself or herself with or without consulting the players),

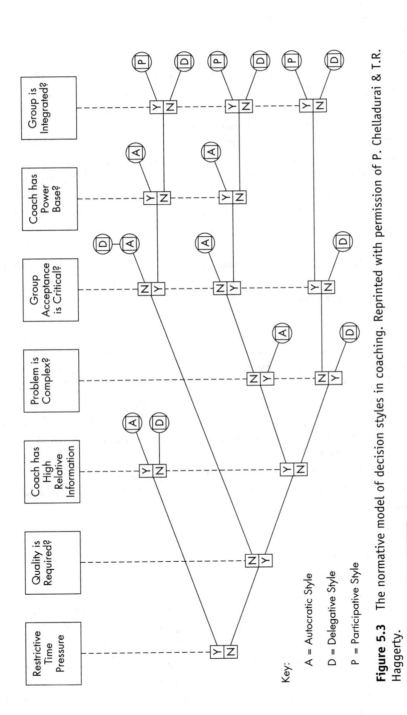

Figure 5.3 The normative model of decision styles in coaching. Reprinted with permission of P. Chelladurai & T.R. Haggerty.

(b) participative style (where every member of the team including the coach jointly make the decision), and (c) delegative style (where the coach delegates the decision making to one or more members of the team).

Pursuant to proposing the model, we and our students—Martha Arnott, Peter Baxter, and Cheng Quek—embarked on some empirical research to verify the extent to which coaches employed different decision styles and whether their choice of a decision style varied from situation to situation. Once again, following Vroom and his associates, we developed a set of cases (scenarios) involving either four or five problem attributes—(a) requirement that a quality decision be made, (b) extent of coach's information pertinent to the problem, (c) relative complexity of the problem, (d) the extent to which the team was integrated, and (e) the extent to which the members of the team would accept the decision if it were to be made by the coach.

In our first study, we asked Canadian university basketball players to express their preferences for a given style of decision making in a given configuration of problem attributes. The cases were described by the first four problem attributes listed above and four decision styles were the choices (autocratic, consultative, participative, and delegative). The results of this study were a rude awakening for us. First, the delegative style was almost totally rejected by the players. Second, both male and female players preferred their coaches to make the decisions more than 50% of the time, with or without consulting the players. In a similar study by Sandy Gordon, with Canadian university soccer players, the results were even more dramatic in that they wanted the coach to make decisions more than 70% of the time.

The explanation for the rejection of the delegative style was simple. In both the autocratic and delegative styles, the influence of the team is minimal. If the players were to forego their influence they would do so in favor of the coach rather than other team members. This is understandable because each player is in one sense competing with the other players on the team and, therefore, would not be comfortable making decisions for others or letting others make decisions for him or her.

As noted earlier, our studies were also concerned with verifying whether the decision style choices or preferences varied with differing configurations of problem attributes. The notable findings from our studies are that the athletes did not prefer to be engaged in decision making when (a) a quality decision was required in a complex problem, or (b) both quality requirement and problem complexity were low. In other words, athletes' preference for participation was minimal in really critical as well as trivial decisions.

The practical implication of this finding for coaches is that it is not fruitful to engage in participative decision making in trivial problems. For example, a basketball coach may allow the players to select the captain for each competition. But does this practice make the coach a democratic one when all that the captain does in a competition is call the toss of the coin? Similarly, the practice of allowing the players to select the starting five for every game does not have much meaning if the coach substitutes the players at the first whistle. I have compared these practices to window dressing by a retailer whose dressed up display windows may or may not reflect the merchandise inside the store.

Many coaches are portrayed as aggressive and loud, and these behavioral tendencies are often equated with autocratic decision making. In contrast, I was supposed to have been different from other coaches: a very pleasant, mild mannered, and socially oriented coach. I realized that despite that image I was as autocratic as any other coach in that I made most of the critical coaching decisions myself. That realization alerted me to the common error of equating a person's mannerisms to that person's style of decision making. What is important is to analyze who made the decision and not to focus on how that decision was communicated.

Yet another confounding issue is the notion of strictness in implementing/enforcing decisions. That is, it is our tendency to consider a strict coach as an autocratic coach. My argument is that strictness in enforcing rules/decisions is independent of how they were made in the first place. A good example is the governance of the United States of America. This country is acknowledged as the most democratic country. All our laws are enacted by Congress, where every issue is hotly debated before a decision is made democratically. But once the decision is made, the bureaucracies (e.g., the Internal Revenue Service, the Immigration and Naturalization Services) take over and strictly implement/enforce it. In a similar manner, the strictness of the coach should be treated apart from the extent to which the coach is participative.

There is also a tendency to confuse the style of decision making with the substance of a decision. I may decide by myself that I would take my wife out for dinner and also choose the restaurant for the occasion. The style was autocratic and the substance was "eating out." In contrast, I could ask my wife if she would like to go out for dinner (seldom does she decline the offer), and I may ask her to decide on the restaurant. Although the style of decision making has changed, the substance remained the same. We should guard ourselves against equating one with the other.

Future Plans

What next? The major task I have set for myself is to revise the Leadership Scale for Sports. The inclusion of transformational leadership in the multidimensional model of leadership makes it necessary to revise the LSS. Further, the development of the LSS was based on exploratory procedures. That is, the five leader behavior dimensions of the LSS were derived from an analysis of a large pool of items purported to reflect leader behavior in sports. A better approach would be to define in advance the relevant dimensions of leader behavior, generate items to reflect those dimensions, and then verify whether those dimensions are supported by data. I propose to consult with athletes and coaches individually and collectively to identify those dimensions of leader behavior that they deem critical to coaching success. I must note that identifying and defining the dimensions of leader behavior is a more critical step than the subsequent conceptually simpler, albeit laborious, processes of generating items and empirically confirming the dimensions.

In a similar manner, I would also like to modify the instrument to assess the choices of and/or preferences for specific decision styles in coaching. Once again, I would like to tap the experiences and expertise of coaches and athletes to gain insight into what attributes of the coaching situation influence such choices and/or preferences. I would also use the narratives of their experiences as the framework for the development of cases. As one can see from the above plans, the topic of leadership in coaching still intrigues and excites me. It will keep me in the "research mill" for quite a while.

Suggested Readings

Bass, B.M. (1985). *Leadership and performance beyond expectations.* New York: The Free Press.

Chelladurai, P. (1978). *A contingency model of leadership in athletics.* Unpublished doctoral dissertation. University of Waterloo, Waterloo, Canada.

Chelladurai, P. (1993). Leadership. In R.N. Singer, M. Murphey, & L.K. Tennant (Eds.), *Handbook of research on sport psychology* (pp. 647–671). New York: Macmillan.

Chelladurai, P. (1993). Styles of decision making in coaching. In: J.M. Williams (Ed.), *Applied sport psychology: Personal growth to peak performance* (2nd ed., pp. 99–109). Palo Alto, CA: Mayfield.

Chelladurai, P., & Haggerty, T.R. (1978). A normative model of decision styles in coaching. *Athletic Administrator, 13,* 6–9.

Chelladurai, P., & Saleh, S.D. (1980). Dimensions of leader behavior in sports: Development of a leadership scale. *Journal of Sport Psychology, 2,* 34–45.

Conger, J.A., & Kanungo, R.N. (1987). Toward a behavioral theory of charismatic leadership in organizational settings. *Academy of Management Review, 12,* 637–647.

Fiedler, F.E. (1967). *A theory of leadership effectiveness.* New York: McGraw-Hill.

Gordon, S. (1988). Decision styles and coaching effectiveness in university soccer. *Canadian Journal of Sport Sciences, 13* (1), 56–65.

House, R.J. (1971). A path-goal theory of leader effectiveness. *Administrative Science Quarterly, 16,* 321–338.

House, R.J., & Shamir, B. (1993). Toward the integration of transformational, charismatic, and visionary theories. In M.M. Chemers & R. Ayman (Eds.). *Leadership theory and research: Perspectives and directions* (pp. 81–107). New York: Academic Press.

Osborn, R.N., & Hunt, J.G. (1975). An adaptive-reactive theory of leadership: The role of macrovariables in leadership research. In J.G. Hunt & L.L. Larson (Eds.). *Leadership frontiers.* Kent, OH: Kent State University.

Riemer, H., & Chelladurai, P. (1995). Leadership and satisfaction in sport. *Journal of Sport and Exercise Psychology, 17* (3), 276–293.

Thompson, J.D. (1967). *Organizations in action.* New York: McGraw-Hill.

Vroom, V.H., Jago, A.G. (1988). *The new leadership: Managing participation in organizations.* Englewood Cliffs, NJ: Prentice-Hall

Vroom, V.H., & Yetton, R.N. (1973). *Leadership and decision-making.* Pittsburgh, PA: University of Pittsburgh Press.

Yukl, G., & Van Fleet, D.D. (1992). Theory and research on leadership in organizations. In M.D. Dunnette & L.M. Hough (Eds.). *Handbook on industrial and organizational psychology* (2nd ed.) (pp. 147–197). Palo Alto, CA: Consulting Psychologists Press, Inc.

Chapter **6**

Cohesion Contagion: Studies of Team Unity by a Cohesive Research Team

Albert V. Carron, Lawrence R. Brawley, and W. Neil Widmeyer

Albert V. Carron (center) is a Professor of Kinesiology, cross-appointed in the Department of Psychology at the University of Western Ontario in London, Ontario. Dr. Carron is also an adjunct Professor in the Department of Kinesiology at the University of Waterloo as well as in the Department of Sport Sciences at Brunel University in London, England. Currently, he is the Editor of the *Journal of Applied Sport Psychology* and a member of the Editorial Board of the *Journal of Sport and Exercise Psychology*. Dr. Carron is a Fellow of the Association for the Advancement of Applied Sport Psychology and the Canadian Psychomotor Learning and Sport Psychology Society and Past President of the Canadian Association of Sport Sciences. Over the past 20 years his research has been focused on group dynamics in sport and exercise. Dr. Carron is the co-author of a number of chapters with (Neil Widmeyer and Larry Brawley) and the author of five books including *Social psychology of sport, Motivation: Implications for coaching and teaching*, and *Group dynamics: Theoretical and practical issues*. He enjoys tennis, jogging with friends, and travel.

Lawrence R. Brawley (left) is a Professor and Associate Chair, Graduate Studies, in the Department of Kinesiology, cross-appointed Professor in the Department of Health Studies and Gerontology, University of Waterloo, Canada. He is also an adjunct Research Professor, Department of Health and Exercise Science, Wake Forest University, Winston-Salem, NC. Dr. Brawley is on the Editorial Board of the *Journal of Sport and Exercise Psychology* and the *Journal of Applied Sport Psychology*. He is the co-author (with Bert Carron and Neil Widmeyer) of numerous book chapters and articles about group cohesion in exercise and sport. He is also well published with respect to research applications of social psychology in health and exercise, particularly social factors influencing adherence and compliance behavior. Dr. Brawley is a Past President and Fellow in the Association for the Advancement of Applied Sport Psychology. Favorite work activities are research with close colleagues and his graduate students. With Nancy, Larry shares a passion for watching his children in competitive aquatics, and he loves good wine, epic novels, and exercise.

Dr. W. Neil Widmeyer (right) is a Professor in the Department of Kinesiology at the University of Waterloo. Dr. Widmeyer has just completed a three-year term as Chair of Social Psychology for the Association for the Advancement of Applied Sport Psychology. In addition to his research articles and chapters (co-authored with Larry Brawley and Bert Carron) focusing on the dynamics of sport teams and exercise groups, Dr. Widmeyer has conducted considerable research in the area of aggression in sport. He is particularly interested in understanding the causes and consequences of the frustration that athletes experience. Teaching has always held high priority for Dr. Widmeyer, and throughout his career he has received considerable recognition for achieving excellence in teaching. Most recently, Dr. Widmeyer has spent a considerable amount of time in the application of sport psychology with Major Junior A hockey players. His loves include his wife, Lynne, his three children and four grandchildren, along with downhill skiing and golf.

For the past 15 years, the three of us have been collaborators in various research programs directed toward, first, the development of a test of group cohesion (*The Group Environment Questionnaire, GEQ*), and then, subsequently, an identification of the correlates of cohesion in sport and exercise groups. This chapter focuses on the dynamics of *our* group during this period.

If you say "15 years" quickly, it hardly seems significant—time flies. But, our 15-year collaboration has required considerable contact including regular commuting between our two universities (which represents a round trip of 200 km), and almost daily telephone conversations and E-mail messages. Researchers who study group dynamics are familiar with the phenomenon of social loafing—the tendency for people to work at less than 100 percent capacity when they are involved in group projects. None of us appreciates a social loafer, so our meetings and our other interactions and communications have been essential for us to plan, carry out and complete our collaborative endeavors.

Our collaborative work has been an important personal and professional constant in our lives. A great quote used by Jerry Kramer to describe the feelings of the Green Bay Packers at the beginning of each new season, aptly describes our own feelings "[at the next meeting], as soon as we saw each other, the old feelings returned, of warmth and affection, respect and admiration" (p. 34).

Originally, we developed our partnership because of a mutual interest in group cohesion. In fact, we have been intrigued by this theoretical construct and it's safe to say that all of our research over the 15-year period has focused on some aspect of group cohesion. As we delved more and more deeply into the theoretical side of group cohesion, we gradually developed greater cohesiveness within our own group.

Two well-known social psychologists, Roy Baumeister and Mark Leary, drew upon research evidence from a wide cross section of areas in psychology and concluded that the need to belong—the desire for interpersonal attachments—is a fundamental human motivation. So, it's not unusual for people to form into groups. However, anyone who has been in a highly cohesive group—a family, a close friendship, a work unit, a military unit, a fraternity, or a sport team—knows that a cohesive group is special. As a member, you have more personal confidence in your own work as well as in the collective output of the group. In a cohesive group, there's also a high degree of satisfaction; you feel less tension; you're more productive personally; there's a feeling of permanence and stability because you and the other group members are less likely to leave; and, finally, the credit for any success and the blame for any failure is accepted equally.

But, of course, group cohesion doesn't appear overnight; it develops slowly over time as the individual members of the group interact, contribute to the group product, make sacrifices for the group, work out their group role(s), share experiences including collective successes and setbacks. Over 30 years ago, Bruce Tuckman suggested that the development of all groups proceeds through common stages: *forming, storming, norming,* and *performing.* Subsequently, a fifth stage was added which was referred to as *adjourning.*

In its development, our group experienced the first four stages identified by Tuckman and, to some extent, the adjourning stage as well. In some cases, we passed through one of the stages more than once. Consequently, in trying to come to grips with the nature of our collective experiences, we thought that Tuckman's model would serve as a useful framework to organize our chapter.

Getting Together: The Forming Stage

The forming stage in a group's development is the period in which the individual members become familiar with one another and some bonds begin to form. The group members identify the group task and the methods that are suitable to carry it out. Naturally, one might think that the cohesion that develops in a group's formative stages might relate to the group's task and strategies to accomplish it—task-related cohesion. Surprisingly, this idea hadn't received a lot of support in the group dynamics literature. This was certainly a question about cohesion that we wanted to answer even when we were forming our own research group. Thus, some perspective on how we finally got around to asking and answering the question might be gained by considering how our research group formed and what led us toward group cohesion research.

Our social bonds began to form in the late 1970s when we met at various scientific conferences in sport psychology. Sport psychology was a small research community in the 1970s. So at the scientific meetings everybody knew each other. This familiarity led Neil and Larry, (who are at the University of Waterloo) to ask Bert (who is at the University of Western Ontario, which is about one hour down the road) if he was interested in teaching Neil's course during Neil's sabbatical leave. Bert agreed and in the fall of 1980, he commuted from London to Waterloo once a week. Part of Neil's sabbatical was spent in Waterloo, so the three of us decided to meet in the mornings prior to the weekly class. The focus of our discussions in those weekly meetings was group cohesion in sport because we had all had a long-standing interest in the subject. Thus, all the conditions were in place for more than a one-time meeting between colleagues with a mutual research interest.

Neil's interest in cohesion stemmed partly from his doctoral research, which was carried out under the supervision of Rainer Martens at Illinois. When Neil began his doctoral studies at Illinois, Rainer had just completed his extensive investigation of the cohesiveness of intramural teams and had helped develop the Sport Cohesiveness Questionnaire. Neil was also influenced by a group dynamics seminar led by the dynamic James Davis (*Group Performance*). As a later influence, his sabbatical leave was spent with Marvin Shaw (*Group Dynamics: The Psychology of Small Group Behavior*), Ivan Steiner (*Group Process and Productivity*), and Alvin Zander (*Group Dynamics: Research and Theory,* which was co-authored by Dorwin Cartwright, *Motives and Goals in Groups, Groups at Work,* and *Making Groups Effective*). Indeed, Zander's writing and his support for our work had a great effect on all of us.

Our discussions on cohesion in 1980 were opportune because Neil had just completed a research project with one of his graduate students and Larry had been a committee member on that student's thesis. Larry also had a long-standing interest in groups. One important factor influencing this interest was the group dynamics work of Carolyn and Muzafer Sherif. Their numerous co-authored publications, which include the classics *Groups in Harmony and Tension* and *Reference Groups,* stimulated Larry's interest in group dynamics generally. In addition, in her role as a Ph.D. advisor at Pennsylvania State University, Carolyn Sherif broadened Larry's views on group dynamics generally and cohesion specifically. The Sherifs' camp studies, which focused on the formation and cohering of groups as well as on their intergroup relations, brought a real-world perspective to the study of groups in Carolyn's courses. For Larry, it provoked an interest in groups that has lasted to the present.

One important factor influencing Bert's interests was the writing of Alvin Zander. A second factor was various research projects in which he had been involved with a colleague, Chella Chelladurai, and a graduate student, Jim Ball. A third influencing factor was serendipitous. Larry, in his role as Conference Program Chairperson of the 1981 North American Society for the Psychology of Sport and Physical Activity (NASPSPA) meeting in Asilmomar, California, had invited Bert to present a keynote address. The focus of Bert's talk was to be the "state of the union" in group cohesion in the domain of sport and exercise.

Quite naturally, then, all of these interests and circumstances generated a considerable amount of discussion at our weekly meetings.

Those weekly meetings with Larry and Neil helped Bert organize his talk for NASPSPA. It was decided that a useful framework for that talk would be to outline what was generally known about cohesion in both mainstream psychology and sport psychology; to discuss the implications of that research; to point out its limitations; and, to propose future directions.

One limitation (and future direction) that was apparent to us was the manner in which cohesion was conceptualized and assessed in both mainstream psychology and sport and physical activity. In general, sport research was not guided by a theoretical framework, which resulted in a real problem for the understanding of group cohesion. This problem can be summarized by a frequently used metaphor—the research facts were like bricks scattered about a brickyard. Ironically, given that cohesion is a construct represented by uniting, there was little organization or plan for organizing the cohesion bricks into a "coherent" whole. The blueprints for the cohesion edifice were never drawn, although numerous architects and draftspersons in group dynamics had proposed some ideas for blueprints. As a consequence, measures were frequently not matched to theories or models, resulting in Peter Mudrack's recent complaint that the measurement of cohesion had become inexcusably sloppy. We believed that if our understanding of cohesion in sport was to increase, the operational measures had to be improved. As a result, we came to the decision that we had to develop a psychometrically sound sport cohesion inventory based upon a conceptual model. Our group task was identified, group cohesiveness was developing, and, for our group, Tuckman's forming stage was substantially complete.

A Harmonious Group to a Group in Tension: The Storming Stage

From a social perspective, the main characteristic of Tuckman's storming stage is that tension develops among group members; from a task perspective, there is resistance to the group's methods and the group task. Although storming does occur early in a group's development, it is not a one-time event. Anyone who has been in a close social relationship knows that storming (or intragroup conflict, discord, disagreement, disharmony, friction, strife—call it what you prefer) periodically arises throughout the life of the group. It's inevitable. So the important factor for group effectiveness is never whether storming occurs but, rather, how it is managed.

It certainly isn't accurate to suggest that any time discord arises in our research group, we immediately draw on our group dynamics expertise and tell each other "relax, it's just that darn storming phase again; it will pass." When conflicts arise, they're unique, unexpected, unpleasant, and unsettling. In every instance, when we realize that the temperature of the discussion has risen to unsettling levels, our respect for each other stimulates us to try to identify the problem and negotiate the contentious issues. For problems that have the potential to be chronic, we come to some agreement on how we can handle the general issue in the future. Some examples might serve to illustrate our approach.

One issue which arose rather early in our group's development involved the editing of the group product. For each of our projects, one of us is responsible for developing what we refer to as a "no-shame draft." The concept was introduced by Neil and we believe it is very effective; we still use it. Systematically (i.e., from project to project), we rotate the responsibility for preparing the first draft of a manuscript. The individual who prepares that draft understands that (a) he is preparing a working document for discussion, (b) that document isn't expected to be ready for submission, and (c) it will be edited extensively by the other two group members.

Our approach has obvious advantages—three heads are better than one. But, this approach also can be a disadvantage, because too many cooks can spoil the broth. If we consider a manuscript to be a broth, each of us brings different ingredients to the kitchen—different writing styles, different personal preferences for communicating an idea, and sometimes different ideas about how the rationale for a problem should be developed. Early in our group's development, we let our personal preferences have free rein with the result that the amount of editing all of us did on a no-shame draft was extensive. When one no-shame draft was completely rewritten by the other two group members, the author expressed frustration and anger at what was apparently a complete waste of time on his part. Through discussions, we agreed that the concept of a no-shame draft was good, that subsequent editing by the other two members produced a better group product, and therefore, that we should retain our protocol. At the same time, we also agreed that any editing of the no-shame draft had to be carried out within the framework provided by the author.

A second issue that also arose rather early was in the item-generating phase of questionnaire development. The items in our questionnaire evolved from a conceptual model, so it is useful to discuss our model's evolution prior to discussing the storming that went on in the item-generating phase.

Our knowledge of the cohesion literature to 1982, led us to conclude that there were recurring themes in the way groups generally and cohesion specifically were conceptualized and investigated. These themes represented two major types of distinctions. The first distinction related to whether the research question was centered around the group's task or social aspects of the group (e.g., "is the group interacting in a way that makes it task-effective, or is it interacting in a way that reflects the social activities and influences among members?").

The second distinction that emerged from our review concerned the way in which the group was examined. In one approach—the group perspective—the collective was the focus. In a second approach—the individual perspective—the input/perspective of each member was the focus. The group versus individual distinction had considerable importance in that it influenced both the type of data analysis group investigators used and their subsequent interpretations of their results.

Bert had presented these issues in an organizational model he used to illustrate the state of the union in sport group dynamics research. Our research group's input into this address and our collaboration led us to agree that these distinctions should be the core for our blueprint for cohesion.

Another important point of agreement after considering the group dynamics research and the "state of the union" in sport group research was what we *would not* include in our blueprint of cohesion. We felt that past investigators had included the things that determine cohesion—the inputs to cohesion (e.g., the sport league, the group task, the coach's management style)—as manifestations of cohesion. They had also included the consequences of cohesion (e.g., player and team satisfaction). Consequently, it was our belief that some researchers and theoreticians had confused the antecedents (i.e., inputs) and consequences (i.e., outputs) of cohesiveness with the actual concept.

To avoid cohesion becoming a grand seining net (i.e., a huge net commercial fishermen drag behind their ocean-going boats which traps both the desired school of fish and everything else it passes), we tried to construct items for our measure which reflected the manifestations of cohesiveness that we had identified (i.e., the task and social attractions of the individual to the group, and the individual's perceptions of task and social group integration). As we realized very quickly, the task of constructing items representative of our cohesion dimensions (a) wasn't easy and (b) didn't lend itself to quick consensus.

Each of us, like investigators who had gone before us, had personal biases about which items best reflected group cohesion. We tried all the sound and recommended procedures of test/scale construction but, nonetheless, our discussions often became heated. At times, tempers even flared—after all, how could those "other guys" even think of discarding "my items." While our approach to research had obvious advantages—more group resources were available—we incorrectly assumed we would have consensus and be cohesive about what best reflected our conceptual ideas. We politely debated, then argued, and then heatedly disagreed about whose items would make the "final cut." Our backgrounds were from competitive sport; all of us have competed and coached at the intercollegiate level—Larry in swimming, Bert in football, and Neil in track and field. Consequently, it's not surprising that each of us battled hard to have his cohesion items included on the "first string."

The most severe storming (i.e., strongest disagreements) occurred in the earliest period of our group's development. Nonetheless, even at that relatively early group stage, there was "resistance to group disruption"—an indication of group or team cohesion. As a research group, we were more interested in pursuing our team research goals than in satisfying our personal preferences. Thus, we agreed on new productive rules for working together. We mutually respected one another, and wanted our research group and friendship to continue. While we still "storm" within our research team, our previously typical patterns of behavior—withdrawing from the discussion, talking over one another, or acquiescing with a martyr's sigh (we're all good at this one)—have disappeared. They are characteristic reactions to conflict that we all recognize. Our norm now is to step back and negotiate a common ground. Our desire to have consensus and stability works to alleviate the anxiety of conflict.

These early attempts at conflict resolution were signs of moving out of Tuckman's group storming phase. As we did this, the productivity of our group increased considerably.

Common Expectations: The Norming Stage

The norming stage of group development is the period in which group norms and roles are established. Increased task cooperation among members is prevalent. Group norms are generalized expectations for the behavior of all group members. For all groups, norms serve an important function. They are (a) descriptive and evaluative (i.e., they represent the group's beliefs about the standards of behavior considered appropriate), (b) informal and unobtrusive (i.e., they are not specifically or overtly set out by the group), (c) internalized (i.e., individual members adhere to them because of the satisfaction this produces), and (d) flexible (i.e., minor deviations are acceptable). Over time, through constant interaction and communication among group members, all groups develop generalized expectations for the behavior of individual group members; our group was and is no exception.

One of our group norms is to develop an agenda and keep the minutes of our meetings. Neil, who has had considerable experience as an administrator, introduced this tradition and assumed the role of recording secretary. The result has been a consistently accurate written record of our group's plans and decisions and, more importantly, which of us is responsible for carrying out a responsibility on behalf of the group.

It has also become the norm for our group to have an annual two-day retreat at Neil's chalet in Northern Ontario at the end of the fall term. This is possibly our most productive meeting of the year. We use the retreat to finish up projects and set out ideas for future group endeavors. Not surprisingly, the retreat serves as a catalyst for the renewal of task and social cohesion.

A role is a shared expectation for the behavior of specific individuals in a group. Roles can be formal (i.e., directly established by the group or organization) or informal (i.e., evolve as a result of the interactions that take place among group members). All of the roles in our group are informal—and dynamic. That is, we do not have one leader, one writer, one research catalyst. Roles and group responsibilities shift with projects and circumstances.

The norms that exist and the role expectations that developed for each member of our three-person research team served to make our activity highly productive during both the norming and performing stages of group development. During a 10-year period from 1983 through 1993, each of us took various leadership roles in investigations that spurred new directions in sport cohesion. The group norm to complete the research and the leadership role went hand in hand. The norm for productivity was characterized by obtaining a research grant, following its work plan, presenting our work at scientific meetings and immediately following up with a research publication. On every project, each of us showed an almost equal work ethic to pursue this pattern of goal directed behavior although there was always a team leader associated with the impetus for a specific research project.

Our overriding objective shortly after we had published a monograph and a journal article on the GEQ in 1985 was to validate the measure, and in so doing, validate the conceptual model of cohesion. Indeed, this is a common pattern in the development of many psychological measures. Nunnally, a well-known expert in the area of research design and statistics, stressed that researchers are never really finished with what he called the validation process. In fact, virtually every study that uses the GEQ as the focal point contributes to the validation process.

Performing to Adjourning to . . . ?: The Next Stage

Performing refers to a stage in group life where relationships are stabilized and the group's focus is on productivity and performance. Our initial performing stage involved developing the GEQ and then carrying out initial validation studies. In those validation studies, we found that the GEQ possessed what is known as concurrent and discriminant validity. We established that GEQ factors represented our four dimensional group cohesion model (i.e., factorial validity), and that it correctly captured the primary aspects of cohesion that we anticipated would be associated with different types of sports groups. Thus, for example, we found that team sports that require performance interaction (e.g., basketball, volleyball) are characterized by stronger group-task integration. Conversely, teams that do not require interaction—teams in sports where team performance results from the simple addition of athlete efforts (e.g., bowling teams, track teams)—are characterized by strong individual-task attraction.

By 1987, we had completed these studies and suddenly were confronted with the realization that our group's *raison d'être* had disappeared. In other words, the adjourning stage of group development was imminent. In the adjourning stage, group members' contact decreases and social dependency among individual members is reduced. The realization that the group might dissolve was a psychological turning point for us. We had completed our group task. The experiences associated with the development of the GEQ had been positive; we had worked well together, we enjoyed each other's company. Consequently, even though we had a feeling of closure, we were unwilling to let our research team disband. Furthermore, we were inextricably linked with the fate of the GEQ. As a result, we sat down and planned programs of research involving the GEQ. Our group had moved back into the performing phase and has remained there to the present day.

After planning a number of programs of research, it became apparent that we were no longer simply validating a measure, we were expanding and clarifying our conceptual model. Today, it seems that our work begs the goal of being integrated into a theory—something that our own thinking and the views of colleagues in various aspects of social psychology have suggested. There appears to be growing consensus among group dynamics theoreticians that the four dimensions of cohesion (i.e., the task and social attractions of the individual to the group, the perceptions of task and social group integration by group members) are central to the idea of a multifaceted group cohesion. By "central," we mean that individual group members psychologically integrate their perceptions of group interactions and their personal attractions to the group. They "gel" these in some cognitive fashion that is probably influenced by their group or team experiences. In so doing, a view of the degree of group unity evolves for each group member. This overall perceived unity is the result of some common influence of one or more of the four cohesion factors we have identified that a team member sees as characteristic of his/her group. Although we suspected this might be the case when we first proposed our conceptual model, the research we have conducted and reviewed since 1987 now suggests it is a real possibility.

In order to appreciate this conclusion, comments about a few of the studies that preceded the conclusion seem in order. The first of these studies concerned group size, a characteristic that Neil suggested would have impact on cohesion because of the way in which interaction and communication occurs among group members. Previous group dynamics research had showed that as the size of the group increases, (a) the number of communication links rapidly increases, (b) the level of member interaction becomes more complicated, (c) equal participation by all members becomes compromised, and (d) satisfaction with participation declines. Consequently, Neil argued that cohesion would be affected. What was unclear, however, was what aspect of cohesion (task? social?) would suffer.

To examine this issue, Neil took a leadership role in getting our group to develop a research design and a grant. Eventually the grant was obtained and this allowed us to conduct studies to manipulate the size of groups. The basic research plan was to vary group size so that small (3 members), medium (6 members), and large (9 members) teams played three-on-three basketball in a recreational adult league. Because the league and game we created were not unusual for recreational/ intramural university participation, the level of salience and involvement for participants was considerably greater than in past group dynamics research where laboratory groups were constructed to perform novel tasks. The results of this experiment showed that smaller-sized teams were higher in task cohesion, whereas medium-sized teams were higher in social cohesion. Thus, an optimal size for the development of different aspects of cohesion was identified. Because group size is central to the way teams interact with one another both on and off the court, the results of this study supported the contention that size is an important moderator of task and social cohesion.

A second example of studies proceeded with Bert as the team leader. Bert's idea was that members in a variety of different groups—sport teams, groups in industry, fitness classes—would consistently exhibit a lack of adherence to the group or its tasks if the group was low in cohesion. Nonadherence was thought to be reflected by the presence of various negative group behaviors, such as drop-out behavior, absenteeism, lateness, early departure, and/or reduced work output. Consequently, we hypothesized that when these behaviors were consistently observed, lower cohesion would also be present. Conversely, maintenance of regular participation, consistent group effort, strong attendance, and early arrival would reflect a united group.

Again, we obtained research funding in order to conduct studies to determine if these hypotheses about the relationship between cohesion and nonadherence were correct. We explored these hypotheses among exercise groups (i.e., where interaction among group members is not necessarily demanded by the group task) and among sport teams (i.e., where interaction in practices and games is necessary for effective functioning). We found that level of cohesion was strongly related to the incidence of nonadherence behavior. In the case of exercise classes, we found that lower perceptions of group task cohesion were associated with a higher rate of dropout from the class, while higher perceptions of class cohesion were related to greater member retention. Subsequently, Bert and his former student and now our colleague, Dr. Kevin Spink of the University of Saskatchewan, extended our research in several studies. They showed that not only did the lower cohesion/lower adherence relationship remain consistent for dropout behavior, it was also observed for absenteeism, lateness, early exit from class, and for the rate of attendance.

Our research team also conducted an initial investigation that examined these same relationships among sport teams (where dropout is a very unusual behavior). We reasoned that the inconsistent adherence of certain team members (the behaviors of absenteeism and lateness at practice used as our dependent measures) might be related to levels of lower cohesion. Our views were verified. In sport teams, lower levels of perceived cohesion were indeed related to a higher incidence of absenteeism/lateness.

A third example was our examination of the relationship between cohesion and resistance to group disruption. We "dusted off" an earlier view of group cohesion advanced by Gross and Martin who argued that resistance to group disruptions was the most conceptually valid definition of cohesion. Larry was team leader in obtaining funding and initiating this project. During Larry's Ph.D. work at Pennsylvania State University, he attended Carolyn Sherif's graduate seminar on group dynamics, where she introduced a social psychology graduate student who provided, in collaboration with a colleague, a thought-provoking discussion of the intimate relationship between resistance to disruption and cohesion.

After considering the arguments pertaining to resistance to disruption, our research group felt that several of the multiple aspects of cohesion we were measuring with the GEQ would be related to a group's perceived resistance toward being disrupted. Our dilemma, however, was that ethically and practically we could neither physically disrupt the group nor wait for significant disruptions to occur. These obstacles to conducting research were likely reasons for the scant research attention paid to the study of resistance to disruption.

In order to get around these obstacles, we decided to have group members identify events that had the potential to be disruptive to themselves or their team. We then asked each member about his/her perception of the group's ability to resist these disruptions. Thus, we obtained a numerical estimate of the strength with which a group member perceived his/her group could resist.

We conducted three studies, two in sport and one in exercise. Our strategy seemed to be effective. In the three studies conducted, aspects of cohesion were strongly related to the perception of resistance to disruption. The higher the perceived level of cohesion, the greater the perception that the team/class could resist potential disruptions, such as cliques, the loss of a key team member, conflict, and loss of or conflict with a team leader (e.g., coach).

In summary, these three areas of research—group size, adherence/absenteeism, and resistance to group disruption—each consisting of several studies, provided a foundation for the assumption that the GEQ possessed predictive validity. They also characterized the early portion of research that was part of the performing stage of our research group. That stage continues to the present and in the eight years since the publication of the resistance to disruption studies, research on group cohesion has gradually increased.

At various times over the past 8 years, each of us has branched out to collaborate with other colleagues on cohesion research projects. These colleagues have included established researchers as well as current and former graduate students. Initially, we struggled psychologically with the reality that each group member had "someone else" with whom he was sharing, adopting, and implementing ideas pertaining to cohesion. Further, it became necessary to discuss the topic of intellectual property as the opportunities for research on group cohesion with colleagues mounted, because our research group had implicitly held the view since 1981 that personal ideas about cohesion (i.e., research projects, position papers) were the property of the group. However, our mutual intellectual respect and the trust and affection we had developed as a group eventually made us view this broader sharing of ideas from a positive "glass is half full" (versus half empty) perspective. Here was an opportunity to bring fresh ideas back to the group and to ensure that our own thinking did not stagnate or become one of a "group mind" such that we failed to challenge our own ideas.

Another Performance Phase: Integration of Research

This sharing of ideas with others, challenges to the validity of the GEQ, and our own collaborative work invigorated the performance phase from 1988 to the present. For example, in 1989, Bert was asked to be guest-editor of a special issue of the *International Journal of Sport Psychology*. This opportunity gave each of us and our collaborators the opportunity to integrate some of the work we had done in the form of a review paper. Rather than the three of us reviewing one literature, we divided our efforts, with Bert choosing to write about group size, Neil to write about group composition, and Larry to write about cohesion. Quite naturally, the phenomenon of group cohesion was also addressed in part in the articles by Bert (group size contributes to cohesion) and Neil (the quantity, variety, and fit of member characteristics contribute to cohesion).

In discussing cohesion, Larry's job became one of not only summarizing our findings but also of (a) further clarifying our group's conceptual ideas about perceptions of team cohesion, (b) suggesting how to overcome consistent problems in cohesion research and (c) suggesting directions for future research. This paper represented our collective viewpoint and provided a somewhat meatier description of our conceptual view of cohesion. It was one of several that we were asked to write or present over a period of years.

What was different about what we began to write (although we had discussed these notions much earlier) was (a) how the social cognitions (i.e., individual attractions to the group—task and social—and group integration—task and social) about cohesion developed, (b) how each changed over time in the group's history, (c) how not all four of the aspects of cohesion we measured were necessarily present in strength at any given point in a group's history, and (d) how all aspects of cohesion were not necessarily observed in all types of groups. We also began to write more about the assumptions behind our conceptual model, in short, about the idea that a group member's beliefs about his/her group are cognitively integrated, held in memory, and are of at least four kinds (i.e., the four cohesion constructs contained in the GEQ).

In this stage, our research group began to integrate more of our thinking while being simultaneously involved in conducting other group research and in addressing challenges to the GEQ's factorial validity. On the research side, we found that the various aspects of group cohesion were related to a broad number of determinants (e.g., social context, communication), consequences (e.g., satisfaction with group performance, performance outcome), and social-cognitions about the group (e.g., perceptions of goal influence, attribution for group success/failure, collective efficacy). Indeed, the generality of the relationships between cohesion and these numerous variables may be a natural consequence of the development of a group around its motivational bases and the shared beliefs of group members about cohesion and other related variables. Many of the relationships we detected, although not previously studied in sport and exercise, were, in hindsight, not surprising. Most of the groups that we studied had a well-developed set of group properties, thereby encouraging social interaction and collective points of view about matters of consequence to the group. As well, the breadth of the findings about cohesion from studies using the GEQ suggested that it was operating in a consistent, predictable fashion—one sign that something reliable and valid was being used.

Relatively recently, we found that the factor structure of the GEQ had been questioned in two studies, one of which had received a great deal of attention from colleagues. We received a considerable number of queries from colleagues who did not normally conduct group dynamics research but were immediately concerned that a well-established instrument had apparently been found to be deficient. It is interesting to note what happened to our research group under these circumstances. When threatened by a force outside the group, the characteristic reaction of a cohesive group is to unite with even greater unity against that outside force.

The reaction of our research group was no exception to this well-established finding. Initially, we were angered, felt threatened, and were anxious to write a rebuttal that would point out the flaws in the challenges to the GEQ. After considerable discussion, we began to look at the challenge to factorial validity as part of a larger problem that we had observed in the research literature—how correctly to observe a phenomenon that is multifaceted and dynamic (i.e., changes gradually over time), how to understand a group phenomenon that does not necessarily reflect all its faces at one time, and, finally, how to choose an appropriate methodological/analytical strategy that clearly answers the group-related research questions being posed. Once we considered the research challenge from this perspective, it forced us to reexamine our conceptual ideas from a theoretical, methodological, and social context perspective. The cohesion that resulted from our reaction to an outside threat now helped us direct our efforts to reconsider our own ideas.

Reconsidering Validity Procedures for the GEQ

A key element of whether a psychological concept can be detected and identified is that it must exhibit characteristics that are measurable *and* that these characteristics reveal themselves in consistent, patterned ways. In order to demonstrate that a measurement instrument has "factorial validity," we count on the foregoing principle. However, when the phenomenon that researchers are trying to detect is fairly dynamic (that is, it doesn't exhibit the same "face" with the same clarity every time it is measured), the approach to demonstrating factorial validity cannot follow a rigid set of rules. A concept cannot be "boxed" in a convenient way to allow for the statistical testing that is generally associated with demonstrating factorial validity. It is the understanding of the concept that should direct the methodological approach taken.

The convenience of a statistical technique or a methodological approach without joint consideration of the phenomenon (in this case, cohesion) being examined can result in a host of research headaches. As Fred Kerlinger put it, "poor measurement can invalidate any scientific investigation" (p. 473). Because our colleagues had given more attention to statistical concerns (therefore, their analyses were conducted very well) but little to the nature of group cohesion, they had committed the error against which Kerlinger had cautioned.

We came to this conclusion because several conceptual features of group cohesion had been overlooked in the analyses of our colleagues. In brief, these features were that (a) the predominant aspect(s) of cohesion (i.e., individual attraction to the group—task and social—and group integration—task and social) can change over time, (b) all aspects of cohesion are not necessarily developed and observable at any given point in a group's history, and (c) all aspects of cohesion are not necessarily found in all sport groups.

This means conceptually that task cohesion and social cohesion are not constantly stable. This also means that investigators seeking to confirm/refute the concept of cohesion must adopt, at minimum, one of two research design strategies. These strategies are compatible and take into account the nature of cohesion. Researchers must (a) follow a number of newly established teams over time, sampling frequently, or (b) sample a wide cross-section of teams that are heterogeneous in their makeup and in their stage of development. The former is what is called a longitudinal, prospective strategy, while the latter is a current, cross-sectional strategy. Neither approach is methodologically easy. The latter approach was what we used first to explore the cohesion factors that the GEQ could measure, and, as a result, we detected four factors. Neither approach was used in the investigations that challenge the GEQ's factorial validity. In fact, the nature of cohesion as a dynamic phenomenon was largely overlooked.

If We Build It, Will Others Come?

Most recently, our research group has discussed future plans for investigating cohesion; these plans are what we refer to as our "Field of Dreams." Each of us has presented the group with a grandiose plan that we would like to explore. In their basic form, each of our personal field of dreams for the group revolves around the integration and further developments of the cohesion construct.

One of our field of dreams involves what, for lack of a better description, can be referred to as theory building. That is, it is our belief that as a research group we need to build a theory about group cohesion that moves beyond the research conducted to date. Central to this theory will likely be our idea of the multi-factored conceptual model of cohesion that has been the foundation for the GEQ and our own research. However, we need to provide leadership in pulling together the potential antecedents and potential consequences identified in our earlier work into a larger framework that offers testable propositions.

Our research group's actions in writing book chapters and delivering symposia over the past 10 years have given us some of the review-type beginnings necessary for theory building. Knowing that others beyond our group agree with a number of our ideas (particularly the centrality of our four aspects of cohesion) provides a supportive social environment in which we could offer this new conceptual work. It also gives us the incentive to tie together some of our colleagues' new ideas with our own. This grand endeavor seems exciting in that it involves the integration of ideas from a number of group cohesion researchers.

Conceptually, theory-building is needed so that cohesion research maintains its rising interest among young investigators. Practically, it suggests that our research group will simultaneously have to do two things. First, we will have to explore the generality of our conceptual model when examining cohesion in other social contexts. We have argued that the four cohesion factors in the GEQ are appropriate for social contexts other than sport—business domains, the military, fire fighters, police units, or health promotion units (e.g., hospital departments, public health units). This avenue of investigation has already begun, but it is too early to draw any useful conclusion.

Second, and probably the more "risky" endeavor, is the investment of our team's collective and individual time and effort to build and publish the theory. Our team, like the central characters in the film, *Field of Dreams*, will have to struggle through discussions of the worth of this investment of time and energy. We are individually and collectively very busy with many other aspects of our professional and personal lives. Like the characters in *Field of Dreams*, there are healthy fields of research corn that we may have to set aside in order to try to build our theoretical playing field. Is there a cost involved in being less involved with our other research crops? Once we build a field/theory, will others come to play and help make the field better? Finally, will we have any spectators who watch and study the game to stimulate their own visions of group cohesion research?

In the closing scene of the film, many spectators are lined up for miles to view and experience whatever appears at the field of dreams. If our research group could offer the potential framework for many more individuals to become involved in conducting group cohesion research (either to criticize, support, or modify the theory), our field of dreams would be worthwhile. These are difficult, but enticing decisions for the future. They are bound to keep us busy in the years ahead.

Regardless of these decisions, however, it seems probable that our research team will not dissolve and adjourn. Although we remain in the performing phase of Tuckman's group development model, we believe that long after our task cohesion declines, our social cohesion will remain intact and important. The processes we experience which help to develop the forms of cohesion that characterize our research group continue to be both challenging and rewarding.

References

Baumeister, R.F., & Leary, M.R. (1995). The need to belong: Desire for interpersonal attachment as a fundamental human motivation. *Psychological Bulletin, 117*, 497–529.

Brawley, L.R., Carron, A.V., & Widmeyer, W.N. (1987). Assessing the cohesion of teams: Validity of the Group Environment Questionnaire. *Journal of Sport Psychology, 9*, 275–294.

Brawley, L.R., Carron, A.V., & Widmeyer, W.N. (1988). Exploring the relationship between cohesion and group resistance to disruption. *Journal of Sport Psychology, 10*, 199–213.

Carron, A.V. (1982). Cohesiveness in sport groups: Interpretations and considerations. *Journal of Sport Psychology, 4*, 123–138.

Carron, A.V., Brawley, L.R., & Widmeyer, W.N. (1997). The measurement of cohesiveness in sport groups. In J.L. Duda (Ed.), *Advancements in sport and exercise psychology measurement.* Morgantown, WV: Fitness Information Technology.

Carron, A.V., Widmeyer, W.N., & Brawley, L.R. (1985). The development of an instrument to assess cohesion in sport teams: The Group Environment Questionnaire. *Journal of Sport Psychology, 7*, 244–266.

Carron, A.V., Widmeyer, W.N., & Brawley, L.R. (1988). Group cohesion and individual adherence to physical activity. *Journal of Sport Psychology, 10*, 119–126.

Cartwright, D. & Zander, A. (1968). *Group dynamics: Research and theory.* New York: Harper & Row.

Cota, A.A., Evans, C.R., Dion, K.L., Kilik, L., & Longman, R.S. (1995). The structure of group cohesion. *Personality and Social Psychology Bulletin, 21*, 572–580.

Davis, J. (1969). *Group performance.* Reading, MA: Addison Wesley.

Escovar, L.A., & Sim, F.M. (1976). The cohesion of groups: Alternative conceptions. Paper presented at the meeting of the Canadian Sociology and Anthropology Association, Toronto, Ontario.

Kerlinger, F.N. (1973). *Foundations of behavioral research.* New York: Holt, Rinehart, & Winston.

Kramer, J., & Schaap, D. (1985). *Distant replay.* New York: G.P. Putnam Sons.

Mudrack, P.E. (1989). Defining group cohesiveness: A legacy of confusion. *Small Group Behavior, 20*, 37–49.

Nunnally, J.C. (1978). *Psychometric theory.* New York: McGraw-Hill.

Shaw, M.E.(1981). *Group dynamics: The psychology of small group behavior* (3rd ed.). New York: McGraw-Hill.

Sherif, M., & Sherif, C. (1953). *Groups in harmony and tension.* New York: Harper & Row.

Sherif, M., & Sherif, C. (1972). *Reference groups.* Chicago, IL: Henry Regnery.

Steiner, I.D. (1972). *Group processes and productivity.* New York: Academic Press.

Tuckman, B.W. (1965). Developmental sequence in small groups. *Psychological Bulletin, 63,* 384–399.

Tuckman, B.W., & Jensen, M.A.C. (1977). Stages of small group development revisited. *Group and Organizational Studies, 2,* 419–427.

Widmeyer, W.N., Brawley, L.R., & Carron, A.V. (1985). *The measurement of cohesion in sport teams: The Group Environment Questionnaire.* London, ON: Sports Dynamics.

Widmeyer, W.N., Brawley, L.R., & Carron, A.V. (1990). The effects of group size in sport. *Journal of Sport and Exercise Psychology, 12,* 177–190.

Zander, A. (1971). *Motives and goals in groups.* New York: Academic Press.

Zander, A. (1977). *Groups at work.* San Francisco: Jossey-Bass.

Zander, A. (1982). *Making groups effective.* San Francisco: Jossey-Bass.

Chapter 7

Coaching Behavior Research in Youth Sports: Sport Psychology Goes to the Ballpark

Frank L. Smoll and Ronald E. Smith

Frank L. Smoll (right) is a Professor of Psychology at the University of Washington. He is Co-Director (with Ronald Smith) of the Sport Psychology graduate program and Husky Sport Psychology Services, which provides performance enhancement training for UW athletes and consultation to coaches. Dr. Smoll's research focuses on coaching behaviors in youth sports and on the psychological effects of competition on children and youth. He has authored more than 90 scientific articles and book chapters, and he has co-authored/edited nine books and manuals on children's athletics. Professor Smoll is a Fellow of the American Psychological Association (APA), the Association for the Advancement of Applied Sport Psychology (AAASP), and the American Academy of Kinesiology and Physical Education. He has extensive experience in conducting psychologically oriented coaching clinics and workshops for parents of young athletes.

Ronald E. Smith (left) is a Professor of Psychology at the University of Washington. Dr. Smith's major research interests are in personality, stress and coping, and sport psychology research and intervention. He has authored more than 100 scientific articles and book chapters, and authored or co-authored 15 books. Dr. Smith is a Fellow of APA, a Past President of AAASP, and the recipient of a Distinguished Alumnus Award from the UCLA Neuropsychiatric Institute for his contributions to the field of mental health. From 1986 to 1996 he directed a psychological skills training program for the Houston Astros and has also served as a consultant to the Oakland Athletics and as Team Counselor for the Seattle Mariners. Dr. Smith is currently a training consultant to Major League Soccer.

In psychology, areas of study often begin with informal observations of naturally occurring events that arouse the interest of the psychologist. In many cases, this occurs in an area that is of personal significance in the life of the investigator. Such was the case with the project about which we wish to tell you.

Sports have been and continue to be a central part of both of our lives. From childhood through college, we participated in several sports and were exposed to a diverse group of coaches, all of whom left their marks on us (sometimes on our backsides). As adults, we became involved in coaching because of our love of the sports in which we participated, and because of our desire to help youngsters derive some of the benefits that we had gained from sport participation.

Our experiences as coaches provided a new vantage point from which to view youth sports. As psychologists, we didn't like everything we saw. At times, we witnessed coaches and parents verbally and psychologically abusing children. We viewed situations in which winning became so important to the adults that children's needs were ignored. It seemed to us that, in some instances, youth coaches had become caricatures of some of the "tough guy" coaches they saw on television, the result being that 8-year-olds were being treated like Marine Corps recruits. Fortunately, these occurrences were the exception rather than the rule, but they happened often enough to make us wonder how youngsters are affected by various coaching styles.

We were aware of the fact that most youth sport coaches are volunteers who know something about the sport they are coaching but who, in most cases, have received no training in how to create a positive psychological environment for young athletes. We also believed that our training as psychologists and our own experiences as athletes and coaches had given us some insights in how to create such an environment. We therefore decided to write a book for youth coaches and help them create a positive sport experience and contribute to the social and psychological development of their young athletes.

As we met and began to draft the guidelines we planned to share with coaches, we began to realize that these guidelines were, in reality, interesting hypotheses that had no direct scientific support. The scientist in us then came to the fore, and we began to discuss how one might go about testing these hypotheses. The more we discussed the issues involved, the more excited we became about embarking on a new line of research that would answer the following question: What kind of coaching behaviors affect what kinds of kids in what kinds of ways? The book was put aside until such time as it could be based on sound scientific evidence rather than our intuitions and speculations. Instead, a grant proposal was prepared and submitted to the National Institute of Mental Health. The grant mapped out a two-phase program of research. In the first phase, we wished to study relations between specific coaching styles and children's reactions to their athletic experience. If significant relations were found, a second phase would involve the development and evaluation of a training program for coaches whose behavioral guidelines were based on those results. Fortunately, our proposal received funding and, over the past 20 years, we have carried out both phases of that research project.

Basic Research: Measuring Coaching Behaviors and Their Effects on Children

In determining *what* to include in a coach-training program, our work was guided by a fundamental assumption that the content should be based on scientific evidence. An empirical (scientifically verifiable) foundation for coaching guidelines not only enhances the validity and potential value of the program, but also increases its credibility in the eyes of consumers. For purposes of illustrating practical issues in program development, we now describe our approach to generating an empirical database for a coach-training program.

Theoretical Model and Research Paradigm

Our deliberations in the early 1970s prompted several questions that we felt were worth pursuing scientifically. For example, what do coaches do, and how frequently do they engage in such behaviors as encouragement, punishment, instruction, and organization? What are the psychological dimensions that underlie such behaviors? Finally, how are observable coaching behaviors related to children's reactions to their organized athletic experiences? Answers to such questions not only are a first step in describing the behavioral ecology of one aspect of the youth sport setting, but also provide an empirical basis for the development of psychologically-oriented interventions.

To begin to answer such questions, we carried out a systematic program of research. The project was guided by a mediational model of coach-athlete interactions, the basic elements of which are represented as follows:

$$\textit{Coach Behaviors} \rightarrow \begin{matrix} \textit{Athletes' Perception} \\ \textit{and Recall} \end{matrix} \rightarrow \begin{matrix} \textit{Athletes' Evaluative} \\ \textit{Reactions} \end{matrix}$$

This model stipulates that the ultimate effects of coaching behaviors are mediated by the athletes' recall and the meaning they attribute to the coach's behaviors. In other words, what athletes remember about their coach's behaviors and how they interpret these actions affects the way that athletes evaluate their sport experiences. Using this preliminary model, we have sought to determine how observed coaching behaviors, athletes' perception and recall of the coach's behaviors, and athletes' attitudes are related to one another. We have also explored the manner in which athlete and coach characteristics might serve to affect these relations.

Behavioral Assessment of Coaches

Coaching Behavior Assessment System. To measure leadership behaviors, we developed the Coaching Behavior Assessment System (CBAS) to permit the direct observation and coding (recording) of coaches' actions during practices and games. The CBAS was developed over a period of several years in collaboration with Earl Hunt, a renowned cognitive psychologist. Like many of our colleagues who have a keen interest in athletics, Professor Hunt has provided us with valuable insights derived from his area of expertise. As a starting point, we observed soccer, basketball, and baseball coaches during practices and games to determine the classes of behavior that occurred. Many days were spent standing in Seattle rain and in steamy gyms. With the use of portable tape recorders, we essentially performed a "play-by-play" description of the coaches' behaviors (as well as the situations in which they occurred) using a time-sampling procedure; that is, random sampling of observation intervals was done with the goal of obtaining a representative sample of coaching behaviors. Each behavior description was transcribed onto a separate index card. The cards were then sorted into categories and content analyzed in light of concepts from social learning theory. An initial set of scoring categories was thus developed from which the present system eventually evolved.

As shown in Table 7.1, the 12 CBAS categories are divided into two major classes of behaviors. *Reactive* behaviors are responses to immediately

Table 7.1   Response Categories of the Coaching Behavior Assessment System

Response Category	Behavioral Description
Class I: Reactive (elicited) behaviors	
Responses to desirable performance	
Reinforcement	A positive, rewarding reaction (verbal or nonverbal) to a good play or good effort
Nonreinforcement	Failure to respond to a good performance
Responses to mistakes	
Mistake-contingent encouragement	Encouragement given to an athlete following a mistake
Mistake-contingent technical instruction	Instructing or demonstrating to an athlete how to correct a mistake
Punishment	A negative reaction (verbal or nonverbal) following a mistake
Punitive technical instruction	Technical instruction following a mistake given in a punitive or hostile manner
Ignoring mistakes	Failure to respond to an athlete's mistake
Responses to misbehavior	
Keeping control	Reactions intended to restore or maintain order among team members
Class II: Spontaneous (emitted) behaviors	
Game related	
General technical instruction	Spontaneous instruction in the techniques and strategies of the sport (not following a mistake)
General encouragement	Spontaneous encouragement that does not follow a mistake
Organization	Administrative behavior that sets the stage for play by assigning, for example, duties, responsibilities, positions
Game irrelevant	
General communication	Interactions with athletes unrelated to the game/practice

Note. Adapted from Smith, Smoll, and Hunt (1977).

preceding athlete or team behaviors—either desirable performance or effort, mistakes and errors, or misbehaviors on the part of athletes. *Spontaneous* behaviors are initiated by the coach and are not a response to a distinct preceding event. The spontaneous class is subdivided into game-related and game-irrelevant behaviors. The system thus involves basic interactions between the situation and the coach's behavior. Linking the behavioral categories to their situational contexts is useful in establishing an observer set. For example, if a desirable performance occurs, the observer is immediately attuned to the kinds of responses (reinforcement or nonreinforcement) that a coach might potentially make and is better prepared to score the behavior accurately. In the case of a mistake or error, there are only five possible behaviors. The spontaneous behavior categories are also, in a sense, situation defined, in that there is no clearly evident stimulus for the coach's behavior in the immediate situation.

Coding and training procedures.   In using the CBAS, observers station themselves at a point (typically in the stands behind the team's bench) from which they can observe the coach in an unobtrusive manner. This means that the observers do not introduce themselves to the coach, nor do they interfere in any way with the ongoing flow of behavior. Observations are recorded by writing behavioral codes (e.g., *R* for reinforcement, *P* for punishment) as the behaviors occur.

Obviously, a behavioral assessment system is only as good as the reliability of the observers. Unless independent observers can agree on how a particular behavior is to be categorized, the system cannot be scientifically useful. A training program was therefore developed to achieve high interrater reliability among observers using the CBAS. The program, which involves 4 weeks of training, includes (a) study of a manual containing an explanation of the CBAS, instructions for its use, and a programmed learning component; (b) group instruction in use of the scoring system, including viewing and discussion of a videotape that provides instruction in the categories and examples of the behaviors; (c) written tests in which trainees are required to define the CBAS categories and score behavioral examples; (d) the scoring of videotaped sequences of coaching behaviors; and (e) a reliability check in the field, in which the accuracy of behavior codings is established in relation to concurrent scoring by a CBAS expert. Before an observer is permitted to collect research data, we require 95% accuracy in the scoring of written and videotaped behaviors and at least 80% agreement for all categories in field assessments.

To obtain CBAS data, we have been fortunate to include University of Washington undergraduate psychology majors in our work. These students have received CBAS training while enrolled in an academic course that provides credit for supervised research experiences. The students not only collected coaching-behavior data, but also assisted with other research-related tasks, such as data entry and analysis.

Reliability studies. Several studies have been performed to assess the reliability of the CBAS coding system as well as to evaluate the effectiveness of the observer-training program. In one study, 19 trained observers used the CBAS to code independently the behaviors of a male Little League Baseball coach. At the same time, we observed the coach and scored each of his behaviors in consultation to provide a basis for assessing the observers' accuracy. Reliability coefficients computed between the 19 observers and our own criterion codings indicated a high level of accuracy in the observers' coding of the data. Reliability coefficients were also computed between all possible pairs of observers to determine interrater reliability (the degree to which different observers gave the same behavior similar codings). The resulting coefficients reflected a high degree of correspondence of coding frequencies across the behavioral categories.

The situation-behavior linkage inherent in the CBAS undoubtedly contributes to its usefulness for field observations. In our research, and that of other sport psychologists, use of the CBAS in a variety of sports indicates that the scoring system is sufficiently comprehensive to incorporate the vast majority of coaching behaviors, that a high degree of accuracy and reliability can be obtained, and that individual differences in behavioral patterns can be identified. It is interesting to note that the CBAS is similar in some respects to a behavioral-coding system developed by Roland Tharp and Ronald Gallimore. They used a 10-category system in analyzing the behaviors of legendary UCLA basketball coach John Wooden. We have often wondered how Coach Wooden's behavioral profile might compare with the styles of other coaches, such as Indiana University's Bob Knight, or former Detroit coach Dick Vitale.

Methodological issues. Although behavioral assessment procedures can provide extremely valuable data within naturalistic settings, there are some potential problems of which researchers should be aware. One problem is reactivity—behavior change occurring simply as a result of being observed. By mere presence, an observer may influence the coach's behavior, resulting in an "artificial" behavior sample. It is difficult to eliminate completely reactivity effects, but observers can reduce them by being unobtrusive. This is why we have instructed student-observers to "blend into the crowd" as much as possible. In addition, reactivity can be reduced by a period of acclimation during which the observer is present and apparently coding the coach's behavior. Most coaches will eventually become accustomed to the presence of the observer, and reactivity effects are reduced. For this purpose, our students have usually observed coaches for one session prior to collection of research data—a dummy observation.

A second potential source of error is the observer's expectations about what will be observed. Biases and expectations can cause observers to attend selectively to certain elements and to erroneously disregard other behaviors that are not consistent with their expectations. For example, if observers expect a coach to be extremely punitive, they may fail to notice instances of encouragement or reinforcement. In training student-observers, we have made them aware of this potential source of bias, and we have instructed them to make every attempt to code coaches' behaviors as objectively as possible.

Observers who are initially trained to a high level of reliability occasionally begin to "drift" away from the system as they start to attach their own meaning to the categories. This typically occurs in situations in which teams of observers work together for a period of time and, through their discussions, develop new interpretations of the scoring categories. To combat this phenomenon, we have held regular meetings with student-observers during the sport season in which they were collecting coaching behavior data. The in-season meetings have focused on reviewing the CBAS categories and specific use of the system.

Coaching Behaviors and Children's Evaluative Reactions

Method. Following development of the CBAS, we used it in several studies to assess relations between coaching behaviors and children's reactions to their sport experiences. This activity is an example of basic research. (Basic research is the quest for knowledge for its own sake rather than to solve an immediate problem; whereas, applied research is the systematic application of scientific knowledge and research principles to the solution of practical problems.) In the largest study, 51 male Little League Baseball coaches were observed during a total of 202 complete games. More than 57,000 behaviors were coded, yielding a behavioral profile consisting of an average of 1,122 behaviors for each coach. Several self-report measures were developed to assess coaches' attitudes, beliefs, and perceptions. These were combined into a postseason questionnaire that the coaches completed. The coaches' self-perceptions of their behaviors were of primary importance. This was assessed by describing and giving examples of the 12 CBAS behaviors and asking

coaches to indicate on a 7-point scale how often they engaged in the behaviors in the situations described.

At the end of the season, 542 boys (8 to 15 years of age) who had
played for the coaches were interviewed and administered questionnaires in
their homes. Included were measures of the youngsters' recall and perceptions of the coaches' behaviors (on the same scales as the coaches had rated
their own behavior), their liking for the coach and their teammates, the degree of enjoyment they experienced during the season, and their general
self-esteem. As for the collection of CBAS data, undergraduate research assistants were trained to conduct the carefully scripted interviews and to ad-
minister the series of questionnaires. None of the 29 interviewers had done
behavioral observations of the coaches. The children were assured that
their data were confidential and that coaches would never be told how their
players responded to the questions. Moreover, the children recorded their
own responses to questionnaire items in such a way that the student-
interviewer could not view them. Only the child's age and the name of his
team were included on the forms to maintain anonymity of responses.

Results. Because we wish to focus on the *process* of scientific inquiry, we will limit our discussion of results to those which bear
most directly on the intervention program that evolved from our basic
research. At the level of overt behavior, three independent behavioral dimensions were identified through a statistical technique known as *factor
analysis.* Factor analysis identifies clusters of behaviors that are correlated
with one another and are therefore assumed to have common psychological meaning. The three major clusters, or factors, that emerged were
(a) Supportiveness (composed of reinforcement and mistake-contingent
encouragement), (b) Instructiveness (general technical instruction and
mistake-contingent technical instruction *versus* general communication
and general encouragement), and (c) Punitiveness (punishment and
punitive technical instruction *versus* organizational behaviors). Relations
between coaches' scores on these behavioral dimensions and player measures indicated that players responded most favorably to coaches who engaged in higher percentages of supportive and instructional behaviors.
Players on teams whose coaches created a supportive environment also
liked their teammates more.

A somewhat surprising finding was that, overall, the team's won-lost
record was completely unrelated to how well the players liked the coach
and how much they wanted to play for the coach in the future. On the
other hand, players on winning teams believed that their parents liked the
coach more and that the coach liked them more than did players on losing
teams. Apparently, winning made little difference to the children, but they

knew that it was important to the adults. It is worth noting, however, that winning assumed greater importance beyond age 12, although it continued to be a less important attitudinal determinant than coach behaviors.

Another important issue concerns the degree of accuracy with which coaches perceive their own behaviors. Correlations between CBAS observed behaviors and coaches' ratings of how frequently they performed the behaviors were generally low and nonsignificant. Children's ratings correlated much more highly with CBAS measures than did the coaches! It thus appears that coaches have limited awareness of how frequently they engage in particular forms of behavior, and that athletes are more accurate perceivers of actual coaching behaviors.

The data from this study were also used to test a hypothesis derived from a self-enhancement model of self-esteem. This model holds that people who are low in self-esteem are particularly responsive to variations in supportiveness from others because they have a strong need for positive feedback from others (or, alternatively, because they find a lack of support to be highly aversive). This hypothesis was verified by the data; the greatest difference in liking for supportive (reinforcing and encouraging) versus nonsupportive coaches was found for children who were low in self-esteem. Also consistent with a self-enhancement model, low self-esteem boys showed the greatest degree of attraction toward (i.e., liking for) coaches who provided abundant technical instruction. Instructiveness should be relevant to self-enhancement because such behaviors are likely to be perceived by athletes as contributing to skill increments that would increase positive self-regard.

Methodological issues.   Prior to their involvement in the study, we had obtained the coaches' informed consent (agreement to participate after being told what is going to happen). Unfortunately, 13 coaches refused to allow coding of their behaviors. Informal observation indicated that several of these coaches were far more punitive than were many of the coaches on whom behavioral data were collected. The self-elimination of the more "animal-type" coaches probably resulted in a range attenuation (restriction) on the punitive behaviors. And, because of the correlational nature of the data analyses, this had important statistical ramifications. Specifically, if coaches displaying a full range of punitive behaviors had been included, it is likely that stronger relations would have been revealed between such behaviors and the players' evaluative reactions. The problem was resolved by appealing to the University of Washington's Human Subjects Review Committee. We emphasized to the Committee that coaches engage in freely-observable, public behavior. Moreover, in collecting CBAS data, coaches' identities are number coded to assure anonymity, and all data are kept strictly confidential. After obtaining the Committee's approval, we have utilized CBAS procedures in subsequent research without the necessity of obtaining coaches' informed consent (but with the consent of the sport programs' directors).

In our Little League Baseball study, CBAS data were obtained only during games. The 10-week league schedules were structured to provide maximum game experiences for the youngsters. Thus, although some preseason practices were held, there were very few opportunities for in-season practices, and the vast majority of coach-athlete interactions took place in actual game settings. Nonetheless, the question of whether coaches' behaviors differ during practices and games is an interesting one that was addressed in a study of 31 youth basketball coaches. CBAS data indicated that the relative frequencies and rates at which specific coaching behaviors occurred during practices were greater than those that occurred during games. But the dimensional structure of these behaviors was similar for practices and games. In other words, the coaches tended to engage in more behaviors during practices than in games, but the patterning of their practice and game behaviors was quite similar.

Studying coaching behaviors and their relations to children's evaluative reactions obviously requires data from two sources—youth sport coaches and athletes. In accordance with ethical principles concerning treatment of human participants, the children's involvement has occurred with both their informed consent and that of their parents. The total of 542 participants represented 83% of the youngsters who played on the 51 teams. At least two factors contributed to the high "hit" rate. First, parents have expressed great interest in the research, which is reflected in their willingness to cooperate. In fact, the student-interviewers consistently reported that, although the actual interview and questionnaire procedures took approximately 20 minutes, they spent a considerable amount of time discussing the project with parents. Second, the duties of interviewers included contacting parents to arrange the data collection sessions in their homes. For each case in which it was not possible to obtain data, the students were instructed to provide a written explanation of the circumstances. In other words, accountability was required.

Developing a Coach-Training Program

Data from the basic research indicated clear relations between coaching behaviors and the reactions of youngsters to their athletic experience. These relations provided a solid foundation for developing a set of coaching do's and don'ts. The data-based guidelines serve two other functions: they allow us to structure the training program as an information-sharing enterprise, and they greatly increase the credibility of the guidelines that we communicate to coaches.

Coach-Training Principles

A set of five core principles underlie the behavioral coaching guidelines communicated in our program, which is called Coach Effectiveness Training (CET). First, we emphasize the important differences between the professional sports model, where winning and financial gain is the bottom line, and a developmental model, where the focus is on providing a positive educational experience for the child. In the latter model, "winning" is defined not in terms of won-lost records, but in terms of giving maximum effort and making improvement. The explicit and primary focus is on having fun, deriving satisfaction from being on the team, learning sport skills, and developing increased self-esteem and lowered fear of failure.

Our second principle emphasizes a "positive approach" to coaching. In such an approach, coach-athlete interactions are characterized by the liberal use of positive reinforcement, encouragement, and sound technical instruction that help create high levels of interpersonal attraction between coaches and athletes. Punitive behaviors are strongly discouraged, as they have been shown to create a negative team climate and to promote fear of failure. We emphasize that reinforcement should not be restricted to the learning and performance of sport skills. Rather, it should also be liberally applied to strengthen desirable psychosocial behaviors (e.g., teamwork, leadership, sportsmanship). Coaches are urged to reinforce effort as much as they do results. This guideline has direct relevance to developing a healthy philosophy of winning and a reduction in performance anxiety. CET also includes several "positive approach" guidelines pertaining to the appropriate use of technical instruction. For example, when giving instruction, we encourage coaches to emphasize the good things that will happen if athletes execute correctly rather than focusing on the negative things that will occur if they do not. This approach motivates athletes to make desirable things happen (i.e., develop a positive achievement orientation) rather than building fear of making mistakes.

The third coaching principle is to establish norms that emphasize athletes' mutual obligations to help and support one another. Such norms increase social support and attraction among teammates and thereby enhance cohesion and commitment to the team, and they are most likely to develop when coaches (a) model supportive behaviors, and (b) reinforce athlete behaviors that promote team unity. We also instruct coaches in how to develop a "we're in this together" group norm. This norm can play an important role in building team cohesion, particularly if the coach frequently reinforces relevant bench behaviors of attention and mutual supportiveness.

A fourth principle is that compliance with team rules and responsibilities is most effectively achieved by involving athletes in decisions regarding the formulation of team rules and reinforcing compliance with them rather than by using punitive measures to punish noncompliance. We believe that coaches should recognize that youngsters want clearly defined limits and structure. By using positive reinforcement to strengthen desirable behaviors, coaches can often avoid the need to use keeping-control behaviors and to deal with frequent misbehaviors on the part of athletes.

Finally, CET coaches are urged to obtain behavioral feedback and to engage in self-monitoring to increase awareness of their own behaviors and to encourage compliance with the positive-approach guidelines.

CET Procedures

In a CET workshop, which lasts approximately 2.5 hours, behavioral guidelines are presented both verbally and in written materials (a printed outline and a 24-page manual) given to the coaches. The manual supplements the guidelines with concrete suggestions for communicating effectively with young athletes, gaining their respect, and relating effectively to their parents. The most basic objectives of CET are to communicate coaching principles in a manner that is easily comprehended, and to maximize the likelihood that coaches will adopt the information. As part of our approach to creating a positive learning environment, we encourage coaches to share their own experiences and associated practical knowledge with the group. CET workshops are thus conducted with an interactive format in which coaches are treated as an integral part of the session rather than a mere audience. The open atmosphere for exchange promotes active versus passive learning, and the dialogue serves to enhance the participants' interest and involvement in the learning process.

The instructional procedures described above contain many verbal modeling cues that essentially tell coaches what to do. To supplement the didactic verbal and written materials, coaching guidelines are transmitted via behavioral modeling cues (i.e., actual demonstrations showing coaches how to behave in desirable ways). In CET, such cues are presented by a live model (the trainer) and by symbolic models (coach cartoons). In addition, modeling is frequently used in conjunction with later role playing of positive behaviors. Coaches are kept actively involved in the training process by presenting critical situations and asking them to role play appropriate ways of responding.

One of the striking findings from our basic research was that coaches have very limited awareness of how they behave. Thus, an important goal of CET is to increase awareness, for no change is likely to occur without it. To this end, coaches are taught the use of two proven behavioral change techniques, namely, behavioral feedback and self-monitoring. To obtain feedback, coaches are encouraged to work with their assistants as a team and share descriptions of each others' behaviors. With respect to self-monitoring, CET coaches are given a brief form which they are encouraged to complete immediately after practices and games. On the form, they indicate approximately what percentage of the time they engaged in the recommended behaviors in relevant situations. For example, coaches are asked, "Approximately what percentage of the times they occurred did you respond to mistakes/errors with encouragement?" Coaches report that they find this form very useful and that it provides a basis for setting behavioral goals for themselves.

Applied Research: Assessing the Efficacy of CET

Sweeping conclusions are often drawn about the efficacy of intervention programs in the absence of anything approximating acceptable scientific evidence. We, therefore, felt it was important not only to develop an empirical foundation for CET but also to measure its effects on coaches and the youngsters who play for them.

Initial Experimental Field Research

Method. In the spring of 1977, thirty-one male Little League Baseball coaches were randomly assigned either to an experimental (training) group or to a no-treatment control group (coaches who did not receive the experimental treatment). During the preseason CET workshop, which we conducted on the UW campus, behavioral guidelines were presented and modeled. In addition to the information-modeling portion of the program, behavioral feedback and self-monitoring procedures were employed. To provide behavioral feedback, 16 observers trained in the use of the CBAS observed experimental group coaches for two complete games. The student-observers were unaware of which coaches were trained and which were controls. Because they were blind to the experimental conditions (unaware of what condition the coaches were in), the students were *blind observers*—a paradoxical, yet technically correct term! Behavioral profiles for each coach were derived from these observations and were then mailed to the coaches so that they were able to see the distribution of their own behaviors. Also, trained coaches were given brief self-monitoring forms that they completed immediately after each of the first 10 games of the season.

To assess the effects of the experimental program, CBAS data were collected throughout the season and behavioral profiles were generated for each coach. Postseason outcome measures were obtained from 325 children in individual data collection sessions in their homes—an 82% participation rate.

Results.   On both observed behavior and player perception measures, the trained coaches differed from the controls in a manner consistent with the coaching guidelines. The trained coaches gave more reinforcement in response to good performance and effort, and they responded to mistakes with more encouragement and technical instruction and with fewer punitive responses. These behavioral differences were, in turn, reflected in their players' attitudes. The average won-lost percentages of the two groups of coaches did not differ, since success at this level is largely determined by the "luck of the player draft." Nevertheless, the trained coaches were better liked and were rated as better teachers. Players on their teams also liked one another more, and enjoyed their sport experience more. In a word, they had more *fun*! These results seemingly reflect the more socially supportive environment created by the trained coaches. Perhaps most encouraging was the fact that a subsample of children who played for the trained coaches exhibited a significant increase on a measure of general self-esteem as compared with scores obtained a year earlier, while those who played for the untrained coaches showed no significant change.

Methodological issues.   The use of a no-treatment control group raised the possibility that the observed and player-perceived behavioral differences between the trained and untrained coaches were the result of a so-called *Hawthorne effect* created by giving the CET coaches special treatment and attention. The extent to which such factors might have combined with the treatment components to produce the obtained differences was not known, because we did not utilize an attention-placebo control group (a group that receives a "theoretically inert" treatment, which is known to have no effect). However, this did not detract from the practical reality that the CET program produced desirable behavioral and attitudinal effects.

The self-esteem results require clarification/interpretation in relation to the manner in which the data were collected. There were indications that the training program promoted higher postseason self-esteem in players who played for CET coaches. However, group comparisons had been conducted for self-esteem data obtained the *previous* year for a subsample of boys who played for the trained and untrained coaches ($Ns = 112$ and 75, respectively). Because a true pretest-posttest design had not been used, no preseason-to-postseason change could be assessed. In other words, the lack of preseason baseline measures of self-esteem presented difficulty in attributing the higher level of self-esteem to the children's athletic experience. This shortcoming was remedied in our later research, which is described below.

Replication and Extension Studies

Method.   A replication of our research on the efficacy of CET was conducted in the spring of 1989. The subjects were 18 coaches and 152 children who participated in three Little League Baseball programs. One league (8 teams) was designated the experimental group. The no-treatment control group included 10 teams from two other leagues. Prior to the season, the experimental group coaches participated in CET. To assess the effects of CET, preseason and postseason data were collected for 62 and 90 children in the experimental and control groups, respectively. The data were collected within two 3-week periods, immediately before and after the baseball season.

In collaboration with our doctoral student, Nancy Barnett, another study was completed one year following the CET intervention. At the beginning of the 1990 baseball season, dropout rates were assessed for youngsters who had played for the two groups of coaches. If a child was not playing baseball, a brief home interview was scheduled. During this session, the children completed a questionnaire designed to assess their reasons for discontinuing participation.

Results.   The replication and extension studies yielded five major results. First, we found that the CET intervention resulted in player-perceived behavioral differences between trained and untrained coaches that were consistent with the behavioral guidelines. Thus, as in previous research, the experimental manipulation was successful in promoting a more desirable pattern of coaching behaviors. Second, the behavioral differences resulting from the CET program were accompanied by player evaluative responses that favored the trained coaches. The trained coaches were better liked and were rated as better teachers by their players, their players reported that they had more fun playing baseball, and a higher level of attraction among teammates was found despite the fact that their teams did not differ from controls in won-lost records. Third, consistent with a self-esteem enhancement model, low self-esteem children who played for the trained coaches exhibited a significant increase in general self-esteem over the course of the season; low-esteem youngsters in the control group did not change. Fourth, the children who played for the CET coaches manifested lower levels of performance anxiety than did the control children. Finally, the follow-up study revealed a 26% dropout rate among children who played for control group coaches, a figure that is quite consistent with previous reports of 30–40% attrition rates in youth sport programs. In contrast, only 5% of the children who had played for CET-trained coaches failed to return to the program the next season. There was no difference in their teams' won-lost percentages between dropouts and returning players; thus, the attrition was not a consequence of a lack of team success. In addition, the questionnaire responses revealed that dropouts in the control group more often reported reasons for withdrawing that were associated with having a negative reaction to their sport experience the previous year.

Methodological issues. In our initial field experiment, coaches were randomly assigned to the conditions; that is, their chances of being assigned to the experimental or control conditions were equal. Fortunately, there was no difference in the mean won-lost percentages of teams coached by the experimental and control group coaches. Team success (winning) was thus ruled out as a plausible explanation for the differences obtained in the outcome variables. In the replication and extension studies, assignment to the conditions was made by league rather than within leagues. This procedure guaranteed that the average won-lost records of the teams in the experimental and control conditions would be an identical 50%.

Use of separate, intact groups (a quasi-experimental design) also helped to reduce the possibility of contamination—communication of training guidelines to control coaches. To reduce leakage of information, we asked the CET coaches not to share their materials with other coaches. This procedure, plus the fact that the experimental and control leagues were separated geographically by more than 10 miles, made it unlikely that contamination occurred. We also wished to rule out the possibility of a halo effect based on players' or parents' knowledge that coaches had participated in a special program. Accordingly, we contacted the eight experimental coaches at the end of the season and asked them if they had told players or parents of their training. All of the coaches indicated that they had not mentioned the program.

After the study was completed, we learned that the control group coaches had attended a preseason clinic on baseball skills conducted by members of the Seattle Mariners baseball team. The coaches in the CET league did not attend the Mariners' clinic. This unplanned (by us) exposure to a high-credibility alternate training experience on the part of the control coaches reduced the likelihood that the favorable group differences could be attributed solely to Hawthorne or attention-placebo effects.

A somewhat related issue is worth noting. In our intervention research, experimental group coaches have been informed of the general purposes and procedures of the studies. This may have fostered desires on the part of these coaches to assist in obtaining favorable results, which, in turn, may have served to increase their motivation to apply the CET principles. In effect then, a possible confound (an unintended, systematically biasing factor) to the experimental treatment may have contributed to the more desirable behaviors exhibited by experimental coaches. Although the preceding is speculative, the practical implication is clear: If coaches are sufficiently motivated to learn and to comply with the positive approach taught in CET, desirable outcomes can be attained in terms of coaching behaviors as well as young athletes' reactions to their sport experiences.

In the initial intervention study involving behavioral assessment of coaching behaviors, we demonstrated that the CET program resulted in parallel effects on both overt and player-perceived behaviors. In the replication and extension studies, differences in coaching behaviors between the two groups of coaches were inferred on the basis of player ratings of their behavior. However, the athletes' perceptions of the coach and sport environment were assumed to be of primary importance, and it is these perceptions that were the target of the intervention. Nonetheless, it would have been desirable to again document differences in overt coaching behaviors.

Community Application and Future Research

Given the favorable outcomes of CET demonstrated in our program evaluation studies, we have applied the program widely in the United States and Canada. More than 15,500 youth sport coaches have participated in some 300 workshops to date. Indeed, CET has been included in the coaching certification modules of several youth sport organizations (e.g., Washington State Youth Soccer Association, Seattle Catholic Youth Organization). The principles of CET have also been applied at the high school, college, and professional levels in staff development projects. We believe that a major factor contributing to the acceptance of CET among coaches and administrators alike is the fact that the program is based on scientific evidence rather than armchair psychology and/or athletic folklore. In this regard, CET has received positive reviews in relation to other coach-training programs. For example, in an article comparing CET with the American Coaching Effectiveness Program and the National Youth Sport Coaches Association program, Bruce Brown and Stephen Butterfield (1992) concluded that "CET is the most convincingly documented program in theory and research-proven effectiveness. The CET program guarantees quality instruction because the developers conduct each training session themselves" (p. 216).

Youth sports is one of several athletic settings that invite the increased attention of behavioral researchers. Our work is one example of research that needs to be extended in several directions. At the basic research level, we have studied only boys' programs and male coaches with direct behavioral measures. Girls' programs clearly deserve empirical attention, and comparative studies of boys' and girls' reactions to specific relationships with coaches could serve to clarify important gender issues. From an intervention perspective, the results from evaluations of CET have been encouraging. The training program has significantly influenced five classes of outcome variables—coaching behaviors, children's attitudes, self-esteem, performance anxiety, and attrition. Nonetheless, a number of research questions remain. For example, studies are needed to assess the relative contributions of the various components of the training program, which include verbal and written instruction, modeling and role playing of desired behaviors, training in self-monitoring of coaching behaviors, and behavioral feedback. Such studies would include experimental conditions in which some of the components were left out. Research of this kind could help to establish the necessary and sufficient components of an effective program and could facilitate the development of improved training programs.

It is also important to note that the evaluations of CET have been done with a limited range of samples, mainly white, middle-class participants. Extension of the program to other populations could have notable benefits if the program is successful. For example, the prevention of sport attrition by training coaches in inner city settings (where dropout rates are especially high) could yield important payoffs by keeping youngsters involved in sports and out of gangs and other unseemly activities. Given the many significant issues yet to be explored, it is our hope that more psychological scientists will come to appreciate the youth-sport setting as a naturalistic laboratory for basic and applied research.

Epilogue

As we noted at the beginning of this chapter, our research arose out of our initial plan to write a book for youth-sport coaches. When we began the project, we never dreamed that the book would not be written for 20 years. But that's what happened. We were so committed to doing the research, and discovering so many things we hadn't anticipated, that we repeatedly decided to put the book on the back burner until "the data are in." It wasn't until 1996 that our book, *Way to Go, Coach!*, finally appeared. We then developed a shorter primer, *Coaches Who Never Lose*, which presents the behavioral guidelines in condensed form and can be used effectively in coaching workshops. We're glad we waited, because our research has given us far more to share than our original intuitions. The process has also given us an even greater appreciation of how important it is to have a strong scientific foundation when we wish to do an intervention that may affect people's lives in important ways.

Suggested Readings

Brown, B.R., & Butterfield, S.A. (1992). Coaches: A missing link in the health care system. *American Journal of Diseases in Childhood, 146,* 211–217.

Smith, R.E., & Smoll, F.L. (1996). The coach as a focus of research and intervention in youth sports. In F.L. Smoll & R.E. Smith (Eds.), *Children and youth in sport: A biopsychosocial perspective* (pp. 125–141). Dubuque, IA: WCB/McGraw-Hill.

Smith, R.E., & Smoll, F.L. (1996). *Way to go, coach! A scientifically proven approach to coaching effectiveness.* Portola Valley, CA: Warde.

Smith, R.E., Smoll, F.L., & Hunt, E.B. (1977). A system for the behavioral assessment of athletic coaches. *Research Quarterly, 48,* 401–407.

Smoll, F.L., & Smith, R.E. (1997). *Coaches who never lose: Making sure athletes win, no matter what the score.* Portola Valley, CA: Warde.

Smoll, F.L., & Smith, R.E. (1998). Conducting psychologically oriented coach-training programs: Cognitive-behavioral principles and techniques. In J. M. Williams (Ed.), *Applied sport psychology: Personal growth to peak performance* (3rd ed., pp. 41–62). Mountain View, CA: Mayfield.

Chapter **8**

Gender Issues: Making a Difference in the Real World of Sport Psychology

Diane L. Gill

Diane L. Gill is a Professor in the Department of Exercise and Sport Science at the University of North Carolina at Greensboro. Dr. Gill also recently served four years as Associate Dean of her School and became Head of her Department in August 1997. She has been President of the North American Society for the Psychology of Sport and Physical Activity as well as the Research Consortium of the American Alliance for Health, Physical Education, Recreation and Dance and became President-Elect of Division 47 of the American Psychological Association in 1997. She is a fellow in the American Academy of Kinesiology and Physical Education, the Association for the Advancement of Applied Sport Psychology, the American Psychological Society, and Divisions 47 (Exercise and Sport) and 38 (Health) of the American Psychological Association. Dr. Gill served as Editor of the *Journal of Sport and Exercise Psychology*, is now Associate Editor of both the *Journal of*

Applied Sport Psychology and the *Journal of Sport and Exercise Psychology,* and is on the Editorial Board of *The Sport Psychologist.* She has over 70 scholarly publications related to social psychology of sport and exercise, and she is now working on the revision of the text, *Psychological Dynamics of Sport.* She takes time to get away from the office for regular jogging and enjoys getting away farther for biking, hiking, travel, and sightseeing, as well as concerts, theater, and arts events.

I did not begin my journey into sport psychology as a "natural" athlete. Sport was not the dominant feature of my childhood, although sport, or perhaps, more broadly, physical activity, certainly was part of my life. I grew up in a small town in upstate New York (my parents still live in the same house) and spent many hours playing backyard baseball, riding bikes, skating and sledding in the northern winters or swimming in the summers. Typical sport and play groups combined sexes, ages, skill levels and attitudes with creative facilities and equipment. Now that I have been in the field of exercise and sport science for over 20 years, my perspective on the role of physical activity remains much as it was in those early years. Perhaps it would be more accurate to say that many years of research and teaching as well as my own continual but varied physical activity participation have brought me back to that perspective. Sport and physical activity is part of and contributes to an active, healthy life.

That same experience and reflection helps me place gender issues within my scholarship and overall perspective on sport psychology. As I reflect, gender always influenced my own sport experience (whether I knew it or not), and gender has always played a major role in the world of sport and physical activity. I have decided that it is not my own gender, or anyone's gender, that makes the important difference. Instead, it is gender in society that opens opportunities, imposes limits, and makes a difference in the real world of sport and exercise.

So, let's return to the baseball game in the Gill backyard and track the moves from there to the office of a university professor in sport and exercise psychology. We played many activities, and I was more skilled than some and less skilled than others. Although we competed, we often changed players, rules, and strategies to accommodate the neighborhood diversity. My backyard baseball career was rudely interrupted one summer when the adjacent city allowed boys in our town (of course, only boys) to join the city Little League. Good-bye to backyard baseball and welcome to the gendered world of sport.

As I moved from the neighborhood to high school fields and courts, sport and activity were still part of my life. But I was much more an academic (even then) than an athlete. I was a strong student, especially in math and science, and sport was simply one of many extracurricular activities that I enjoyed. Of course, one reason I did not seek out competitive athletics was because competitive athletics weren't there. Girls teams did not have the same resources (barely any resources at all) that boys teams had, but we practiced and had occasional games or play days with other schools.

I decided to major in physical education rather than math because I knew I would teach (teachers were my educated role models), and by teaching physical education I could stay active. Also, at that time, the only women who seemed to engage in sport and activity were in PE.

I attended the State University of New York (SUNY) at Cortland, majoring in physical education. Cortland had a strong program and admission was selective. The curriculum was demanding academically, but focused on training teachers, and included many skill- and teacher-preparation classes. I was much stronger at the academically-demanding part of the program (e.g., exercise physiology, a barrier for many of my friends, was easy for me, and I chose statistics as an elective) than at the skills, although I continued to participate in as many different activities and intramural sports as I could. At that time, Cortland's program, like most others, did not have a sport psychology course, and sport psychology did not exist as an identifiable area. One of my instructors, Dr. Margaret Robb, used the then newly published Kenyon and Loy reader in sociology of sport in one of our methods courses and that introduced me to some of the social-psychological topics that are now central to my work. Dr. Robb also offered a graduate course on motor learning during my senior year. She encouraged me to take the course; I did; and, using Bob Singer's new motor learning text, I got a research-oriented introduction to psychology and motor behavior.

The time of my undergraduate education, from 1966 to 1970 and continuing into the 1970s, was a time of social change, including changes in women's roles. The sport setting was one site for challenging gender roles. Kathy Switzer jumped into the Boston marathon in 1967; Billie Jean King made points for women's sport by defeating Bobby Riggs in the "Battle-of-the-sexes" tennis match/media event; and several girls made headlines challenging Little League, as women and girls were challenging exclusionary practices throughout society.

Those challenges to male-dominated sport expanded during the 1970s, and gender and sport issues became real to me as part of my life as a public school teacher. During the two years that I taught high school physical education (1970–72), my colleagues and I coached several girls teams, organized events ourselves, and received no added pay. I was also a volleyball and basketball official, and our women's officials organization was engaged in legal action to remedy sex discrimination and gender inequities for officials.

1972 was a landmark year for gender and sport with the passage of Title IX, the federal act that mandated nondiscrimination in federally funded educational programs. Although Title IX was an educational act, not specifically directed at sport, the sport implications attracted the most attention and controversy. High school and college sports are educational programs, and covered under Title IX, but changes did not come immediately. Instead, sport programs and administrators (overwhelmingly men) resisted changes, and even 25 years after passage of Title IX, challenges continue.

Two years of public school teaching confirmed that I was a better student than teacher and that I was more suited to the libraries and labs of academia than the fields of competitive sports. I had not specifically focused on sport psychology when I applied to graduate school; in fact, there was no sport psychology program to which to apply. While I was teaching, I had taken a short summer course with Dorothy Harris. Dorothy managed to introduce me and everyone else in that class to gender issues as well as sport psychology.

That same year, Dan Landers, who was then teaching at SUNY at Brockport, organized a conference on sport and social issues (before Dan got into his current psychophysiological work at Arizona State). That two-day conference included presentations by several sociology of sport scholars and influential papers on competition by Rainer Martens and Carolyn Sherif. (Current sport psychology colleagues Penny McCullagh and Dan Gould were undergraduates at Brockport who worked at the conference.) Taking personal days from my teaching to attend that conference turned out to be an influential move. The presentations were just the inspiration I needed to apply to graduate school, and the conference steered me in the social psychology direction. Although I now see the influence of that conference and the scholars who were there, I applied to Illinois with only a very vague direction toward social psychology.

I focused quickly when I entered graduate school at the University of Illinois in 1972. As soon as I took Rainer Martens' course on social psychology and physical activity, I found my direction. Rainer, who was then a relatively recent Ph.D. himself, was an ideal mentor who introduced me to the content, experimental methods, theory, and academic culture of our field. Rainer was a great role model as an active researcher, teacher, and advisor, as well as a major player in the emerging sport psychology discipline.

Our lab also included other motor behavior and social psychology scholars who were beginning their careers. For example, during my first year at Illinois, I assisted Karl Newell with a motor learning experiment as he was completing his doctoral work. During my graduate program I shared office space and traveled to conferences with fellow graduate students, including Tara Scanlan and Dan Gould. We spent many hours working together and discussing research topics, theories, and professional issues as well as developing networks that continue to sustain us through our careers. The experimental social psychology model, with emphasis on social psychology theory and experimental control, was dominant in the 1970s, and I developed research skills and my social psychology knowledge base. I took courses with top scholars in social psychology and statistics as well as exercise and sport science, but the work with Rainer and my other colleagues at the motor behavior lab had the most influence. I did my own thesis and dissertation research (social reinforcement and motor performance for my thesis, individual-group performance for the dissertation), but also worked on other research continually and developed research as a habit and an integral part of my academic life.

During my graduate program Rainer shifted from his earlier experimental lab research to his field-based research on competition and development of the Sport Competition Anxiety Test (SCAT). I was involved in that work. The experience of working through all the stages of that project (with careful development of the measure following high psychometric standards and several validation and subsequent research studies on competitive anxiety) helped me see the benefits (and problems) in developing sport-specific measures, as well as the challenge of developing a line of research. Martens's SCAT has been a model for others to develop sport-specific measures, but the hands-on experience and involvement with all the unseen steps gave me skills and appreciation that made my own later work on competitive orientation much stronger.

My research direction within sport psychology followed that experimental social psychology model during my graduate program. But, occasionally gender issues did enter my thoughts and work. One incident in particular stands out. For part of the competitive anxiety work, I was testing middle-school students on a competitive maze task. The motor maze was set up in a mobile van, which I drove to the school for testing. The competition was controlled so that, although we had bells and whistles to show a competitor's performance, the outcome was contrived to manipulate win-loss. I brought individual students to the van, explained the competition set up (a scripted scenario), gave them some practice with the task, and asked them if they were ready for the competition. Most were enthusiastic and quickly responded that they were ready to go. Then one day one girl hesitated and responded, "I don't know; I'm not very good at games like this." Title IX was in place, girls had opportunities, and I didn't understand why this one wasn't following the script. But, she was not an isolated case, several others (all girls) also approached the task with low confidence and little enthusiasm.

However, the most striking responses were not the approaches to competition, but the reactions to the outcomes (which I was manipulating in true social psychology deceptive style). Youngsters did 10 trials of the task and those in the losing condition lost 80% of the time, so, by the tenth trial, it was quite clear that they were losing. One day, one child in the losing condition—a boy—started crying before the competition was over. I resisted the urge to tell him it was all deception and we would allay his concerns with our elaborate debriefing story after we got our final measures; like any true researcher I managed to convince him to continue after he wiped away some tears.

Although I protested that I wasn't going back to the schools if I had to do any more "losing" conditions, I did. A few more children cried and became overly emotional in the losing condition—all boys. That experience taught me something about gender issues, and those images have stayed with me longer than the specific research results (the specific results are documented in publications and generally supported the validity of SCAT and our competitive anxiety models; i.e., SCAT, a measure of competitive trait anxiety, was a strong predictor of competitive-state anxiety, and once competition was underway, win-loss had a powerful effect on state-anxiety responses.):

- Girls can be just as competitive and physical as boys can. For example, I bypassed one girl because she had a cast on her arm. Her teacher cornered me later to tell me she really wanted to do the game. I relented, she did very well on the task, and was just as enthusiastic a competitor as the most competitive boys.
- Title IX did not solve everything. More boys than girls were eager to compete and more girls expressed doubts and hesitation.
- Boys can cry. Although we stereotype males as non-emotional, this competitive activity seemed to bring out more emotional extremes in boys than in girls. In fact, my continuing personal observations and reflections tell me that sports generally brings out or permits emotional responses in boys and men that are re-

stricted in other domains. Michael Messner's 1992 work on men, masculinity and sport, *Power at play*, provides evidence confirming my observations as well as an insightful, provocative analysis of gender issues of men in sport.

I completed my Ph.D. in 1976 and took my first academic position in the Department of Kinesiology at the University of Waterloo, specializing in psychology. Waterloo emphasized the research/science base of kinesiology more than most programs in the U.S., and my research orientation fit well. Waterloo did not have a Ph.D. program at that time, but, as the only specialist in sport psychology (we had several specialists in motor behavior, physiology, and biomechanics), I worked with several excellent undergraduate students on senior research projects and masters students on theses within sport psychology. Three years later I moved to the University of Iowa where my main role was in the sport and exercise psychology graduate program.

My research, and that of my students (who were really colleagues more than students) covered a range of sport psychology topics from the group performance and cohesion issues of my doctoral research into more social cognitive topics, such as attributions and self-efficacy. During my seven years at Iowa I also extended into the applied area. I consulted and did psychological skills training with women's basketball and softball teams, and several of my students did even more of that work. I always encouraged my students to follow their own research interests and to seek out other faculty and resources. By doing that, many developed their own research lines and gained recognition, and, moreover, I have expanded my knowledge and interests by working with them.

During my years at Iowa, I not only developed my sport psychology research and graduate program, but I also developed a feminist consciousness of gender issues in sport. Some students and colleagues in my department were influential (Susan Birrell, a sociocultural sport studies scholar who joined Iowa's faculty shortly after I did, and who continues to do fine feminist scholarship, deserves special note). But, the strongest influence came from the wider community of women and feminist scholars outside my department. The Women's Studies program at Iowa was strong, and I was a dedicated member of that program. Contact with scholars from English, history and other areas helped me put a feminist framework around my thinking about gender and sport. Gender in sport was not simply Title IX and getting more women into athletics. Gender in sport, like gender everywhere, is a sociocultural process. Overt discrimination is rare, but more subtle gender influences are everywhere, and even more resistant to change.

I began teaching "women and sport" at Iowa, actively supported women's programs and women's issues, and joined a softball team (associated with the Women's Resource Center) that *really* did not care about winning (I haven't found one since then, but have focused on my personal running and health-oriented activities).

My major research line at Iowa was on competitive orientation. I spent several years developing a multidimensional measure of competitive orientation, and investigating competitive orientation with participants in varied sport and exercise settings. I incorporated many of the procedures and standards that I had learned from the SCAT work with Rainer, along with some psychology models of achievement orientation, particularly the work of Janet Spence and Bob Helmreich. Several doctoral students worked on that project, and Tom Deeter and David Dzewaltowski made particularly important contributions, and initiated some projects. We developed the Sport Orientation Questionnaire (SOQ), which assesses three dimensions of competitive orientation: (a) competitiveness—the tendency to enjoy sport competition, to seek out and strive for competitive achievement (e.g., I look forward to competing; I thrive on competition); (b) win orientation—the tendency to focus on win-loss outcomes and strive to win (e.g., winning is important; I hate to lose); and (c) goal orientation—the tendency to focus on personal goals in competitive sport (e.g., I set goals for myself when I compete).

We used the SOQ with several samples of college and high school students, as well as with athletes; and others have used it with many varied samples around the world. In our work, one of the clearest findings, which supports the validity of the sport-specific achievement measure, is that athletes score higher than nonathletes on all three dimensions, and the athlete-nonathlete difference is much stronger and clearer for the SOQ than for general achievement measures. The overall greater competitiveness is expected, but a more unexpected and interesting finding relates to the dimensions of competitive orientation. With the SOQ, athletes are higher than nonathletes on all three scores, but it's the basic competitiveness—achievement orientation for competitive sport that really differentiates them from nonathletes.

In some of our work we used a different measure of competitive orientation developed by Robin Vealey. That measure has outcome and performance scores that are similar to the win and goal SOQ scores. But Vealey's scores are opposites and the measure forces a choice between outcome and performance. Popular thought suggests athletes are especially win-oriented, but our results clearly indicated that athletes were more focused on performance and less on winning than were nonathletes. That particular finding, which seemed surprising at the time, conforms with much of our current sport psychology practice. Top athletes focus on performance and immediate performance goals—they focus on what they can *do*, and work for that. Top athletes and coaches know this well—the thrill of competition is in the event; the gold medal is a reminder, but is not the achievement.

Gender issues emerged in the competitive orientation work. As one might expect, males were more competitive than females with almost all the samples we tested. Male college and high school students were more competitive and especially higher on win orientation than were females, but females were just as high, and sometimes higher, on goal orientation.

Also, with high school samples, we asked students if they participated in competitive sports, noncompetitive sport activities, and nonsport activities. Boys were more likely than girls to participate and have experience in competitive sports, but girls were just as likely or more likely to participate in noncompetitive sports and nonsport activities, and scored as high or higher on general achievement orientation. Overall, then, the gender differences in competitiveness did not seem to reflect either achievement orientation, or an interest in sport and physical activity per se, but a specific emphasis on competitive, win-oriented sport competition.

After the initial development of the SOQ, we used it with Iowa's men's and women's athletic teams, and later with international samples of elite athletes in Taiwan and with ultramarathoners. With the Iowa sample, we found that athletes scored much higher than nonathletes on all dimensions, and overall, men scored higher than women on competitiveness and win orientation. But, those gender differences were minimal with the athletes. The women athletes were higher on all SOQ scores than male nonathletes, and similar to men athletes. Gender differences were greater for nonathletes. Similarly, in Taiwan, intercollegiate athletes scored higher than nonathlete students, and international-caliber athletes scored even higher. Moreover, gender differences were minimal in Taiwan.

The ultramarathoners were a particularly interesting sample. All were participants at the challenging Western States 100, and had qualified by completing previous ultramarathons. The ultramarathoners, a unique sample in many ways, were competitive, extremely high on goal orientation, but quite low on win orientation in comparison to our other samples. We did not find gender differences as in other samples. In fact, the women ultramarathoners were slightly higher than the men on competitiveness and win scores.

Overall, the gender message from the competitive orientation work is that experience and opportunity have a much greater influence on competitive orientation than does gender. When women and men have similar sport experiences, competitive orientation is similar. But the catch is that women and men rarely have similar sport experiences, even when it appears that they do.

The research on confidence and gender illustrates the influence of social context. Considerable research suggests that females typically display less confidence than males across varied settings (and sport is certainly one of those settings). Ellen Lenney, in the 1970s, after reviewing literature and contributing her own research, concluded that the social situation was the primary source of gender differences. Gender differences emerged with masculine tasks, in competitive settings, when clear, unambiguous feedback was missing. Several studies with motor tasks by Chuck Corbin and his colleagues confirmed Lenney's propositions. In our lab at Iowa, several of my students and I set up a competitive situation (using noncompetitive baseline scores, we matched males and females of similar ability on a pegboard task), and found few gender differences. Males were slightly more likely to predict a win, but performance expectations were similar. Females performed slightly better in competition, and expressed positive perceptions and responses. But all of this research involved experimental studies with novel motor tasks in controlled lab settings that purposely strip away social context. In the real world, sport is typically seen as masculine, competition is the norm, and males and females develop their confidence along with their sport skills and behavior patterns through radically different experiences and opportunities—in different worlds.

If experience and opportunity are the keys to competitive orientation and, in turn, to participation and behavior in physical activity, then we might expect few gender differences after over 25 years of mandated nondiscrimination. The number of girls' and women's sport teams in public schools has exploded since 1972, and we see athletic shoe ads promoting the benefits of sport and exercise activities for girls and women (not to mention benefits for the company). But the real world, with its pervasively gendered social context, continues to exert strong influence on both women and men in sport. The real world, and particularly the real world of sport, is not gender-neutral. Noted sociologist, Jessie Bernard, made this point in her 1981 book, *The Female world*. According to Bernard, women and men live in different worlds, even when the situation seems to be the same. For example, the world is different for starting centers on the men's and women's basketball team, for the boy and girl pitching the Little League game, and for the woman and man jogging in the park.

Although the number of females in high school and university athletics has increased about six-fold since 1972, to about one-third of the total number of participants, the numbers are not equal. More telling, the numbers of females in other sport roles has not increased so dramatically, and in several ways women and girls have lost ground. Most dramatically, the number of women coaches and athletic administrators has decreased since Title IX. Competitive sport retains a gendered, hierarchical power structure which maintains the emphasis and channels resources to competitive, elite sports, reducing the options and alternatives for both females and males.

Even a casual review of media reports on sport reveals gender influence, and research evidence confirms the bias. Females received less than 10% of the media coverage in terms of column space, photographs or television time. Moreover, coverage is different; athletic ability and accomplishments are emphasized for men, but femininity and attractiveness are emphasized for female athletes. For example, as I prepared this chapter, I noted a *USA Today* (March 20, 1997) report on figure skating, with the opening line, "Tiny Tara Lipinski, figure skating's high-jumping sweetheart, can become the youngest world champion in history Saturday." The emphasis on young and petite contrasts with the photo insert caption reporting that "Elvis Stojko hits quad, triple jump and wins third world title."

This emphasis on social context, and consideration of gender as part of the dynamic, complex sport process matches my general research orientation at this point in my career. Although I continue with some research projects, more of my work is devoted to reviewing others' work (as an advisor, reviewer or editor), pulling together varied information and perspectives, reflecting, and attempting to develop integrative scholarship. From a larger, integrative perspective, the tremendous influence of social context and the futility of attempting to pin down a phenomenon with isolated studies of individual behavior at one time in one context are clear. Gender is part of the social context, an ever-changing dynamic process. Within sport, gender has some unique manifestations, but we should not lose sight of the big picture of gender in social context if we are to understand gender and sport.

Considering gender from this social dynamic perspective has expanded my perspective to broader diversity issues. Gender is one part of the social dynamic, and other diversity issues, such as ethnicity, sexual orientation, age, and especially physical abilities and characteristics are culture issues for sport psychology that further complicate and enrich the real world of sport.

My specific research over the past few years has involved older adults, and that work has expanded my thinking about the social dynamics of sport for all participants. We talked with over 100 women age 65–95 about activity and general health and well-being during our research. Although these women developed their thoughts and behaviors about sport long before Title IX, I found these women much more active than I expected, and, most notably, they clearly saw a role for activity in their lives in terms of promoting their overall well-being.

Activity is multidimensional for these older adults; that is, activity has social and psychological benefits that are just as important as the physical and health benefits. The balanced approach stands in contrast to the over-emphasis on elite, competitive sport in most of our programs. If we organized programs and offered more alternatives that fit more diverse women and men, we would likely realize more of the overall benefits of activity for everyone.

For example, noncompetitive programs focused on participation and individual health goals are the model for many cardiac rehabilitation or other health-oriented activity programs. Certainly that model serves most participants better than a competitive athletics model (although some competitive activities would entice some participants). Recent, long-overdue moves by the American College of Sports Medicine (ACSM) and leading exercise science scholars and professionals to promote health-oriented exercise are positive steps in a direction that fits more people's lives. The most recent guidelines call for *lifestyle* activity, emphasizing common activities, such as walking and yard work, and the *accumulation* of at least 30 minutes of moderate activity most days of the week. Previous guidelines that called for 30+ minutes of continual aerobic activity (e.g., running) fit the lives of the young men who typically conducted and participated in the exercise studies, but did not so easily fit the lifestyle constraints and preferences of most people, especially most women. We could expand even further and make more specific attempts to accommodate more diverse participants and potential participants. For example, Capri Foy, a doctoral student here at UNCG, is developing an exercise program with an emphasis on cooperative activities and a sense of community to accommodate African-American women in the community.

As I continually try to take a more social perspective and diversify my thinking, research, and actions, I have become more committed to putting scholarship into practice. Translating gender scholarship into sport psychology practice is a challenge, but the expanding literature on sociocultural sport studies and feminist practice in psychology provide some guidance.

To translate gender scholarship into feminist practice we must first avoid sexist assumptions, standards, and practices. Then we might follow the lead of psychologists who have moved beyond nonsexist practices to more actively feminist approaches. Feminist practice incorporates gender scholarship, emphasizes neglected women's experiences (e.g., sexual harassment), and takes a more nonhierarchical, empowering, process-oriented approach that shifts emphasis from personal change to social change.

To take a more active feminist approach, we might consider going beyond gender awareness in our research issues and methods, and in our professional practice. For example, a coach or sport psychology consultant might encounter an intercollegiate soccer player who is overly aggressive and often out-of-control, or one who is tentative and lacks confidence. The aggressive soccer player could be male or female, but a male soccer player is more likely to grow up in a world that reinforces aggressive behavior, and a male athlete is more likely to continue to have such behaviors reinforced. The less aggressive, more tentative approach is more typical of female athletes. Even talented, competitive female athletes are socialized to keep quiet, be good, and let others take the lead. Moreover, most female athletes have a male coach, trainer, athletic director, professors, and deal with males in most other power positions.

Overly aggressive, uncontrolled behavior is not exclusively male, nor tentative styles exclusively female. Still, we will work more effectively if we recognize gender influences in the athlete's background and situation. Anger control or confidence building has a different context, and likely requires different strategies for female and male athletes. For example, a consultant might examine the media and public relations for the women's team as well as the status of women's sport in general. How does sport fit into the player's life? How do others (coach, teammates, family, spectators, friends) react to the player? Behavior is not just within the athlete, but within a particular sport context, and within a larger social context, and both the immediate situation and larger context are gender-related.

Let's consider a scenario with clear gender implications—a figure skater with a potential eating disorder. Information on psychological disorders and diagnoses indicates that females are nine times as likely as males to exhibit anorexia or bulimia. Moreover, the incidence is increasing, more prominent in adolescence and early adulthood, and participants in certain activities including dance and sport may be at higher risk. The figure skater is much more likely to be female than male (as well as white, middle to upper class, and adolescent). But, personality and gender are not the only considerations; eating disorders are social phenomena and body image plays a major role.

Females in certain sports may have exaggerated body image concerns related to appearance and performance. Judges do look for a "line," and appearance does affect endorsements. For such cases an educational approach stressing proper nutrition, without discounting the athlete's understandable concern for body image, might be effective. Sport psychology consultants might take a more active feminist approach and move to social action—educate others and try to change the system that leads athletes to pursue an unhealthy body image.

When I discuss gender in classes or incorporate gender in my research and practice, I do not focus on gender differences, and I certainly do not encourage students and colleagues to do so. But over 20 years in my sport and exercise psychology career have confirmed what I recognized in my backyard baseball days—*gender makes a difference*. Gender is a pervasive social force, and the real world of sport and exercise reflects society's gender hierarchy. Gender is so ingrained in our sport structure and practice that we cannot simply treat everyone the same. But, neither can we assume that male and female athletes are dichotomous opposites and treat all males one way and all females another way. Gender is a dynamic influence that varies with the individual, situation and time, as well as with other sociocultural characteristics. Gender makes a difference in the real world—in my own sport psychology work, in working with students and colleagues, and in all our lives.

Suggested Readings

Carpenter, L.J., & Acosta, R.V. (1993). Back to the future: Reform with a woman's voice. In D.S. Eitzen (Ed.), *Sport in contemporary society: An anthology* (4th ed., pp. 388–398). New York: St. Martin's Press.

Gill, D.L. (1992). Gender and sport behavior. In T.S. Horn (Ed.), *Advances in sport psychology* (pp. 143–160). Champaign, IL: Human Kinetics.

Gill, D.L. (1993). Competitiveness and competitive orientation in sport. In R.N. Singer, M. Murphey, & L.K. Tennant (Eds.), *Handbook of research on sport psychology* (pp. 314–327). New York: Macmillan.

Gill, D.L. (1995). Gender issues: A social-educational perspective. In S.M. Murphy (Ed.), *Sport psychology interventions* (pp. 205–234). Champaign, IL: Human Kinetics.

Gill, D.L. (March, 1997). *Gender and competitive motivation: From the recreation center to the Olympic arena.* Paper presented at the Nebraska Symposium on Motivation, Lincoln, NE.

Messner, M.A. (1992). *Power at play.* Boston: Beacon Press.

Messner, M.A., Duncan, M.C., & Jensen, K. (1993). Separating the men from the girls: The gendered language of televised sports. In D.S. Eitzen (Ed.), *Sport in contemporary society: An anthology* (4th ed., pp. 219–233). New York: St. Martin's Press.

Tavris, C. (March, 1997). *The science and politics of gender research: The meanings of difference.* Paper presented at the Nebraska Symposium on Motivation, Lincoln, NE.

Chapter 9

Spectators, Hostility, and Riots

Gordon W. Russell

Gordon W. Russell is Professor Emeritus in the Psychology Department at the University of Lethbridge in Alberta, Canada. Among his 60-plus publications are several books including *The Social Psychology of Sport* (1993). Professor Russell is a member of the Council of the International Society for Research on Aggression and served as its Treasurer from 1988 to 1994. During this same period, he was also the book review editor for the journal *Aggressive Behavior*. Since his retirement in 1995, he has remained active in research, writing articles for scientific journals. In addition to travel, he enjoys watching his favorite sports, curling and golf.

Over the years I have had an off-again, on-again affair with crowd behavior. My curiosity was initially sparked during my freshman year at The University of British Columbia. The late Dr. Edro Signori had been invited by a Vancouver newspaper in the late fifties to be its guest at the first home game of the newly formed British Columbia Lions of the Canadian Football League. In return, Dr. Signori was to give its readers his impressions of the game. In addition to being a clinical psychologist, his qualifications for the assignment included having been named "All-Canadian" lineman during his earlier career in varsity football.

The interview was prominently featured in the weekend edition. Essentially, Dr. Signori suggested that those who attend football games are generally more hostile than the rest of us and that watching the violence on the field of play provided them with an outlet for their pent-up aggressive urges. This interpretation did not sit well with football enthusiasts, many of whom were UBC students. Monday morning's Psychology 101 class promised some excitement.

Dr. Signori entered the lecture theater to find all 200 plus seats occupied. While he was adjusting his microphone, some students registered their displeasure by covertly hissing. Others joined in and the din shortly reached a crescendo. The unflappable Dr. Signori expressed mock alarm that there was apparently a snake loose in the room and made a short pretense of looking for it. The hissing slowly subsided.

At the time, the prevailing view in clinical circles was that the observation of aggression acted as a safety valve, a vent by which hostility or aggressive impulses could be safely discharged. The whole idea struck me as entirely reasonable and I filed it away in my collection of psychological gems from Psychology 101.

During the summer of 1963, I was working in Washington, D.C., for the Bureau of Social Science Research, a private research group that did contractual research projects for various government and private organizations. Earlier that year I had read a review chapter on collective phenomena that dealt in large part with the structure of various types of crowds. It was still fresh in my mind when the country was told of plans for a March on Washington to be led by Dr. Martin Luther King, Jr. The windup to the civil rights demonstration was to see tens of thousands of protesters march from the Washington monument along the avenue bordering the reflecting pool to the steps of the Lincoln memorial. It was there that Dr. King was to deliver his famous "I have a dream" speech.

Only days before the march, word came down from the Bureau's director that money was available to conduct some pilot research on the crowds expected to be drawn to the nation's capital. Having just read the chapter on collective phenomena and with time running out, I was suddenly thrust into the role of an "expert" on crowd behavior. It was a heady experience for someone still in graduate school.

One topic in particular had caught my attention. It dealt with the physics of a moving crowd and suggested that a procession moves much like the water in a stream. The faster flow is in the center of the stream and slower movement is found closer to the edges where friction with the banks occurs. A research team comprised of Dr. Frederick Pauling, myself and several research interns took on this aspect of the overall project.

The flow of demonstrators was to be recorded from a roof top overlooking the route using a rented camera that took a picture every 15 seconds. Tracking the flow of the procession was made easier by having the interns wear large white hats and "attach" themselves to marchers either at the center or near the edges. After spending most of the final 3 days prior to the march traveling from one government office to another obtaining permissions, we were finally issued a permit for the roof of a U.S. Navy building alongside the route.

On the morning of the march, we took up our position on the roof along with a network television crew. Our assistants, who were about a block away, were given the signal to join the march. But, it was not to be. Two or three frames into our data collection, the camera jammed. Despite our best efforts and some help from the television crew, we couldn't get the bloody thing to work. Our part in the project crashed and I was left with little to show for the effort except a nasty sunburn and a lesson from life. Researchers should always have Plan B in reserve, in this case a second camera.

Other research interests and responsibilities took me away from crowd phenomena until 1971. Then, a widely cited article by Dr. Jeffrey Goldstein and his graduate student Robert Arms rekindled my interest in crowds. They conducted a field study that sought to establish the effects of viewing a violent competition on spectators' hostility.

The study was conducted on the occasion of the Army-Navy football game held annually in Philadelphia. Their research design pitted several rival positions against each other. A cathartic view predicted that those witnessing aggression would experience a beneficial venting of their pent-up hostility (Dr. Signori's interpretation was being put to the test). On the other hand, a frustration-aggression view predicted an increase in hostility, but only in the case of spectators whose favorite team was defeated. A third position, a social learning view, argued that there would be an overall increase in the aggression of observers irrespective of which team won.

Men were intercepted on a random schedule as they entered the stadium and asked their age and which team they were supporting. They also completed a hostility inventory. An equivalent group was interviewed immediately after the contest. In keeping with basic design principles, the same procedures were followed at an equally competitive but non-violent control event, i.e., an intercollegiate gymnastics meet.

The results were straightforward. Men watching the football game experienced an increase in hostility from before to after the game. The hostility of those men attending the gymnastics event remained constant over the course of the program. The sole beneficiary of the study was Social Learning theory. From the theory's perspective, witnessing aggression on the gridiron weakened inhibitions and led to an overall increase in the aggression of observers. On that occasion, at least, neither the cathartic model nor the frustration-aggression position found support in the results.

Support for a link between player violence and crowd violence was also seen in an influential paper by the late Michael Smith of York University. He examined the events that precipitated hostile outbursts among sports spectators. His was an archival study that analyzed media accounts of crowd violence in a variety of sports from around the world. Smith found that 74% of all violent outbursts were immediately preceded by player violence. Parenthetically, controversial calls by game officials (15%) and spectators baiting players (11%) were identified as lesser causes.

In a fortuitous turn of events, Robert Arms was offered and accepted an appointment in our department at the University of Lethbridge. Before long, we began to talk crowds. As impressive as Goldstein's study was, we wondered if the same results would be found on the Canadian frontier, with different subjects and other violent sports.

At the time, a suggestion had been floated in the aggression literature to the effect that a fictional or stylized display of aggression was a special circumstance that provided observers with a cathartic outlet for their aggressive impulses. Thus, where the aggression is recognized as a spoof (e.g., cartoons, roller derby, professional wrestling), it was thought that observers would be purged of their aggressive urges. Fortunately, I had friends in the wrestling community dating back to an earlier stint selling tickets to matches in a Calgary cigar store. Pro wrestling became the obvious choice to represent the category of fictional aggression.

Mark Sandilands joined our effort and we set about to design a systematic replication of the Army-Navy football study. Football holds little interest for sports fans in Lethbridge, so we substituted an equally violent sport, ice hockey. To summarize our procedures, we took large numbers of our students to a hockey game, a professional wrestling card or a non-violent control event, i.e., a provincial swim meet. The students were randomly assigned to one of the venues and to complete our measures either just before or immediately after their event.

The results were straightforward. Just as in the Army-Navy football study, the hostility of males (and females) increased over the course of the hockey game. Fictional aggression did not prove to be a special circumstance offering a cathartic experience insofar as our student spectators also showed an increase in hostility at the wrestling match. Watching the competitive swim meet had no effect on spectators' hostility.

Although these studies were consistent in showing before-to-after increases in spectator hostility at violent sports events, we could only speculate about the course of hostility over the entire three hours of a football or hockey game. To answer this question, we conducted a further study in which we administered our hostility measures to real-life spectators not just before and after a hockey game but also at the end of the first and second periods.

The result was not a linear increase in hostility, but a curvilinear relationship. Spectator hostility rose steadily through the first and second periods followed by a slight decrease at the end of the game. This inverted-U function closely paralleled the frequency of on-ice player violence that also peaked near the end of the second period. As suggested by Michael Smith's earlier data, spectator hostility closely tracks player aggression. What happens on the playing surface has immediate emotional consequences for those in the stands.

Throughout the decade of the sixties, seventies and on into the eighties, a virtual consensus was building among aggression researchers to the effect that witnessing aggression generally increases aggression in the observer. There was little or no evidence to suggest a reduction in viewer aggression through some sort of cathartic mechanism. Thus, the studies above merely paralleled findings from the wider body of experimental and other investigations of viewer effects.

The Long Arm of Sports Violence

The effects of people witnessing violent sports has far-reaching implications for the well-being of a community. Not only is there a general increase in hostility at the sports venue, but some carry their heightened emotional state back into the community with tragic consequences for others. Consider the results of a 1992 study by Garland

White, Janet Katz, and Kathryn Scarborough. These researchers examined the admission records of emergency wards in Washington, D.C., area hospitals both before and after Sunday afternoon NFL Redskins football games. Home games were followed by increases in the number of women admitted for injuries in the categories of gunshot wounds, assaults, stabbings and "accidental" falls. The obvious implication is that the effects of witnessing violence on the field of play extend into the community with women becoming a principal target for heightened male aggression.

There was an intriguing wrinkle in these results that calls for an explanation. The increase in emergency ward admissions occurred only after Redskins wins! Neither the frustration-aggression view nor Social Learning theory would have predicted the result. The authors speculated that wins lead to an increase in power motivation among spectators. The result is that domestic disputes that might normally be resolved by negotiation or compromise are instead settled by force. However, the Redskins study is only a part of the story. The harmful effects of staging violent sports contests extend much further into society, sometimes with lethal consequences.

Sociologist David Phillips conducted a series of archival investigations examining the effects of heavily publicized media events. What was sought was evidence that major news stories (e.g., plane crashes, suicides, and executions) had adverse effects on members of the general public. One study in the series examined the impact of heavyweight championship prize fights on homicides.

How might a researcher track changes in the well-being of a citizenry? Phillips consulted the U.S. national registry for the information recorded on death certificates (e.g., the cause of death, age, sex, race, etc.) of the deceased. In the case of heavyweight championship prize fights, Phillips recorded homicide rates for the days leading up to the match and for a time following the match. This was done for all championship bouts from 1973 to 1978.

His findings should give even the staunchest defender of boxing pause for thought. In short, there was a significant increase in homicides 3 days after the fight. This 3-day lag is common to all studies in Phillips' program and invites the question, why? Perhaps it takes about 3 days to plan and find the opportunity to dispatch someone.

Equally intriguing questions are raised by the additional finding that the homicide victims resembled the losing boxer. For example, if a White fighter defeated his Black challenger, the homicide victims tended to be young Black males. On the other hand, the loss by a White boxer to his Black opponent was followed by a jump in the homicide rate among young White males. Some evidence suggests that simply having characteristics in common with a recent victim makes us a more likely target for aggression.

Other lines of investigation also highlight the lethal implications of staging major combatant sports events. One such study tested the hypothesis that important National Football League games would be followed by increases in the local homicide rate. To this end, all playoff games from 1973 to 1979, including the Superbowl, were examined, as were the homicide rates for the metropolitan areas in which the franchise teams were located. An increase in homicides occurred consistently 6 days after the playoff game. However, the increase occurred only in those cities whose team had been *eliminated* in the playoffs 6 days earlier.

As the researchers observed, the sixth day following a playoff game is on the eve of the next round of the playoffs. Whereas last week's winner is still in contention, fans of last week's losing team are forced to confront the realization that "their" season is over. There will be no game tomorrow, only an emotional void. Whether the lethal outcomes occur as a result of fans having their hopes so cruelly dashed or because of problems associated with gambling losses remains open to speculation.

Toward a Psychological Profile of Rioters

But, now to a current interest. I think it was a series of highly publicized disasters at several European football stadia that first focused my research interest on those individuals who instigate or are to be found at the center of riots or crowd disturbances. A fire and subsequent panic in 1985 at Bradford, England, left 56 dead and 200 injured. Shortly thereafter 95 young football fans at Hillsboro lost their lives in a crush of spectators celebrating their team's promotion to the second division of the English Football League. More than anything else, it was the Heysel Stadium tragedy in Belgium that rekindled my interest in crowd violence.

The Heysel tragedy was a disaster waiting to happen. Preparations for the European Cup final between Juventus of Italy and Liverpool were wholly inadequate and as a result, authorities were unable to maintain any semblance of order (see Russell, 1993, for an account of the incredibly sloppy arrangements for the match). Shortly after the match began the English fans charged a section of Italian supporters in what is traditionally called "the taking of the ends." The Italian fans were sent scurrying for safety and in the ensuing panic they were pushed up against a concrete retaining wall. The wall collapsed, killing 39 and injuring 470 others. Against the background of this and the almost weekly outbursts of hooligan violence, it dawned on me that we knew relatively little about the sorts of people who instigate or escalate crowd disturbances.

Certainly, there was already a wealth of theory and research available on the topic of football hooliganism. Due primarily to the efforts of sociologists, trouble makers in Britain and elsewhere were generally characterized as young, single males who were marginalized, often unemployed and in some sense alienated from the larger society. At the time, I thought this research literature could be carried a little further.

While a demographic profile of those causing disorders before, during, and after football matches has made a valuable contribution to our understanding of the phenomenon, for me there was a large gap. I wanted to know more about the people who stand ready to involve themselves in public disturbances, in actions that most of us would judiciously avoid. What type of personality lends itself to this behavior and how might their personal history, social habits, perceptions and thought processes differ from those of others?

The idea of administering personality measures to spectators was not new. Jeffrey Goldstein and others before him had done just that in regard to hostility. Our objectives were merely an extension of previous work inasmuch as we intended to assess spectators in a more in-depth fashion, using an assortment of social-personality measures.

The research strategy we adopted called for would-be rioters to identify themselves through their answers to questions worded along the lines of: "If a fight or other disturbance were to erupt in the stands, how likely is it that you would join in?" Identifying people who would escalate crowd disturbances in this way is not without its weaknesses. However, neither is the procedure of interviewing participants in the aftermath of a riot. Retrospective accounts are subject to several biasing influences, most notably the selective recall and selection of events. Moreover, given the illegal nature of their actions, many of those involved in acts of public disorder are unwilling or unable to cooperate with researchers.

Initially, I had some concerns about the intrusive nature of some of the questions in the proposed battery of social-personality measures that we were considering. Spectators had been entirely willing in the past to reveal something about their aggressive tendencies and the things that make them angry, but how would they react to requests for even more personal information, i.e., their love life, personal habits, etc.? Consequently, we started slow.

As it turned out, my concerns were misplaced. Our student interviewers were carefully trained in making tactful approaches to their prospective subjects. This, and the anonymity and assurance of confidentiality, allowed spectators to tell us a great deal about themselves, in many cases with enthusiasm. Of course, a handful declined our interviewers' tactful requests, but always with a polite comment.

Our first attempt sought answers to some very basic questions regarding those who would involve themselves in a crowd disturbance. Taking our lead from the European literature on football hooliganism, we surmised that those in the vanguard of a riot would, above all, be young, single males. We further speculated that they are attracted to combatant sports mainly by the prospect of watching player fights.

Our choice of a combatant sport was, quite naturally, ice hockey. However, the format of hockey games presented us with an initial difficulty. The intermissions between the periods of play are only 15 minutes in length. It is also a time when many spectators are looking for a cup of coffee or attending to pressing bodily functions. However, the most important implication of these time constraints was that our proposed battery of personality measures would have to be administered piecemeal in a series of studies. Of course, it also meant that any one interviewer had time to conduct only 3 or 4 interviews over the course of a game.

After committing ourselves to a series of field investigations, we introduced the project as the research component in our senior level social-experimental and sports psychology courses. Next, we developed procedures that provided an approximation of a random sampling of those spectators in attendance on any given evening. Fifteen to twenty of our students were randomly assigned to occupied sections of the hockey arena. Within their assigned sections interviewers worked out a procedure that allowed them to sample spectators somewhat randomly. For example, they might start with row 11 and seat 3. The occupant becomes their first subject. If the seat is empty they move further along the row to the first occupied seat. People who were seen to be deeply involved in conversation or those who were obviously intoxicated were bypassed. The interviewers then moved to another row and seat location previously chosen at random. Not perfect, but we think it is a rough approximation of a random sampling of those in attendance.

There was considerable enthusiasm for the project particularly as, unlike term projects in other courses, their data were neither destined to end up in the waste basket nor collecting dust on their professor's shelf. Interviewers' data were combined with that of their classmates to be analyzed and individually written up as a research report (APA format, of course).

Our rationale for each study in the series of nine was ". . . an interest in the reasons why different types of people attend hockey games." Of course, at the outset we were not certain that people attended because they like to watch on-ice fights nor were we certain that a significant number of people would join in a developing riot. Our first two studies reassured us on both counts.

"I like to watch the fights" was third in importance for males, a position it has held throughout the entire series. Females show little interest in watching men fight. At the same time they rate "to please someone else" as a somewhat stronger reason than males for their attendance.

The second study used exclusively male subjects and established that a substantial number of men were willing to escalate a disturbance. In this and subsequent studies, approximately 47% of men indicated at least some likelihood of involving themselves in a crowd disturbance (ratings of 1 or more on a scale ranging from zero to 6). Those indicating a strong likelihood (ratings of 6) make up approximately 8% of our sports audiences.

Over the next half dozen studies, we administered personality measures one or two at a time. These included a measure of public self-consciousness that reflected the subjects' concern with how others will evaluate them. A sample item is "One of the last things I do before leaving the house is look in the mirror." Trait measures of anger and physical aggression were also administered early in the series. We also included in our battery a measure of psychopathy or anti-social tendencies. An example of an item is "People who never lie are suckers."

Impulsivity was also predicted to be related to a willingness to escalate a crowd disturbance. The tendency of some people to take precipitous action without giving due thought to the consequences is seen in one's agreement with an item, such as "Do you do things on the spur of the moment?" A final measure in the test battery tapped sensation-seeking tendencies. Some among us actively seek out thrilling, sometimes risky, experiences. Agreement with such items as "I would like to try skydiving" capture this tendency.

To return to the question of the battery's overall success in predicting those willing to join in a disturbance, all of the foregoing measures were found to be related. Where our findings were tested cross-culturally, they were found to be robust. For example, the measure of psychopathic tendencies was related to the likelihood of involvement both with Canadian hockey spectators and Dutch soccer fans. Further evidence of cross-cultural consistency was provided by a study conducted with our Finnish colleague, Anu Mustonen. Hockey fans in Finland and Canada who scored high on the measure of sensation seeking also foresaw a strong likelihood of their involving themselves in a crowd disturbance.

Part of our broad approach to an understanding of those individuals who show a proclivity for involvement in crowd disorders involved a cognitive phenomenon, that of "the false consensus effect." The effect refers to people's tendency ". . . to see their own behavioral choices and judgments as relatively common and appropriate to existing circumstances, while viewing alternate responses as uncommon, deviant, or inappropriate." For example, an audience listens to a safety expert stress the importance of driving with our headlights on over the upcoming holiday weekend. Those who are persuaded by her arguments and who express their intention to have their lights on will generally estimate that a larger percentage of the driving public will also have their lights on than will those not persuaded by the expert.

Our predictions were that those attracted to hockey games by the prospect of watching on-ice fights would believe that a disproportionately larger number of other spectators are in attendance for the same reason. Also, those willing to join an altercation were also expected to estimate that a disproportionately large number of others in the stands are similarly inclined to violence. Both predictions were supported.

These findings have several implications for understanding the dynamics involved in the initial stages of some riots. Those who believe that a disproportionately large number of other spectators also like to watch player fights may be prompted to involve themselves in a disturbance emboldened by the belief that many in the audience will applaud their intervention. Similarly, a sense that others are approving of violence may also tend to weaken inhibitions that would normally be engaged when one considers a deviant or risky course of action. Finally, those likely to riot who believe that a disproportionately large number of other fans are similarly inclined may act precipitously in the belief that other fans will follow their lead and also join in.

Personal background factors were also thought to be potentially predictive of involvement in a riot. Specifically, we asked spectators about their fight histories. Each subject was asked how many fights (i.e., pushing, shoving, punching) he had been involved in during the past year. The results provided strong support for the hypothesis that men with a history of fighting are more willing than others to escalate a disturbance.

A further prediction was derived from the literature on European football violence wherein acts of public disorder are almost invariably committed by groups of young supporters. Rarely are solitary individuals seen to commit acts of hooliganism. A number of controlled experiments and field studies make the same point.

My favorite example of a group-antisocial relationship is a 1976 field investigation conducted by Ed Diener and several colleagues. Candy and money were momentarily left unattended when trick-or-treaters arrived at households on Halloween eve. Youngsters traveling in groups stole more than those going door-to-door by themselves. For our purpose, then, we hypothesized that spectators attending hockey games with male companions would be more willing to participate in a disturbance.

As noted earlier with regard to the personality measures, *all* of the foregoing variables (i.e., the false consensus effect, fight history, liking to watch the fights, and group size) were found to be related to a willingness to join a riot in progress. The exception to this uniform pattern of significant findings was the group-aggression relationship. While the relationship was found to be significant in one study, it fell short of significance in Mustonen's comparison of Finnish and Canadian hockey spectators.

Bringing It All Together

No doubt it has already occurred to you that this series of piecemeal studies has involved a fairly large number of personality, social and other variables, all shown to be predictive of spectators' participation in a crowd disturbance. It is also apparent that some of the variables are themselves intercorrelated. For example, impulsivity and psychopathy are undoubtedly related inasmuch as one facet of the psychopathic personality is an impulsive nature. What was needed to bring order to all of this was a single study wherein all previous measures could be *simultaneously* administered to sports spectators.

Robert Arms and I were at a choice point in developing our plans for an overarching study. Should we use real-life spectators found in attendance at a game as we had done before? If so, we would somehow have to entice 60 to 100 men to stay after a game to complete our lengthy battery of measures, an expensive and not really feasible choice in our circumstances. Instead, we chose to recruit avid hockey fans from our Introductory Psychology subject pool.

Our self-selected sample of volunteers seemingly lived mainly for hockey. When asked about their interest in the sport, they indicated that they attend one game per week and watch at least two others on television. They were in effect the sort of men that one would expect to find at a game on any given evening. The major drawback to this means of recruiting "spectators" was the much lower and limited age range of a student sample. That is, all previous results were obtained with samples whose mean ages were slightly over 30 with a large standard deviation rather than a mean age of 21 years with little variability.

We were heartened by the results. Even using a very young university sample who we assumed would normally be found attending games, we replicated all of our previous results save one. The measure of public self-consciousness was unrelated to the likelihood of joining in a crowd disturbance.

Having simultaneously administered all measures used in previous studies, we were now in a position to conduct a multiple regression analysis. The goal was to identify those variables within the battery that were, overall, the best predictors of involvement. Our measures were found to account for fully 65% of the variance, with the time since the respondent's last serious fight (a new measure), and liking to watch player fights emerging as the best two predictors. Thus, those who have recently been embroiled in a fight or those who are attracted to on-ice violence are considerably more likely than others to be found at the center of a riot.

It is interesting to note that the recency measure of fighting had not previously been used and was only added to the battery at the last minute. It was while attending the meetings of the International Society for Research on Aggression that a colleague urged me to consider including it in our battery. The suggested measure turned out to be the best single predictor we have used! The experience has reinforced my view that almost any proposed investigation stands to be improved by suggestions from others working in the same field. For me, it is standard practice to seek constructive criticism from colleagues.

There were several surprises in the results. Despite the fact that our sample was comparatively young and fell within a very narrow range, age was nevertheless strongly (negatively) correlated with most other measures. Within our sample, it is the youngest of the young who have fought often and recently, like to watch fights, are aggressive, run in packs and react impulsively in social situations.

The series produced a further surprise that came to light as I was examining the results of an early study in an exploratory, post-hoc fashion. The reason "I like to watch the fights" was uncorrelated with any of the other reasons for spectators' attendance. In fact, the finding has held up across all nine studies in the series. Seemingly those individuals who are strongly attracted to violence attend for that reason and that reason only. It would suggest that were gratuitous player violence to be minimized or eliminated in a sport, this element of the audience would have little interest in attending. Of course, their absence would also have the effect of reducing the likelihood of crowd disturbances in the sport.

Future Directions

While the series has produced answers to some of the questions associated with people's involvement in crowd disorders, other questions remain. Would similar results be found among spectators attending other sports? Are there major cross-cultural differences in the response of spectators to a fight erupting in their midst? Would similar results be obtained in investigations of other types of crowds (e.g., rock concerts, protest demonstrations)? Presently, these are questions about which we can only speculate.

One of the related questions we are presently pursuing is that of how people react to an unexpected outburst of violence in the stands. It would seem that at best there are only five responses available to audience members. They can stand by and watch, stand by and applaud or incite others, leave the sports facility or, of course, join the melee. However, a fifth possibility intrigues me the most, that of joining in for the purpose of attempting to quell the disturbance by verbal and/or physical means. An obvious first step is to determine if there is a sufficient number of such "peacemakers" in a crowd to allow an investigation of their motives and psychological profile using the present paradigm (recent data collected by Anu Mustonen indicates that 26% of Finnish males would intervene to dissuade fellow spectators).

Certainly, there are anecdotal accounts of peacemakers who have joined violent outbursts with a view to restoring order. Moreover, we have the splendid example of Danish football fans who have taken the name "Roligans" to describe their efforts in being good role models for youngsters and others in the international football community. They are no less enthusiastic in support of their teams than the British, Dutch or Germans, but do so in a spirit of friendly competition. Regardless of the circumstance, whether their team wins or loses, taunting by rival fans or unpopular decisions, the Danes keep a close reign on their emotions and behave in a nonviolent fashion.

Peacemakers intrigue me. What prompts them to risk their personal safety and possible involvement with the legal system? Are they intervening in an attempt to preserve the good name of their team or sport, or do they have especially strong views about law and order? It seems unlikely that they simply exhibit the opposite traits to rioters. They would predictably be older rather than younger and involved in fewer rather than more fights. However, they may be equally impulsive, jumping in without due regard for the consequences. It is such questions as these that we are presently pursuing. The answers lie ahead.

Suggested Readings

Arms, R. L., & Russell, G. W. (1997). Impulsivity, fight history and camaraderie as predictors of a willingness to escalate a disturbance. *Current Psychology: Research & Reviews, 15*, 279–285.

Diener, E., Fraser, S.C., Beaman, A.L., & Kelem, R.T. (1976). Effects of deindividuation variables on stealing among Halloween trick-or-treaters. *Journal of Personality and Social Psychology, 33*, 178–183.

Goldstein, J.H., & Arms, R.L. (1971). Effects of observing athletic contests on hostility. *Sociometry, 34*, 83–90.

Guttmann, A. (1986). *Sports spectators.* New York: Columbia University Press.

Kerr, J.H. (1994). *Understanding football hooliganism.* Philadelphia: Open University Press.

Mann, L. (1989) Sports crowds and the collective behavior perspective. In J.H. Goldstein (Ed.), *Sports, games, and play* [2nd ed., pp. 299–331] Hillsdale, NJ: Erlbaum.

Milgram, S., & Toch, H. (1969). Collective behavior: Crowds and social movements. In G. Lindzey & E. Aronson (Eds.), *The handbook of social psychology* (Vol. 4, pp. 507–610). Reading, MA: Addison-Wesley.

Mustonen, A., Arms, R.L., & Russell, G.W. (1996). Predictors of sports spectators' proclivity for riotous behaviour in Finland and Canada. *Personality and Individual Differences, 21*, 519–525.

Phillips, D.P. (1986). Natural experiments on the effects of mass media violence on fatal aggression: Strength and weaknesses of a new approach. In L. Berkowitz (Ed.), *Advances in experimental social psychology* [Vol. 19, pp. 207–250] New York: Academic Press.

Russell, G.W. (1993). *The social psychology of sport.* New York: Springer-Verlag.

Russell, G.W., & Arms, R.L. (1998). Toward a social psychological profile of would-be rioters. *Aggressive Behavior, 24*, 219–226.

Russell, G.W., & Mustonen, A. (1998). Peacemakers: Those who would intervene to quell a sports riot. *Personality and Individual Differences, 24*, 335–339.

Smith, M.D. (1983). *Violence and sport.* Toronto: Butterworths.

White, G., Katz, J., & Scarborough, K. (1992). The impact of professional football games on women. *Violence and Victims, 7*, 157–171.

Chapter **10**

Drugs and Coping in Sport

Mark H. Anshel

Mark H. Anshel is Associate Professor in the
Department of Psychology at the University of Wollongong in New
South Wales, Australia, where he conducts much of his research in the
area of drugs and coping with acute stress in sport. Born and raised in
Chicago, Dr. Anshel immigrated to Australia in 1988, where he is a
member of the Australian Psychological Society, the College of Sport
Psychologists, the College of Counselling Psychologists, and a registered psychologist with the New South Wales Board of Psychologists.
Dr. Anshel has authored close to 70 articles in refereed journals, six
book chapters, and authored the textbook, *Sport Psychology: From Theory to Practice*, now in its third edition. He is an editorial board member for *The Sport Psychologist* and the *Journal of Sport Behavior* and is
a regular reviewer for the *Journal of Sports Sciences, Journal of Sport and
Exercise Psychology, Perceptual and Motor Skills, The Australian Psychologist*, and the *International Journal of Sport Psychology*. He is the sport
psychologist (formal title, "mental skills coach") for the (professional)

Steelers Australian Rugby League club and has consulted with several college teams, primarily U.S. football, during his six years at New Mexico State University. He has been an invited speaker and consultant in several countries, particularly throughout Asia in recent years. For relaxation, he enjoys a daily jog and an occasional weekend "bush walk" along the beautiful south coast of New South Wales, Australia.

Early Thoughts and Experiences

I am uncomfortable writing about myself, preferring to let my written work do the "talking" for me. However, in this case, I may have something to contribute to students, athletes, and other readers who dream of future success, no matter what their endeavor, and want to make the commitment to achieve it. After all, isn't that what all high quality athletes must do to reach *their* lofty aspirations—dream and then commit? Of course, dreams and aspirations often change as we grow older. During childhood and adolescence, like many athletes, I aspired to be a professional baseball player. However, this was not to be. My lack of physical stature and the genetic predisposition necessary to hit a baseball with the required power or to throw it with the required velocity made that dream highly unrealistic. So, I redirected my love for sports towards majoring in, then teaching, physical education.

During my college years at Illinois State University, two types of experiences shaped my thinking about future interests and goals. One type of experience was my course work. My psychology, philosophy, and education courses were challenging and stimulating, and helped me understand and appreciate human behavior and thinking. I continue to use these skills as a university educator and sport psychology consultant.

The other type of experience that altered my future aspirations concerned my summer employment at a childrens overnight camp in Lake Delton, Wisconsin, from ages 19 to 22 years, as a group counselor, counselor supervisor, and program director. During this time, I worked with and learned from trained social workers and psychologists. Nothing can replace "hands on" training with the most sophisticated minds one could imagine. Understanding the sources of behaviors and emotions of children and adolescents, then planning and implementing cognitive and behavioral strategies that would favorably change these behaviors and emotions, while often promoting group cohesion, prompted me to re-think my future as a physical educator (taking nothing away from the many superb physical education teachers who comprise this field).

There was much to learn about human behavior that could be applied in sport and exercise settings—information I wish I had as a high school and college baseball player.

Developing a Research Ethic

Rather than enter graduate school immediately after graduation, I fulfilled a two-year scholarship commitment to become a Director of Physical Education in community recreation. From the Centers that offered me a position to meet my commitment, I selected Montreal, Quebec, Canada. I stayed at this position for five years, and, along the way, took courses toward my master's degree at McGill University in Montreal. I completed my master's degree on the psychology of motor performance. My thesis advisor was Dr. Dan Marisi, a very talented, warm, and giving individual. In addition to spending many hours with me and other graduate students over coffee, Dan provided a non-threatening and pleasant environment in which to learn the research process and develop my writing skills.

From the start I aspired to gain the necessary skills to publish my work in journal articles and even to write a book. Dan and I published two studies. One study, based on my master's thesis on the effects of music and rhythm on physical endurance, stemmed from my community recreation days where I learned from my Swedish colleagues to give aerobic exercise classes to music. Not surprisingly, I observed that exercisers would be far more motivated and energetic when moving in rhythm to musical accompaniment than in the absence of music. However, this effect had never been scientifically proven. In addition, I was not certain if background music would affect the exerciser similarly. The genesis of this study reflected "hands-on" experience rather than the more common way researchers get ideas—from previously published theories and models, or from the lack of research in some area of study. It was particularly gratifying to conduct a study that reflected previous experiences and had real-world implications. I was especially pleased to see this study published in 1978 in the journal, *Research Quarterly*, now called *Research Quarterly for Exercise and Sport*. Like so many graduate students, I never envisioned myself as a future researcher. So my first publication was very gratifying and provided me with the incentive to make research an important part of my career. While I still enjoy teaching immensely, contributing to the academic literature through research has become a particular source of pleasure over the years.

Perhaps the motive to publish my work is partly based on an anonymous quotation I came across: "If the tree falls, but no one hears it, did it make a sound?" Said another way, if you don't report your work, no one will ever know you did it. You will not have contributed to the body of knowledge. This philosophy was reinforced at the next step in my career.

The decision to pursue my Ph.D. and my wish to make a permanent career change and become a university professor happened at the same time. But where to go? Doctoral programs in the sport sciences, especially sport psychology, were rare in the mid–1970s. During my master's degree, I read the first textbooks in sport psychology written by the prolific Dr. Robert (Bob) Singer, a well-published professor at Florida State University (FSU). I was attracted to the applied nature of Bob's writing and, given my ambition to pursue an academic career, wanted to learn from his superb writing skills and professionalism. I was pleased to be accepted in the FSU graduate program in September, 1976, despite no promise of financial assistance (that came in the second and third years of the program as his laboratory assistant).

I completed the program in exactly three years. During this time, I was exposed to the greatest challenges, the most rapid intellectual growth, and at times, the most intense stress of my life. Doctoral students have the awesome responsibility to master skills in research design and statistical procedures, create a coherent written narrative for the thesis and future journal publications, enhance their oral presentation skills, and, of course, develop extensive knowledge in an academic discipline—in my program, psychomotor behavior (i.e., the combination of motor learning and sport psychology, a common structure in those days). There is a massive amount of material that doctoral students are asked to master in a relatively short time (so much for a social life). Either a person is committed to a Ph.D. or he or she is not. It's no wonder that so many individuals who enter doctoral programs fail to complete them.

My doctoral thesis concerned the effectiveness of cognitive strategies and adjunct questions on learning and remembering a series of motor skills of varying complexity, all of which concerned juggling (who said a doctoral thesis can't be fun?). Adjunct questioning is a teaching strategy in which the performer is asked to recall information about the skill or task before (pre-adjunct questions), during (embedded adjunct questions), or after a practice session (post-adjunct questions). In my study, the purpose of adjunct questions was to help performers to focus on the most relevant aspects of the juggling skills during the skill acquisition phase. Participants were asked to learn several juggling skills (e.g., two beanbags with one hand, three beanbags with two hands) with or without the use of cognitive strategies (e.g., self-verbalized rhythm, imagery, chunking). My study also compared the effectiveness of traditional (live instructor) versus programmed teaching (use of a self-contained instructional package). One group learned the series of skills with a live instructor and another group used the written instructional (self-contained) materials. Results of the study, published in *Research Quarterly* in 1980, indicated that subjects who used the self-contained, modular instructional package, combined with cognitive strategies, performed significantly better on the combined learning and retention trials than subjects in the traditional (live) instructional groups. Further, while no measurable differences were found on the retention test—retention differed as a function of skill complexity—performance was markedly poorer on the two most complex juggling skills, but not on the less difficult skills under both instructional methods. The primary value of this study, in addition to examining a real-world problem, was that motor skills can be taught by written instruction, although no one is suggesting that physical education teachers and coaches are easily replaceable. This early research in the cognitive strategies area has proved to be very useful to me in working with athletes as a sport psychology consultant and teaching sport psychology.

The Start of My Academic Career

As I indicated earlier, one intangible outcome of completing the FSU doctoral program was developing a strong research ethic and a commitment to contribute to sport psychology through my teaching, graduate student supervision, and writing. I brought this commitment to my first full-time position at New Mexico State University (NMSU) in Las Cruces. While the Physical Education Department was devoted almost exclusively to teaching and published virtually no research, I was grateful for the resources made available to me to begin formally my career as an educator and scholar. Soon after my arrival in August, 1982, I also founded the university's (and community's) first summer sports day camp. The focus of the camp was to have our physical education majors teach sports skills to children, ages 5 to 12, in a low-competitive, non-threatening environment. The camp remains a strong summer program for the community to this day, 14 years later. Since the graduate program in physical education at NMSU was being phased out in 1988, I was compelled to find another position in which graduate education and research efforts would be strongly endorsed. In 1988, the University of Wollongong in Australia made me an offer I could not refuse. But before discussing

Australia, I turn to one very important aspect of my work at NMSU that led to my research on drugs in sport.

In 1984, NMSU hired a new football coach, Fred Zechman. Fred was a very affable person and, coming from Ohio State University under the legendary coach, Woody Hayes, was also very capable. During his first season, I asked Fred if he would allow me to attend practice sessions and football games as a casual observer and an academic in sport psychology, then to meet with him in a couple of weeks and to give him my impressions. I did not stress the need for his team to have a sport psychologist, nor did I critique his performance. Instead, I focused on areas in which coaches often agree they can use some assistance in their teaching skills—especially among the younger, less experienced coaches assistants. This was the path of least resistance to gain entry into the program, and, indeed, an area that needed immediate help by a trained observer. My background in motor learning and sport pedagogy, rather than sport psychology, actually provided me with the expertise to gain trust and acceptance, albeit slowly, by the coaching staff and to begin my consultancy (voluntarily) with the NMSU football team. A three-year relationship with the team followed—until Fred's departure in 1987. During this time, I became increasingly aware of the forces that propel some athletes to behave in a way they would regret the rest of their lives. I also learned how coaches actually contribute to the problem.

Drugs in Sport

To be candid, drug-taking in sport, especially for the purposes of building strength and enhancing performance, is common. Because I have lived in Australia since mid–1988, I cannot speak first hand about the use of drugs in U.S. college sport now. However, my reading of the literature indicates that the problem has not gone away. In fact, steroids are now found in body-building gyms and among high school males in greater numbers than ever. Perhaps this problem is inherent in the ever-increasing use of mind-altering drugs in the U.S., particularly marijuana. Athletes are not exempt from the increased use of banned drugs, particularly in less-detectable form among elite performers. So, despite warnings about the long term harmful effects of performance-enhancing drugs and the tragic deaths of a few professional athletes, ostensibly due to prolonged drug abuse, the practice continues.

Research is strictly defined as an attempt to solve a problem. If there is no problem, there is no research (Note: You don't go to the library to "do research"; you go to the library to gather information). The research problem I wanted to undertake, based primarily on my involvement with the NMSU sports teams and through reading about the premature deaths and diseases of young elite athletes, was *why?* Why would young and extremely healthy athletes, particularly males, make a conscious decision to ingest substances that would place their physical and mental health at risk? Why would an athlete practice for hundreds of hours over months, even years, in preparation for sport competition, then decide to cheat in order to obtain a desirable outcome? Finally, why would athletes risk being expelled by their team or a sport organization by taking banned substances?

From 1985 through 1987, I interviewed as many athletes on the NMSU campus as I could find to determine the extent of drug-taking by their teammates. I decided not to ask them about their own drug habits, because I would not expect them to be candid if there were a problem. Underreporting of drug-taking is a major limitation of the published research in this area. But, if I asked about what "other athletes" were doing (not by name), the participants might be more willing to disclose what they actually knew. So I conducted a study based on the structured personal interview technique with college male and female athletes. As a university academic staff member in a physical education department and a sport psychology consultant to an array of teams, mostly with the university's football team, I was fortunate to interview more elite (intercollegiate) athletes (94 males and 32 females) than are usually accessible to sport psychology researchers.

Since statistical techniques would be inappropriate for this kind of data, I decided to use an approach to analyzing data that has grown quite popular in recent years, deductive content analysis. Content analysis (CA) organizes raw data, in this case, the athletes' open-ended responses to my questions, into interpretable and meaningful categories. CA can be inductive or deductive. *Inductive* content analysis requires the formation of themes or categories based on the participants' statements. *Deductive* content analysis, on the other hand, requires that these categories are determined before, not after, the interview. Deductive CA is preferred if a researcher has a preconceived notion in which categories the respondents' answers will fall.

Based on my reading of the anecdotal (print media) and sports medicine literature—almost nothing was available in sport psychology journals at this time—I generated two main drug categories, performance-enhancing and recreational. The athletes' statements were further divided into three likely causes of drug use: physical, psychological/emotional, and social. An example of a performance enhancement statement for physical purposes was "Steroids help me bulk up." A psychological/emotional example was "Steroids make me feel mean" or "The coach expects me to overpower my opponent." A social reason was "All the pros do it and it doesn't hurt them" (modeling). Examples of physical, psychological/emotional, and social causes under the recreational drug category, respectively, were "A 'joint' helps me forget the pain," "I get bored doing the same thing all the time," and "Everyone does it at parties."

The data, published in the *Journal of Sport Behavior* in 1991, showed that athletes were taking drugs that were both banned (e.g., anabolic steroids) and illegal (e.g., marijuana). Perhaps not surprisingly, the main reason for drug-taking—for both males and females—was to "be competitive." My data also showed that their motive to take performance-enhancing drugs was in response to the tremendous pressure to succeed and to live up to their coaches' expectations of an athlete on scholarship. However, taking performance-enhancing drugs was not their only reaction to pressure; recreational (mind-altering) drugs, such as marijuana, was another way of dealing with the pressure of being a competitive athlete. Other reasons for taking recreational drugs included relief from pain and overcoming boredom.

One strategy to combat drug abuse in sport (and out of sport) over the years has been drug education. How effective were such programs? My colleague, Dr. Ken Russell, and I decided to find out. We wanted to determine whether the athletes' knowledge about the harmful effects of taking anabolic steroids for a long period of time was related to their attitudes toward taking this banned substance. Said another way, does drug education in sport, particularly about the harmful effects of steroids, really lead to more negative attitudes about taking steroids, as drug education is intended? Ken and I asked State-level track and field athletes in New South Wales, Australia, to complete two self-generated inventories.

One inventory addressed the athletes' *knowledge* of the effect of taking steroids and one inventory concerned their *attitude* toward taking steroids—by them or any other athlete. The main results of our study showed very low relationships between the athletes' knowledge and their attitude about taking steroids. These results confirmed past studies that indicate very limited effectiveness of drug education programs—in this case, on the harmful effects of steroids. So, despite efforts to provide information about steroids on one's health and well-being, attitudes (especially the attitude of rejecting drugs) are not markedly influenced. One implication of this study, in support of past research with nonathletes, is that drug education effectiveness is questionable, at least in terms of the way it is currently carried out. Other studies will have to examine different strategies that more effectively change attitudes about drug-taking, particularly among athletes.

I made another discovery about drug-taking in competitive sport that has gone unreported in the literature—the role of coaches. Too often, I have found that coaches are part of the problem, not part of the solution, of reducing drug-taking among athletes. This may appear cynical and perhaps even a bit unfair to coaches, many of whom believe that they are unable to control—and hence should not be responsible for—the behaviors of their athletes away from the sport venue. In addition, many coaches do, in fact, have very restrictive team rules about ingesting any banned drug. However, in general, coaches could do much more.

These conclusions are based on two primary issues. First, unless there is a drug-testing program in the league or organization, few coaches warn their athletes about the negative consequences of taking steroids. Second, relatively few teams have anti-drug (including steroid) policies—and carry them out. According to many athletes, and confirmed by my own observations, coaches know the strength-enhancing effects of taking steroids. If added strength and power will improve performance, and, therefore, enhance the chance of winning, coaches will hesitate before placing the athlete at a disadvantage. This is especially true in those sports in which strength is a primary component of performance, such as American football and weight lifting, and if opponents are perceived to be taking steroids. Although many coaches genuinely care about the physical and mental, short-term and long-term, health of their athletes, too many coaches have simply ignored the problem.

The unspoken sentiments of many coaches appear to be that, if steroid ingestion would improve the athletes' performance, whether they take these drugs is not the coach's business. I disagree. Athletes need coaches' protection and support in actively *preventing* drug use. Protection is needed by instituting a team policy which the coach is prepared to enforce. Support is needed by reminding athletes, in group and individual settings, that drug-taking is unnecessary, unhealthy, and undesirable. If the coach communicates a negative attitude toward drug-taking, it is more likely that athletes will follow. However, it is the rare coach, especially at elite sport levels, who communicates this necessary point of view. Knowing that the coach is not applying pressure to succeed at any cost will eliminate one common reason for taking performance-enhancing drugs.

My belief that coaches could do a lot more to prevent drug abuse generated one published study, one (non-research) journal article, and two book chapters in which I discuss what these coaching strategies could—and should—be. The study, conducted in 1991 with my doctoral student, Michael Martin, measured the attitudes of adolescent, elite Australian athletes (53 males and 41 females) towards taking different types of drugs under two hypothetical conditions: whether the drugs were detectable or undetectable. We found that the athletes generally agreed that using alcohol and tobacco products, especially during the off-season was acceptable, and that anti-inflammatory drugs were okay to use in response to an injury. But, perhaps the most interesting finding was their support for using performance-enhancing drugs *if they were undetectable by drug testing*. If the drug was detectable, then they disagreed with such drugs. Instead, they preferred that their peers help them stay away from banned substances. Not surprisingly, then, drug testing was viewed as a deterrent from using performance-enhancing drugs, anabolic steroids in particular. The one person who has greater influence than any other person over the athletes' behaviors is their coach.

Athletes need, but have not been getting, protection by sport leaders and administrators from the constant pressures of winning, virtually perfect performance, and from peers and teammates. Examples of coaching strategies that offer this protection include instituting a team drug policy; communicating the need to avoid drug-taking, particularly steroids which athletes would more likely take for their potential performance-enhancing properties; pointing out the problems associated with drug use, perhaps having expert guest speakers on the issue; and working with each athlete in dealing with the pressures and expectations that predispose a competitor to take drugs in the first place.

Discussions with parents about the team's policy and the coach's insistence that athletes' adhere to it are also warranted. Other ideas include being aware of the athletes' lifestyles away from the sport venue (as much as one can, at least), looking for signs of drug use (e.g., heightened aggression, short attention span, rapid muscular growth, or other changes in physical features), instituting a drug testing program, having an athlete support group and other individuals who are trained to offer professional counsel (e.g., psychologist, religious leader) in case the athlete has a drug problem, and offering educational materials and lectures. Finally, the coach must not only have a drug policy but also have a plan of action if it must be enforced. Once a coach turns a blind eye to a positive drug test or fails to recognize drug use on the team, his or her credibility no longer exists—and neither does the drug policy in any meaningful sense.

I also made another important discovery from my research on drug-taking in sport: one reason athletes ingest drugs—both performance-enhancing and recreational—is to cope with the pressure and stress of sport competition. This finding led me to another, more current, area of research—coping with stress in sport.

Coping With Acute Stress

Coping is an athlete's attempt, through thoughts or actions, to reduce stressful feelings following an unpleasant event. Since athletes experience stress all the time (mostly through making errors, opponents' successes, receiving penalties, among other examples), they have to be able to use effective coping techniques. Perhaps my most vivid memory of developing this area of research was the difficulty with which players were able to overcome the reprimands of their football coach. I saw adult males, many with great athletic talent, become emotional "basket cases" after being ridiculed, berated, and embarrassed by their head and assistant coaches. The one experience that most stands out in my mind was when an assistant football coach grasped a player's faceguard, and yelled—only inches from the player's face—a string of personal obscenities. I found it difficult to believe that this player could maintain his composure and play anywhere near his capability after this experience.

I discovered a large body of literature on coping with stress in general psychology, but was surprised to see how little coping literature was available—research and nonresearch—in sport psychology. In fact, in the 1980s, no literature on coping with stressful events in sport (i.e., acute stress, as opposed to chronic stress) could be found. So I proceeded to generate a model based on my readings, discussions with successful university-level athletes about how they cope with stressful events (especially with coach reprimands), and my own intuitiveness on coping effectively—which I did *not* do as a high school and college (bench-warming) baseball player. The outcome of this effort was the COPE model, published in the *International Journal of Sport Psychology* in 1990. The model consists of a series of structured thoughts and actions by the athlete almost immediately after experiencing the stressful event. I thought that the model could best be remembered if it consisted of an acronym, with each stage represented by a letter. COPE, in sequence, was represented by *c*ontrolling emotions, *o*rganizing input into meaningful and nonmeaningful categories, that is, knowing when to listen to and when to ignore the coach's message, *p*lanning the next response, then *e*xecuting the next task as quickly as possible after the stressful event.

The effectiveness of this model was tested on college tennis players in response to contrived negative feedback from their coach. The coach informed her players that she would assess their performance based on their scores from a tennis task. The task consisted of hitting a series of tennis balls, forehands and backhands, projected across the net by an automatic ball machine. Their scores were based on the ability to return each ball to a targeted location near the baseline. In response to performance errors, the athletes received negative verbal feedback, such as, "you can do better" or "I am not happy with that." The athletes' performance and mood state following the last trial were recorded. All athletes experienced the same treatment, because the coach wanted all of her athletes to benefit from learning the COPE model in coping more effectively with stressful events, particularly performance error. Over the next six weeks, the players learned the COPE model of intervention and then were retested. Pre- and postintervention comparisons showed that the athletes' performed significantly better and reflected markedly lower negative mood states following use of the COPE model. I am pleased to learn that the model is presently being used by sport psychologists in several countries.

In more recent years, I have been asking another research question in the coping area. Are we predisposed to using certain types of coping strategies following stressful events in sport? For example, are some athletes inclined to cope by seeking information about, or confronting, the source of stress, while others distance themselves from or ignore sources of stress? The first category of coping strategies, called *approach coping*, consists of analyzing or reviewing the stressful event, or gaining social support, seeking information, or arguing and expressing feelings. The second category of coping strategies, called *avoidance coping*, concerns the use of techniques that desensitize the individual to the stressful event. Examples of avoidance coping techniques are psychological distancing, discounting, physically removing oneself from the situation, or quickly moving on to the next task at hand. My research concerns whether coping *styles* (a disposition) among athletes can be identified, if athletes' coping strategies can be predicted from their coping style, if these predictions are stronger for some types of stressors than others, and if stress management intervention programs would be more effective if coping strategies that took into account the athletes' coping styles were taught.

In 1996, I published a study in the *Journal of Social Psychology* supporting approach and avoidance coping styles among 421 adolescent competitive athletes. I developed a 128-item inventory that consisted of

16 approach and avoidance coping strategies for each of eight stressful events. These included making a mental or physical error, being criticized by the coach, receiving a "bad" call from the referee or umpire, being injured, poor performance because of unfavorable environmental conditions, the opponent's successful performance, cheating by an opponent, and unpleasant spectator reactions. The athletes were aged 14 to 18 years, and moderate- to high-skilled—all had to make their team. They represented basketball ($n = 221$), field hockey ($n = 66$), soccer ($n = 59$), rugby ($n = 53$), and volleyball ($n = 22$). Statistical analyses showed that coping style was more evident in some stressors than others. Approach coping was more common in stressful events that were under the athletes' control, such as making an error, or environmental factors that hurt performance. Less controllable stressful events, such as an angry coach or a cheating opponent, warranted avoidance coping.

Future Directions in My Research

I am blessed with a job that has given me great pleasure in sharing my knowledge and expertise with thousands of students, athletes, coaches, and colleagues over the years. In attempting to link theory with practice, my writing has taken a highly applied direction. This is reflected by my book, *Sport Psychology: From Theory to Practice* (3rd ed.), and in my research, which has dealt with "real life" issues, such as drug-taking and coping in sport.

Coping with stressful events in sport remains an underexplored area of research in sport psychology. To date, the results of my studies, together with those in the non-sport literature, indicate evidence of coping styles among athletes. That is, athletes tend to have preferences, or tendencies, in their use of certain types (categories) of coping strategies, usually designated as approach and avoidance. It appears that we are "approachers" or "avoiders" in our reactions to unpleasant events during the contest. However, are athletes consistent with their use of coping styles after experiencing different types of stressful events? Will an athlete use approach coping styles following a performance error and after receiving a penalty due to the referee's "bad" call? Or will the athlete approach-cope in one instance, becoming highly self-critical and analyzing the performance error, and avoidance-cope following another type of stressor, for instance, discount the importance of the penalty, quickly forget about the incident and move on, or not take responsibility for the penalty? The trait-coping model is supported if athletes demonstrate similar types of coping styles following different types of stressful events, while the transactional coping model is supported if coping styles vary according to the type of stressful episode.

Why is it important to know how competitors cope in sport? Sports participants experience a huge amount of stress. Performance errors, success of or interaction with an opponent, committing infractions (we all make mistakes), weather conditions, equipment failure, pain or injury, and many other types of stressful events occur all the time during the contest. It's essential that athletes develop skills to react to (cope with) these unpleasant situations.

As I found in my drug-in-sport research, one ineffective way of coping with the stress and pressure of sport, especially at more advanced levels, is taking recreational drugs (e.g., marijuana, cocaine). This is especially true for hallucinogenic (mind-altering) drugs. When athletes cannot cope with the pressures of winning, training, expectations of others, and maintaining high-quality performance, they may mentally escape by ingesting hallucinogenic drugs.

Performance-enhancing drugs (e.g., steroids) also reflect maladaptive coping in that the athlete endangers his or her health and future involvement in sport (if they get caught through a positive drug test). Examining the consistency with which athletes cope with stress during the contest, and the effectiveness of using these coping styles, will allow coaches, sport psychology consultants, and even the athletes, themselves, to apply better stress management techniques. In addition to reducing stressful feelings, the result of effective coping will likely lead to improved performance and more enjoyment as a participant.

In my future work, I will continue to examine the coping tendencies of athletes, especially in the child and adolescent age groups. I'll also be investigating different factors that might influence the coping process, such as gender (males and females do cope differently in nonsport research), the athlete's skill level (limited research suggests that better athletes are more closely linked to avoidance coping than their less-skilled peers), sport type (contact and noncontact sports, team and individual sports), and cultural differences (an area of study virtually ignored in sport psychology).

Until this research is completed, let me share some practical advice on coping with stress to readers who are athletes or are the parents and coaches of athletes. First, I have never known an athlete to admit *wanting* to make an error or lose the contest. As human beings, we are all imperfect. Let's allow ourselves the right to fail, as long as we've tried our best to succeed. This is an *avoidance* coping style called rationalization. Second, remember there are many types of events during the contest that are not under our control. Among the most important of these is our opponent. Let's not be so quick to blame athletes for their opponent's success, again an *avoidance* coping style. When something unpleasant happens, the best athletes usually avoidance cope; they get past the negative feelings and remain on the task at hand. However, on the side of an *approach* coping style, athletes must not always assume the role of victim. Learn from mistakes. When time allows, analyze what went wrong and ask for advice to improve your mental and performance skills. What's the best strategy to overcome a superior opponent? What is working and what is not? Be prepared, and adapt. Mentally rehearse your strategy with confidence. That's *approach* coping.

Finally, while winning and playing well is preferred to losing and playing poorly, not everything in life should be taken so seriously. After losing or performing below expectations, life goes on. Remember the good experiences about every contest, as well as (but not only) the not-so-good points. I have seen many athletes (most of whom suffer from low self-confidence), who think of what went wrong during the game—the errors, penalties, opponent's scoring, missed opportunities, and so on. They struggle with recalling the good things about the contest, their performance successes, their improvement, and the fact that they did their best. Coaches and parents, help your sons and daughters learn from their mistakes. Separate your emotional reactions, especially anger, from a more subdued approach in providing feedback and instruction. At the end of the day don't forget to have some fun, maybe even a good laugh. Now, that's effective avoidance coping.

Suggested Readings

Anshel, M.H. (1990). Toward validation of the COPE model: Strategies for acute stress inoculation in sport. *International Journal of Sport Psychology, 21*, 24–39.

Anshel, M.H. (1991). A survey of elite athletes on the perceived causes of using banned drugs in sport. *Journal of Sport Behavior, 14*, 283–307.

Anshel, M.H. (1991). Cognitive-behavioral strategies for combating drug abuse in sport: Implications for coaches and sport psychology consultants. *The Sport Psychologist, 5*, 152–166.

Anshel, M.H. (1998). Drug abuse in sport: Causes and cures. In J.M. Williams (Ed.), *Applied sport psychology: Personal growth to peak performance* (3rd ed.) (pp. 372–397). Mountain View, CA: Mayfield.

Anshel, M.H. (1993). Drugs in sport. In R.N. Singer, M. Murphey, & K. Tennant (Eds.), *Handbook on research in sport psychology* (pp. 851–876). New York: Macmillan.

Anshel, M.H. (1996). Coping styles among adolescent competitive athletes. *Journal of Social Psychology, 136,* 311–324.

Anshel, M.H. (1997). *Sport psychology: From theory to practice* (3rd ed.). Needham Heights, MA: Allyn & Bacon.

Anshel, M.H. & Marisi, D.Q. (1978). Effect of music and rhythm on physical performance. *Research Quarterly, 49,* 109–113.

Anshel, M.H., & Russell, K. (1997). Effect of an educational program on knowledge and attitudes toward ingesting anabolic steroids among track and field athletes. *Journal of Drug Education, 27,* 143–157.

Anshel, M.H. & Singer, R.N. (1980). Effect of learner strategies with modular versus traditional instruction on motor skill learning and retention. *Research Quarterly, 51,* 451–462.

Anshel, M.H., Williams, L.R.T., & Hodge, K. (1997). Cross-cultural and gender differences on coping style in sport. *International Journal of Sport Psychology, 28,* 141–156.

Martin, M.B., & Anshel, M.H. (1991). Attitudes of elite adolescent Australian athletes toward drug taking: Implications for effective drug prevention programs. *Drug Education Journal of Australia, 5,* 223–238.

Zaichkowsky, L.D., & Perna, F.M. (1992). Certification of consultants in sport psychology: A rebuttal to Anshel. *The Sport Psychologist, 6,* 287–296.

Chapter **11**

The Psychology of Athletic Injury

Jane Crossman

Jane Crossman is a Professor of Kinesiology at Lakehead University in Thunder Bay, Ontario, Canada where she was Chair for six years. She teaches sport psychology, sport sociology and research methods at the graduate and undergraduate level. Dr. Crossman has more than 40 refereed publications and 3 chapters in books and is an Associate Editor of the *Journal of Sport Behavior*. She is a Fellow of the Association for the Advancement of Applied Sport Psychology and a Member of the Canadian Mental Training Registry. As a clinician, she has worked with the Canadian National Cycling Team and high-performance athletes in running, ski jumping, alpine skiing, and swimming. During sabbatical leaves, she has been a Visiting Professor at the universities of Exeter and Brighton (United Kingdom) and the University of Otago (New Zealand). Her hobbies and interests include creative writing, reading contemporary fiction, traveling, racquet sports, running, and shoveling snow.

I do not consider myself a *natural born* researcher. As a child, I did not stand among rows of corn pondering the wonders of cross-pollination. Nor did I give a second thought, as I played catch with my father after dinner, of how to maximize the velocity of a baseball as it left my hand, hurled toward his glove, and made a satisfying smack upon impact. At the time, I was too busy "doing." This may be somewhat comforting to readers who do not perceive that they were born to research.

For many senior university and graduate school students, research may be regarded as a necessary evil—a means to an end. For a lucky few, parts, if not all, of the research experience are indeed enjoyable and satisfying. For me, the research process has been a challenging and sometimes puzzling process—a love/hate relationship. Whatever negative feelings I encountered along the way were almost always overridden by the tremendous sense of satisfaction I felt upon opening a newly-arrived journal, finding my article, and seeing hundreds of hours of work in print. This is much like the feeling I get after a round of golf: numerous lousy shots seem to be overridden by that one good one; and it is that one good one that brings me back time after time.

The process of arriving at a research specialty can be akin to molding clay. Each successive move determines the next until the final goal is reached. Following high school, I decided to study Kinanthropology (the science of human motion). I had always been an active person but was quite sure that I did not want to become a physical education teacher. So off I went to the University of Ottawa in 1970 to do a Bachelor of Science degree. In my fourth and final year, a young and dynamic professor named Dr. Terry Orlick joined the faculty. After enduring the wrath of the Krebs cycle and Newton's laws of motion, I finally found the area that kindled my interest. In our sport psychology seminar, I was particularly drawn to an article by Dr. Brent Rushall at Dalhousie University in Nova Scotia about the application of behavioral principles to sport. This branch of psychology was rooted in the idea that behavior was determined by its consequences. For example, positive reinforcement following a behavior increases the likelihood that the behavior will occur on subsequent occasions, whereas punishment has the opposite effect. In retrospect, I can see that I was attracted to behaviorism and to Rushall's work, with its application to sport, because it suited my underlying analytical nature. Cause-effect relationships made perfect sense to me.

Knowing that I enjoyed going to university and wanted to further my education, I applied to become Brent Rushall's graduate assistant for the next academic year. Some of the most important events that shape one's life aren't a result of careful planning and consideration, but of chance. Dr. Rushall called me that summer to announce that he would be transferring to Lakehead University in Thunder Bay to head a new graduate program and, if I wanted to study with him, I would have to go there. I remember looking at a map to see where Thunder Bay was located. As a child growing up in southern Ontario, for me Thunder Bay (then Port Arthur and Fort William) was a place you drove through to get out West. Little did I know that I would spend the majority of my career living and working in this small port city cut out of the bush in Northwestern Ontario.

The two years I spent studying with Brent Rushall were, at times, anxiety-provoking but, for the most part, enlightening. Dr. Rushall was a stickler for detail and error-free assignments. The late nights spent redoing mediocre work until it passed his high standards are etched in my memory. I have tried to take the lessons learned from Brent Rushall into my own teaching and research. Settle for sloppy, rushed work and that is what you get. Quality research involves painstaking attention to detail and the willingness to write numerous drafts until the final product reflects a polished effort.

My Master's thesis, which was my introduction to hands-on research, investigated the effects of cognitive strategies on the running performance of varsity wrestlers. We asked our subjects to think of different things (e.g., their technique, running in the countryside) while on a treadmill. The object was to run as long as possible and I remember vividly having to catch some highly-competitive subjects as they virtually fell off the end of the treadmill in an effort to stay on as long as possible. This initial research effort made me aware that the process of doing research is best learned by actually having to perform the varied tasks involved (planning, data collection, analysis and reporting) and cannot be learned just by reading a textbook.

A natural progression for me was to pursue my doctorate with Dr. Daryl Siedentop at Ohio State University. Drs. Rushall and Siedentop had co-authored a book that applied behavioral principles to teaching and coaching. Dr. Siedentop allowed me the latitude to do the majority of my doctoral course work in psychology. Two excellent counseling psychology courses enabled me to hone my clinical skills that would, in time, become invaluable when interviewing injured athletes.

For my doctoral dissertation, I studied feedback and its effect on the practice behaviors of athletes. With the assistance of a few fellow students, I documented the subjects' behavior (objectively and systematically) and, after having established a baseline, gave them feedback regarding how they were spending their time while in practice. Using a single-subject design, I found that the behaviors became more productive after the feedback intervention was implemented.

After a one-year stint as an Assistant Professor at the College of William and Mary, I was invited to return to Lakehead University, this time as a faculty member. After I had my courses well in hand, I began to consider on what area of sport psychology I should concentrate. Orlick had made his mark researching children in sport and then mental preparation; Rushall (who eventually transferred to San Diego State), in mental preparation; and Siedentop, in teacher education. Even though I had completed a Master's thesis and a doctoral dissertation, I was still a neophyte researcher. The good news is that even the most prolific researchers have to start somewhere. People who are graduating today with their Ph.D.'s come with more street smarts about the process of getting research published than I did. For example, it took me a while to learn the importance of sending manuscripts to quality, refereed journals. Unfortunately, I learned much of what I know about research by trial and evaluation. There is much to be said for a mentor system that links novice researchers with more established ones.

At the time I was considering what my research niche could be, I was befriended by the university's sports therapist. Based on his experience as a trainer for a professional football team, he told me stories of the impact a coach can have on injured players as he slowly walks through the training room inspecting the casualties. He might be inadvertently sending the message, "Get back on the playing field or lose your place on the team." As one athlete said to me, "It always feels like, once injured, you are the trainer's commodity and the coach wants you only when you are able. . . . Coaches shouldn't make athletes feel that way."

Often coaches are ambivalent towards their injured athletes and the pain they must endure as a result of being injured. My friend and I discussed why some athletes get injured more frequently than others and why some recover faster. I had long held an interest in what is loosely referred to as the mind-body relationship. From casual observation it seemed to me that there were some people, albeit a small minority, who always had something wrong with them. These people were constantly preoccupied with dashing from doctor to doctor until they found one who would give whatever they were complaining about a label and usually some remedy to treat it. Similarly, almost everyone from time to time gets a cold or the flu. It is how individuals react to illness that I find interesting. Some get on with their regular routine and, in due course, the virus disappears. Others are out of commission for days.

My interest in the influence of the mind on injury and illness motivated me to learn what had been written about the psychological dimensions underlying athletic injury. I found very few sources, and most were anecdotal in nature. The three empirical studies that I located pertained to the relationship between life change and injury. I then perused numerous textbooks and journals devoted to sports medicine, only to find that psychological aspects of injury were not considered or, at best, were given a cursory overview. The lack of available research in this area further motivated me to select it as my specialty.

In my quest to find an area of sport psychology where I could make a contribution, two factors were important: (1) I wanted it to be a subject in which I was truly interested, and (2) I wanted my work to be groundbreaking. This was important to me, as I was not interested in studying a subject that had already been researched ad nauseam (thereby adding more bricks to the brick pile). I wanted then, and still want, the outcome of my research to have real-life implications for practitioners; in the case of athletic injury, these are athletes, coaches, and medical professionals. I become quickly uninterested in a project when an enthusiastic student strides into my office proclaiming a desire to research motivation, visualization, or goal setting. A plethora of research has already been published in these areas, evidenced by the meta-analyses that have been conducted. I direct my students towards choosing subjects whose coals haven't been raked over until light from the ash has burned out.

I learned that it is wise to consider the phrase *know thyself* before embarking upon a research project. In my experience, most researchers don't possess all the tools necessary to complete a research project. Therefore, it is advantageous to collaborate with colleagues who possess the traits and/or abilities in which you are deficient. Acutely aware that my knowledge of statistics was rudimentary, I approached one of my thesis advisors, who happened to be a crackerjack statistician in the Department of Psychology at Lakehead. Dr. John Jamieson also had a keen interest in sport psychology and was very receptive to working on a project involving the perceptions of the seriousness of injury as viewed by the injured athlete and his/her trainer. The value of linking up with experienced, positive role models is well established in the psychological literature, and the research process provides an excellent forum to put this strategy to use. It was John who told me that a well-established research portfolio of refereed publications in quality journals was the most expedient route to tenure and, indeed, promotion. During my six year stint as Chair of my school, I kept my research going, even if it meant years of twelve- to fourteen-hour workdays.

By no means am I downplaying the importance of quality teaching. Those who are actively involved in researching subjects which they also teach are undoubtedly relaying to their students the most up-to-date information. It is no surprise to me that two professors at Lakehead who have won the Distinguished Researcher Award also have won the Distinguished Teacher Award.

Our first research project involved determining whether there were differences in the perceptions of the seriousness and disruption of the injury between the affected athlete and his/her trainer. Using standardized tests that measured anxiety and mood, in combination with our own questionnaire, we found that lower level athletes (i.e., novice or recreational) tended to overestimate the seriousness and disrupting impact of their injury and experienced more anxiety, anger, loneliness, and apathy. A follow-up study, this time incorporating the injured athletes' coaches and physicians, found a similar pattern. When the seriousness of the athlete's injury was considered, medical professionals, who were accustomed to seeing injuries daily, tended to underestimate and coaches tended to overestimate the impact.

At this initial stage of my research, I began counseling some athletes who had been injured and who were in the process of recovering both physically and psychologically. One such person was a young woman who had torn her anterior cruciate knee ligament in a skiing accident. Following the injury and subsequent rehabilitation, she had a fear of skiing down hills similar to the one on which she was injured (i.e., narrow, icy, and steep), felt she wasn't skiing as aggressively, and she didn't have as much confidence in her ability. This, for her, was a potentially debilitating experience because she was a ski coach and a skilled skier, and she did not want to limit her future involvement. Consequently, we embarked on a program of systematic desensitization.

This psychological process is commonly used for treating people with phobias (irrational fears), and initially involves listing anxiety-provoking situations on a hierarchy from least fearful to most fearful. For my client, a nonthreatening situation would be skiing down a wide hill with few moguls under ideal snow conditions. She ranked increasingly threatening skiing situations by narrowing the hill, changing the snow from packed to icy, and increasing the number of moguls and the steepness of the hill. The scene she envisioned that was the most fear-rendering (and, thus, at the top of the hierarchy) was to ski down a hill that was narrow, icy and extremely challenging.

Once we had determined her fear hierarchy, I taught her progressive relaxation which involved the systematic contraction and relaxation of sixteen muscle groups. Following a few sessions, we shortened the number of muscle groups to seven, after which she was able to get into a relaxed state in a matter of minutes. We then paired this feeling of relaxation with imagining the least threatening scene in her fear hierarchy. When she reported feeling relaxed while imagining the skiing scene, we moved to the next most threatening scene. Over time, we worked through all the scenes until she was able to imagine the most fear-provoking one while in a relaxed state. Following our series of meetings, she gradually attempted to ski progressively more challenging hills until she was able to ski down the hill where she was injured. There are many other athletes with whom I have spoken who have or could have overcome their fear of reinjury using the process of systematic desensitization. For example, I interviewed a varsity hockey player who had severely injured his knee as a result of colliding with a goal post (before the advent of mag-nets). When his hockey career resumed, following surgery and extensive rehabilitation, he had a tremendous fear of reinjury that was manifested in his inability to skate toward the net.

I include these case studies here to illustrate the point that, more often than not, sport psychology applications have their roots in the psychology literature per se. People were relaxing, visualizing, and being motivated and aggressive before sport psychology came into its own. We have adapted the theories, principles, and strategies for our purposes in sport and physical activity.

Because I believe it is important to have a solid understanding of the literature before embarking on a new project, I devoted the summer of 1984 to finding all the published literature concerning the role psychology plays in the occurrence of and recovery from athletic injury. I began by doing a computer search. From there I tracked down copies of all relevant studies, then cross-referenced them until I was confident I had found all the research that had been published pertaining to the psychology of athletic injury. The outcome of my investigative efforts was the publication of two papers, one written primarily for sports medicine practitioners and the other for coaches. My efforts reinforced what I had already suspected: there was much empirical work to be done concerning the relationship of psychology to injury.

From my discussions with medical professionals around the world who treat athletes who are injured, and from a formal survey of 11 physiotherapists in Thunder Bay, I became aware that sport therapists and physicians were generally receptive to the use of psychological strategies in injury rehabilitation. More specifically, goal setting and positive self-talk were understood and used more than mental imagery and relaxation training. The problem, however, was that many believed they lacked the necessary skills and training. At the time I began my research, I noted that the number of overuse-type injuries sustained every year was rising. Sports medicine clinics were flourishing throughout North America and sport-developed nations.

Casual observation led me to wonder whether athletes who gravitated to the sports medicine clinic were really there for an injury-related purpose. It seemed to me that our university's sports medicine clinic was a hub of social activity on campus. Music played, hot whirlpool baths were available, and hands-on attention seemed to be the norm. As a scientist, I wanted to objectively and systematically find out how athletes were spending their time while in sports medicine clinics. To achieve this, I developed a Sports Medicine Observation Code (SMOC) that consisted of eleven possible behavior categories. These behaviors were then designated as either productive, unproductive, or concurrent.

With the help of a research assistant, we observed the behaviors of 20 clients using one of two sports medicine clinics. We found that 58% of the time in the clinic was spent in behaviors directly related to injury rehabilitation, 29% of time was spent in unproductive behavior, such as waiting, and 13% was spent managing equipment or getting ready for treatment. Managers wanting to improve the efficiency of their rehabilitation clinics must first know what their clients are doing while there. Are they on task? Do they wait too long for treatment? An observation instrument such as SMOC could now be utilized to get an accurate picture of how clients are using their time.

From my conversations with injured athletes, I realized that an understanding of the emotional responses accompanying injury would be advantageous. While many athletes spent many hours and much energy each day physically preparing for competition, more often than not they were unprepared psychologically to handle the stress associated with an unforeseen or unexpected injury. As one injured athlete said to me, "An injured athlete is suddenly taken away from her daily routine, her goals and hopes and, more often than not, feels alone as the rest of the team moves on." Injury is a stressor and stress impedes the healing process. How the athlete responds to stress caused by an injury can, to a great extent, influence progress in rehabilitation. Medical professionals observe that the negative emotions experienced by their clients as a result of injury can influence attitude toward and subsequent recovery from injury.

Early attempts at explaining the emotional reaction to injury were largely anecdotal. Several authors equated the stages through which injured athletes progress to those proposed by Kubler-Ross in her renowned book, *On Death and Dying*. With the help of two willing students, I embarked on two research projects to ascertain the emotions that injured athletes experience at various times following injury. The emotional responses of 55 injured athletes competing at various levels, from recreational to semiprofessional, were monitored. A three-part questionnaire was used. The first section of questions pertained to the background information of the injured athlete (age, gender, level of participation and number of athletic injuries sustained). The second segment focused on the specific athletic injury sustained in the last year. Questions about the seriousness of the injury and the level of importance of participation and commitment to rehabilitation were included here. In the last section we asked subjects to check adjectives (from 48 possibilities) that described how they were feeling on four separate occasions (the day of the injury, the following day, halfway through rehabilitation, and the day of return to practice). One study consisted solely of football and hockey players, and the other of a more varied sample of athletes.

We found in both studies that the postinjury reactions were complex and varied. Injured athletes vacillated through a series of emotional highs and lows on their way to recovery. One triathlete likened the emotions he experienced following the onset of shin-splints to "being on a roller coaster ride."

We found that the three emotions athletes experienced most often following injury were frustration, anger, and depression. They also reported feeling irritable, miserable, discouraged and uncomfortable. Generally, the more severe the injury, the more intense was the response. Keep in mind that most athletes are mentally healthy individuals and mood disturbances are a departure from the norm.

In both studies, we found that the negative emotions experienced after the injury were gradually replaced with more positive feelings. However, some athletes reported lingering feelings of frustration after returning to practice because of the disappointment of not being able to perform to a preinjury level and of having fallen behind the progress of teammates.

With the limited number of athletes, coaches, and medical professionals specializing in sports injuries in Thunder Bay, I realized the need to expand data collection outside the city. A graduate of our program approached me about doing some collaborative research on injuries in ballet. At the time, she was studying with the Royal Winnipeg Ballet, had a chronic lower back injury, and wanted to understand more about the psychological dimensions underlying her injury. Ballet dancers, sometimes referred to as "artistic athletes," were an excellent group to survey because injury is pervasive in their activity (the most frequent injuries are ankle, back, toe and foot sprains, and knee and Achilles tendinitis). We developed an interview schedule and then interviewed 26 dancers with the Royal Winnipeg Ballet school. We asked them about their reactions and feelings following injury, how they coped, the reactions of significant others and the impact the injury had on their lives.

Similar to the two studies previously mentioned, we found that the emotions experienced following the onset of injury were quite negative. Fear of the reactions of others (teachers, staff, parents, and other dancers), and of the effect the injury would have on their dancing careers predominated. As they progressed through rehabilitation, reactions varied from optimism that they would be able to resume their dancing careers, to pessimism about the severity of the injury and the amount of time it would take to heal and get back into preinjury performance. These varied reactions were consistent with other studies being published at the time, which found that athletes react in different ways. Generally, however, the dancers replaced their negative feelings with more positive ones as recovery occurred. A myriad of reactions occurred when the dancers returned to training. Some felt as if they were starting all over again. Half indicated that they were more aware of ways to avoid reinjury, such as stretching and modifying exercises. Most felt that the injury had slowed their short-term progress, but few thought it negatively affected their long-term progress.

The strategies that the dancers adopted to cope with their injuries were also varied. Some pursued hobbies for which they had previously had no time; others did more socializing. Fellow ballet dancers seemed generally very supportive and empathic about the injury, but the injured dancers' reports about their ballet instructors were mixed: some were viewed as very understanding, while others were not. Mothers clearly were the parents who were the most concerned and supportive of their children's injuries. The majority of dancers also felt that their therapists were positive throughout rehabilitation. Physicians did not fare as well. Half the dancers with whom we spoke felt that their physicians were impersonal and did not provide enough information about the injury. Clearly, what the dancers told us about the reactions of significant others towards their injury led us to believe that social support is an important dimension in dealing and coping with the stress of injury.

Ironically, in June of 1991, I experienced a potentially debilitating injury. In the process of training for a marathon, I developed tingling sensations first in my hands, then my legs. Over time, I began to lose my motor coordination. I consulted general practitioners who, at the time, convinced me that I was either overtrained or under stress (my mother had recently passed away). It was my masseuse who convinced me that I needed to see a specialist. I was very fortunate that two excellent neurosurgeons practiced in Thunder Bay. After a thorough examination, they referred me (ironically on the same weekend that I was to run the marathon) to a hospital in Duluth, Minnesota that had magnetic resonance imaging (M.R.I.) equipment. This amazing machine produces pictures of the interior of the body, in my case the brain and spinal column, that are much clearer and more detailed than an X-ray. They warned me that, on the basis of my symptoms, I might have multiple sclerosis (M.S.). Curiosity got the better of me and I arrived early at the hospital, went into their library and read all that was available on the disease. By the time I was rolled into the M.R.I. cylinder, I was convinced that I had M.S. and had even planned the remaining years of my life. Just a few weeks previously my immediate goal had been to run my first marathon in less than four hours. How quickly priorities change when life throws a curve ball! I was prepared to hear the worst from the radiologist on duty. To my great relief, he told me I had two herniated disks that were pinching the spinal cord. I was fixable! So a week later I was fixed.

I went into the experience with a "mind over matter approach." Get up, get out, and get moving was my attitude. Through my research with injured athletes, I have observed that, for many, being injured had allowed them the opportunity to grow in other areas of their lives. This was indeed the situation for me. During my stay in the hospital and during recovery, I became aware of some writings that reinforced my belief in the power of the mind to influence recovery from injury and illness. Dr. Bernie Segal (*Love, Medicine and Miracles*), an oncologist, uses imagery and positive attitude to help his patients with cancer. Dr. Norman Cousins (*Anatomy of an Illness*) uses humor as a vehicle to enhance recovery. As a result of his influence, many hospitals now have humor rooms where patients can go to watch videos, read material, and involve themselves in activities that will bring a smile to their faces, and laughter to their voices.

During the weeks and months that followed my surgery, each day I visualized my body healing, and encouraged myself about the fast progress I was making. I was fortunate to have an opportunity to put into effect the belief I had in the power of the mind to affect the body. Six weeks after my operation, I was a bit depressed because I wasn't recovering as fast as I had hoped. My neurosurgeon reminded me that a normal recovery time for my operation was from three to five years. I had other plans. I returned to the classroom in September (albeit a little rough around the edges) and that winter put five hundred kilometers on my cross-country skis. I looked at my own injury as a chance for personal growth and an opportunity to stop and evaluate what is really important at the end of the day. When I speak with others who have been injured, I can truly say, "I have walked in your shoes."

In 1993, while on sabbatical, I had the opportunity to teach and research at the University of Brighton (England) and the University of Otago (New Zealand). While at both of these institutions, I linked up with colleagues interested in my field of research. Having worked at a relatively small, isolated university, I was really looking forward to working with associates who had conducted research in the psychology of injury. Dr. Adrian Taylor was one such colleague. Adrian was doing work in goal-setting interventions for injured athletes and compliance to sport-injury rehabilitation, and had also developed a satisfaction scale for clients frequenting sports-injury clinics. He organized a session at the annual United Kingdom Sport Science Conference in November of 1993 pertaining to the psychology of injury. Five years previously, there wouldn't have been enough interest in the subject to organize such a session, which was now filled to capacity. The response we received reinforced for me that injury was definitely a "hot" topic in sport psychology. At this time, it seemed to me that each issue of most sport psychology journals had at least one article devoted to injury. What had begun as mere speculation based on casual observation in the early 1980's was now, ten years later, undergoing more rigorous scientific investigation.

I was equally fortunate to connect with Dr. David Gerrard. David had been an Olympic swimmer turned physiotherapist turned physician specializing in sports medicine. He reinforced my impression that physicians specializing in sports medicine were aware of and receptive to the use of psychological strategies to enhance recovery from injury. The problem, as he saw it, was that they wanted and needed to know more. While at Otago, I lectured in his sports medicine class and interviewed several athletes who had been injured about the impact the injury had had on their lives. I wrote a paper specifically for medical professionals, i.e., physicians and sports therapists, who treat injured athletes. In the paper I outlined what impact the injury may have on their clients from a psychological perspective and discussed strategies to deal with the varied reactions.

Wherever I travel, lecture, or teach, I seek out athletes who have been injured. All have been willing and sometimes grateful for the opportunity to share with me their injury stories. I have interviewed runners, wrestlers, triathletes and volleyball, hockey, basketball, netball and football players, to name a few. For this purpose, I developed an interview schedule. I ask them about what effect their injury has had on their athletic careers, their life outside of sport, how they felt during various stages of recovery and the reactions of significant others. As an outcome of these interviews, it is tempting to proclaim that I have developed a "model of recovery," but such is not the case because of the variability in reaction. However, some interesting patterns have emerged.

As a result of being injured, the athlete often feels a loss of status exemplified by loss of playing time, fitness level, and attention from the coach, teammates, and sometimes the media. This is particularly true for athletes who possess a strong self-identity through sport (e.g., "I am a runner."). Oftentimes, this loss of self-identity can adversely affect self-esteem, which can result in withdrawal from the team. One wrestler told me that, as a result of his career-ending injury, all he did was spend his time watching TV, while his school work and social life suffered. Success in coping with the injury and working hard at rehabilitation seem to be a function of several factors. The athlete's attitude toward the injury and motivation to recover are of paramount importance. What became increasingly evident to me was that the athlete is not powerless to influence his/her attitude toward the injury and recovery. Athletes who are willing to learn and practice strategies to assist in their recovery, such as visualization, goal setting, and relaxation, seem to cope more effectively.

No doubt, injury can have a profound influence on the athlete's life. One athlete told me that her series of injuries "strained every aspect of my life outside of sport. It even put a strain on my faith and belief in God." Most injured athletes, at some point, have asked themselves, "Why me?" (Why did the injury happen to me?) One runner, when describing the impact of her injury, said, "It becomes something in the pit of your stomach that you'd just rather forget about but it's constantly on your mind."

Certainly, those who have positive social support from significant others, such as parents, coaches, teammates, partners, friends, and the medical professionals treating the injury, tend to have a more optimistic outlook about their recovery. Effective communication between these people and the injured athlete also seems to be an essential ingredient. One basketball player told me that she "liked the relationship with my physiotherapist because he helped me believe I would heal, understood the pain and frustration I felt, and seemed to have a way of listening and helping me focus on the positive." Athletes also want their physicians to talk to them honestly about the nature of their injury and prognosis for recovery in terms they can understand. One volleyball player reported that her physician told her that he had "real patients to treat" and that her injury was "all in her head." One consistency among those

I have interviewed is that they remember vividly getting injured and their reaction to the injury. It is an indelible experience.

Research concerning the psychology of athletic injury is still in its infancy. Many interesting problems still warrant investigation. I am convinced that athletes, coaches, and medical professionals want and need to learn more about how to treat the mind when injury occurs.

As a result of shrinking health care dollars, a shift towards prevention as opposed to intervention will occur. The outcome will be a greater need to understand the psychological dynamics influencing injury and disease. With this realization, I recently coauthored a study that examined factors influencing motivation to return to work and effort in rehabilitation among injured clients on a worker's compensation scheme. Interestingly, and contrary to popular belief, we found that clients were highly motivated to return to work. In addition, a positive correlation existed between the client's perception of his/her motivation to return to work and the therapist's perception. In other words, clients and their respective therapists were generally in agreement with regard to how motivated the client was to return to work. Females were significantly more motivated than males to return to work. Therapists did not perceive their clients were working as hard at their rehabilitation as their clients did.

The study of how our psyche influences the body when we are injured is indeed a fascinating one. It is this fascination that has changed me from a reluctant researcher to one who relishes the opportunity to put down on paper what I have learned from investigation. It is my continuing wish that my research will help injured athletes and medical practitioners to understand better the psychological dimensions of injury. I am, perhaps, also fortunate to have been able to have applied what I have learned from years of research to my own healing and recovery from a debilitating injury. I have learned, first hand, that the mind can help to heal the body.

Acknowledgment

The author is grateful to Trish McGowan for her critique of the initial drafts of this manuscript.

Editor's Note

With great joy, Jane completed the London (UK) Marathon on April 26, 1998.

Suggested Readings

Brewer, B. (1994). Review and critique of models of psychological adjustment to athletic injury. *Journal of Applied Sport Psychology, 6,* 87–100.

Crossman, J. (1997). Psychological rehabilitation from sports injuries. *Sports Medicine, 23* (5), 333–339.

Crossman, J. (1985). Psychological factors and athletic injury. *The Journal of Sports Medicine and Physical Fitness, 25,* 151–154.

Crossman, J., Gluck, L., & Jamieson, J. (1995). The emotional responses of injured athletes. *New Zealand Journal of Sports Medicine, 23,* 21–22.

Crossman, J., & Jamieson, J., (1990). Perceptions of athletic injuries as viewed by the athlete, coach and medical professional. *Perceptual and Motor Skills, 71,* 1–3.

Crossman, J., & Roch, J. (1991). An observation instrument for use in sports medicine clinics. *Canadian Journal of Physical Therapy,* 10–13.

Crossman, J., Zuliani, A., Preston, J., & Gluck, L. (1996). Factors influencing motivation to return to work and effort in rehabilitation amongst injured workers. *Physiotherapy Canada, 48* (4), 263–265.

Heil, J. (Ed.) (1993). *Psychology of sport injury.* Champaign, Il.: Human Kinetics.

Kerr, G., & Goss, J. (1996). The effects of a stress management program on injuries and stress levels. *Journal of Applied Sport Psychology, 8,* 109–117.

Lamba, H., & Crossman, J. (1977). The knowledge of, attitude toward and use of psychological strategies by physiotherapists as a tool in injury rehabilitation. *Physiotherapy in Sport, 20* (1), 14–17.

Larson, G.A., Starkey, C., & Zaichkowsky, L. D. (1996). Psychological aspects of athletic injuries as perceived by athletic trainers. *The Sport Psychologist, 10,* 37–47.

Macchi, R., & Crossman, J. (1996). After the fall: Reflections of injured classical ballet dancers. *Journal of Sport Behavior, 19* (3), 221–234.

Pargman, D. (Ed.) (1993). *Psychological bases of sport injuries.* Morgantown, WV: Fitness Information Technology.

Quackenbush, N., & Crossman, J. (1994). Injured athletes: A study of emotional responses. *Journal of Sport Behavior, 17* (3), 178–187.

Smith, A.M. (1996). Psychological impact of injuries in athletes. *Sports Medicine, 22* (6), 391–405.

Smith, A.M., Scott, S.G., O'Fallon, W.M., & Young, M.L. (1990). Emotional responses of athletes to injury. *Mayo Clinic Proceedings, 65,* 38–50.

Udry, E. (1997). Coping and social support among injured athletes following surgery. *Journal of Sport and Exercise Psychology, 19,* 71–90.

Epilogue

After reading *The Sport Scientists: Research Adventures*, I hope that you feel the excitement that characterizes the exploration of important issues in sport. More important, though, I trust that you have gained insight into the research process and the people who engage in that process.

I have devoted a great deal of energy to the preparation of this book and would appreciate your feedback. If you have any comments or suggestions for improvement, I would like to hear from you. Please forward your comments to me at the Department of Psychology, State University of New York at Plattsburgh, Plattsburgh, NY 12901 (Email: Brannigg@SPLAVA.CC.Plattsburgh.Edu)

Thanks,
Gary G. Brannigan